Lecture Notes in Computer Science 4765

Commenced Publication in 1973
Founding and Former Series Editors:
Gerhard Goos, Juris Hartmanis, and Jan van Leeuwen

T0223169

Ana Moreira   John Grundy (Eds.)

Early Aspects: Current Challenges and Future Directions

10th International Workshop
Vancouver, Canada, March 13, 2007
Revised Selected Papers

 Springer

Volume Editors

Ana Moreira
Universidade Nova de Lisboa
Faculdade de Ciências e tecnologia
Departamento de Informaática
2829-516 Caparica, Portugal
E-mail: amm@di.fct.unl.pt

John Grundy
University of Auckland
Department of Electrical and Computer Engineering and
Department of Computer Science
Private Bag 92019, Mail Centre, Auckland, 1142, New Zealand
E-mail: john-g@cs.auckland.ac.nz

Library of Congress Control Number: 2007941794

CR Subject Classification (1998): D.2, D.3, I.6, H.4, K.6

LNCS Sublibrary: SL 2 – Programming and Software Engineering

ISSN	0302-9743
ISBN-10	3-540-76810-6 Springer Berlin Heidelberg New York
ISBN-13	978-3-540-76810-4 Springer Berlin Heidelberg New York

Springer is a part of Springer Science+Business Media

springer.com

© Springer-Verlag Berlin Heidelberg 2007
Printed in Germany

Typesetting: Camera-ready by author, data conversion by Scientific Publishing Services, Chennai, India
Printed on acid-free paper   SPIN: 12192458   06/3180   5 4 3 2 1 0

Preface

Celebrating Five Years of Early Aspects

The early aspects community had its origins in the "Early Aspects: Requirements Engineering and Architecture Design" workshop organized during the first international conference on Aspect-Oriented Software Development (AOSD), in March 2002. Since then, the early aspects community has grown rapidly. At the time this project started, the Early Aspects Steering Committee (www.early-aspects.net) had organized nine editions of the Early Aspects workshop in conferences such as AOSD OOPSLA, ICSE and SPLC and edited two special issues in international journals. Workshop attendance has exceeded 200, and from these more than 60% were different individuals. This number corresponds to just over 20 participants per workshop, despite the fact that participation was allowed only to authors of accepted papers or invited researchers.

However, the early aspects community is much larger than that. A considerable number of papers have been published regularly in journals, books and conferences where the early aspects workshop has not yet been organized. The number and range of submissions to the workshop series have demonstrated that the field has a solid base of continuous research being done by established groups around the world.

The early-aspects community is now self-sustaining and continuously expanding. Therefore, we felt that the fifth anniversary of the first early aspects workshop was an appropriate juncture to upgrade the autonomous standing of the community by providing it with its own formal publication. In this way, relevant new work can be showcased in a dedicated publication, instead of being dispersed across several different events with more informal proceedings.

What Are Early Aspects?

Traditionally, aspect-oriented software development (AOSD) has focused on the implementation phase of the software lifecycle: aspects are identified and captured mainly in code. Therefore, most current AOSD approaches place the burden for aspect identification and management on the programmer working at low levels of abstraction. However, aspects are often present well before the implementation phase, such as in domain models, requirements and software architecture.

Identification and capture of these early aspects ensure that aspects related to the problem domain (as opposed to merely the implementation) will be appropriately captured, reasoned about and available. This offers improved opportunities for early recognition and negotiation of trade-offs and allows forward and backward aspect traceability. This makes requirements, architecture, and implementation more seamless, and allows a more systematic application of aspects.

Early aspects are crosscutting concerns that exist in the early life cycle phases of software development, including requirements analysis, domain analysis and architecture design activities. Early aspects cannot be localized using traditional software development divide-and-conquer functional decomposition techniques and tend to be scattered over multiple early life cycle modules. This reduces modularity and reusability, potentially leading to serious maintenance and evolution problems.

Whereas conventional aspect-oriented software development approaches are mainly concerned with identifying aspects at the programming level, early aspects work focuses on the impact of crosscutting concerns during earlier activities of software development. Identifying, modularizing and managing aspects early in the software development process has a large and positive impact on the whole software system.

About This Volume

The tenth edition of the Early Aspects workshop was a success. The quality of the technical program, marked by three special moments, attracted some 50 participants in all. We began with a brilliant keynote given by Anthony Finkelstein on "Aspects, Views and Processes" where he emphasized the need to step away from considering aspects purely in terms of representation and start exploring the tangled relationship between processes and aspects.

The International Programme Committee selected ten high-quality papers for presetnation at the workshop. These were presented in four single-stream sessions with a discussant and emphasis on audience participation and debate. In a second, post-workshop phase, the authors were requested to produce a new version of their work to address the comments received from PC members and also specific points that were raised by their paper discussant and other participants during the workshop. These revised papers were submitted to a subset of the original PC members for a second review, each paper in this volume thus going through a two-stage revision process.

Finally a panel entitled "Early Aspects: Are There Any Other Kind?" was run at the conclusion of the workshop. The panel leader was Awais Rashid (University of Lancaster) and the panelists were Anthony Finkelstein (University College London), Gregor Kiczales (University of British Columbia), Maja D'Hondt (INRIA) and Ana Moreira (Universidade Nova de Lisboa). This panel attracted to the room not only early aspects researchers but also a whole set of software engineers usually more interested in later activities of software development. A summary of the discussions closes this volume with an editorial authored by Awais Rashid.

We would like to thank all the Programme Committee members for evaluating the papers, the authors for submitting their work and for improving it according to comments received from reviewers and discussants, and the AOSD-Europe project for sponsoring the workshop. We also would like to thank the papers discussants: Paul Clements, Ruzanna Chitchyan, Monica Pinto and Bedir Tekinerdogan. A special word of thanks is due to Anthony Finkelstein for his superb keynote and to Awais Rashid for making the panel a success. Many thanks to Gregor, Anthony, Maja and Ana for providing the participants with an enthusiastic and lively discussion. No doubt remains about the fundamental role played by early aspects in aspect-oriented software development.

September 2007
Ana Moreira
John Grundy

Organization

Program Committee

Alessandro Garcia (University of Lancaster)
Anthony Finkelstein (University College London)
Awais Rashid (University of Lancaster)
Bashar Nuseibeh (Open University)
Bedir Tekinerdogan (University of Twente)
Charles Haley (Open University)
Christa Schwanninger (Siemens)
Dominik Stein (University of Essen)
Elisa Baniassad (Univerity of Hong Kong)
Jaelson Castro (University of Pernanbuco)
Jean-Marc Jezequel (IRISA)
Jeff Gray (University of Alabama at Birmingham)
João Araújo (Universidade Nova de Lisboa)
John Hosking (University of Auckland)
Jon Whittle (George Mason University)
Juan Hernandez (University of Extremadura)
Julio Leite (PUC, Brazil)
Krzysztof Czarnecki (University of Waterloo)
Len Bass (Carnegie Mellon University)
Lidia Fuentes (University of Malaga)
Michael Jackson (Open University)
Oscar Pastor (University of Valencia)
Paul Clements (SEI, USA)
Robert Walker (University of Calgary)
Ruzanna Chitchyan (Lancaster University)
Siobhan Clarke (Trinity College Dublin)
Stan Sutton Jr. (IBM T. J. Watson Research Center)
Stefan Hanenberg (University of Essen)

Table of Contents

Aspect-Oriented Requirements

A Taxonomy of Asymmetric Requirements Aspects 1
  Nan Niu, Steve Easterbrook, and Yijun Yu

Flexible and Expressive Composition Rules with Aspect-oriented Use
Case Maps (AoUCM) 19
  Gunter Mussbacher, Daniel Amyot, Jon Whittle, and Michael Weiss

Improving Functional Testing Through Aspects: A Case Study 39
  Paolo Salvaneschi

Aspect Requirements to Design

DERAF: A High-Level Aspects Framework for Distributed Embedded
Real-Time Systems Design 55
  Edison Pignaton de Freitas, Marco Aurélio Wehrmeister,
  Elias Teodoro Silva Jr., Fabiano Costa Carvalho,
  Carlos Eduardo Pereira, and Flávio Rech Wagner

On the Symbiosis of Aspect-Oriented Requirements and Architectural
Descriptions 75
  Lyrene F. Silva, Thais V. Batista, Alessandro Garcia,
  Ana Luisa Medeiros, and Leonardo Minora

Aspect-Oriented Architecture Design

AO-ADL: An ADL for Describing Aspect-Oriented Architectures 94
  Mónica Pinto and Lidia Fuentes

Composing Structural Views in xADL 115
  Nelis Boucké, Alessandro Garcia, and Tom Holvoet

Using Aspects in Architectural Description 139
  Rich Hilliard

Aspect-Oriented Domain Engineering

Mapping Features to Aspects: A Model-Based Generative Approach 155
  Uirá Kulesza, Vander Alves, Alessandro Garcia, Alberto Costa Neto,
  Elder Cirilo, Carlos J.P. de Lucena, and Paulo Borba

Metamodel for Tracing Concerns Across the Life Cycle 175
  *Bedir Tekinerdoğan, Christian Hofmann, Mehmet Akşit, and
  Jethro Bakker*

Panel

Early Aspects: Are There Any Other Kind? 195
  Awais Rashid

Author Index 199

A Taxonomy of Asymmetric Requirements Aspects

Nan Niu[1], Steve Easterbrook[1], and Yijun Yu[2]

[1] Department of Computer Science, University of Toronto
Toronto, Ontario, Canada M5S 3G4
{nn,sme}@cs.toronto.edu
[2] Computing Department, The Open University
Walton Hall, Milton Keynes, UK MK7 6AA
y.yu@open.ac.uk

Abstract. The early aspects community has received increasing attention among researchers and practitioners, and has grown a set of meaningful terminology and concepts in recent years, including the notion of *requirements aspects*. Aspects at the requirements level present stakeholder concerns that crosscut the problem domain, with the potential for a broad impact on questions of scoping, prioritization, and architectural design. Although many existing requirements engineering approaches advocate and advertise an integral support of early aspects analysis, one challenge is that the notion of a requirements aspect is not yet well established to efficaciously serve the community. Instead of defining the term once and for all in a normally arduous and unproductive conceptual unification stage, we present a preliminary taxonomy based on the literature survey to show the different features of an asymmetric requirements aspect. Existing approaches that handle requirements aspects are compared and classified according to the proposed taxonomy. In addition, we study crosscutting security requirements to exemplify the taxonomy's use, substantiate its value, and explore its future directions.

1 Introduction

The many early aspects researchers and practitioners have grown a set of meaningful terminology and concepts, of which the most prominent is the distinction made between code-level and early aspects. Early aspects are concerns that crosscut an artifact's dominant decomposition, or base modules derived from the dominant separation-of-concerns criterion, in the early stages of the software life cycle [5]. "Early" signifies occurring before implementation in any development iteration, and embodies the key activities of requirements engineering, domain analysis, and architecture design, as indicated in the early aspects Web portal [12].

It is probably not a coincidence that one of the earliest descriptions of early aspects appeared in the proceedings of the premier requirements engineering (RE) conference in 1999 [14]. And the fact that the most recent RE conference

A. Moreira and J. Grundy (Eds.): Early Aspects 2007 Workshop, LNCS 4765, pp. 1–18, 2007.

(RE'06) presented the best paper award to an early aspects paper [17] demonstrates the strong connection between RE and early aspects communities. In fact, many existing RE approaches advocate and advertise an integral support of early aspects analysis, e.g., use cases [20], scenarios [3], viewpoints [28], and goals [36].

Aspects at the requirements level present stakeholder concerns that crosscut the problem domain, with the potential for a broad impact on questions of scoping, prioritization, and architectural design. A thorough analysis of early aspects in requirements offers a number of benefits:

- Explicit reasoning about interdependencies between stakeholder goals and constraints;
- Improving the modularity of the requirements structure;
- Identification of the impact of early aspects on design decisions can improve the quality of the overall architectural design and implementation;
- Conflicting concerns can be detected early and trade-offs can be resolved more economically;
- Test cases can be derived from early aspects to enhance stakeholder satisfaction; and
- Tracing stakeholder interests throughout software life cycle becomes easier since crosscutting concerns are captured early on.

Despite the growing awareness of these benefits and the continuing endeavor to achieve them, one challenge RE and early aspects communities currently face is that the notion of a requirements aspect, i.e., aspect at the requirements level, is not yet well established. We seek to explain and clarify the requirements aspects phenomena. The goal is to provide requirements analysts and other stakeholders a foundation for discussing specific challenges they might face in aspect-oriented RE projects. To this end, we conduct literature survey and domain analysis, thus presenting a taxonomy to show the different features of a requirements aspect. The sources of our survey focus mainly on asymmetric approaches and come primarily from the publications and reports in the literature, which can be found in [12].

Reference models with the unifying taxonomy represent prototypical models of some application domain, and have a time-honored status. One well-known example is the OSI 7-layer reference model, which divides network protocols into seven layers: physical, data link, network, transport, session, presentation, and application. The taxonomy of protocol layers is in widespread use, and is discussed in virtually every basic textbook on computer networks. The OSI 7-layer model is successful because it draws on what was already understood about the networks domain, thus codifying the core knowledge to be flexible.

Not every domain is sufficiently standardized to allow for a reference model or a unified taxonomy. In a blooming research field such as early aspects, people explore and tackle recognized problems complementarily, based on different mindsets and traditions. Various perspectives may not converge in a short period of time, which makes the conceptual unification process arduous and unproductive most of the time. As an example, the term "component" is used to describe rather different concepts in software engineering: subsystems, JavaBeans, ActiveX controls, .NET assemblies, CORBA components, and more. As we shall see in section 2, the term "requirements aspect" saliently resembles in this respect the notion of a component.

Moreover, approaches like the one followed by the OSI 7-layer model are not necessarily supportive of change, especially when this change goes beyond the initially covered domain. However, at least experience on how to get to the model and the taxonomy should be recorded and shared [29], as undeniably a contribution to knowledge. Along this line, we present an initial attempt to identify reusable resources in the domain of requirements aspects. In section 3, We document our domain analysis results – a taxonomy of requirements aspects – using feature diagrams [21], and then apply the taxonomy to compare existing approaches that deal with aspects at the requirements level.

To exemplify the taxonomy's use and substantiate its value, in section 4, we present a reified requirements aspect – security, one of the most mentioned crosscutting concerns in the current literature. We then review related work in section 5, and conclude the paper with a summary and some directions for future work in section 6.

2   A Teaser Description for Requirements Aspects

There exist several definitions and descriptions for the term "requirements aspect", one of them by the initiators of research in early aspects: Elisa Baniassad, Paul Clements, João Araújo, Ana Moreira, Awais Rashid, and Bedir Tekinerdoğan:

> "A requirements aspect, then, is a concern that cuts across other requirement-level concerns or artifacts of the author's chosen organization. It is broadly scoped in that it's found in and has an (implicit or explicit) impact on more than one requirement artifact." [5]

We will use it as a starting point for our further discussion. Let's consider some parts of this description in detail:

- "a concern": Calling a requirements aspect a concern develops strong ties with stakeholders of the intended software system. A requirements concern is a matter of relevance that conveys the problem domain's property of interest to specific stakeholders. Therefore, any requirements aspect has its intent or purpose of existence, and needs to be traced to some stakeholder interest. Addressing requirements concerns thus enhances the stakeholder satisfaction and the overall software quality.
- "cuts across": No matter how stakeholder concerns are structured, a requirements aspect crosscuts the dominant decomposition, i.e., the author's chosen organization. This view assumes that the author has chosen some dominant organizing decomposition structure at the requirements level first, and makes the crosscutting concern a second-class object. Actually, aspect has become an equivalent substitute for a crosscutting concern in the literature.

– "author's chosen organization": Current requirements techniques offer a variety of structures for organizing the requirements, such as (structured) natural languages, use cases, scenarios, viewpoints, goal models, features, etc. [26]. The requirements analyst (author) develops a relatively well-organized set of requirements based on some dominant decomposition criteria and chosen structures. Requirements aspects emerge as a result of the lack of additional decomposition dimensions of the author's chosen organization.

– "broadly scoped": The authors of the original article [5] stated that broadly scoped properties can be quality attributes (nonfunctional requirements) as well as functional concerns that the requirements engineer must describe with relation to other concerns. These broadly scoped properties manifest as scattered and tangled concerns in the author's chosen organization of requirements.

– "impact on": Requirements aspects do not exist in isolation. They need to contact other requirement-level concerns or artifacts to provide some service according to their purpose of existence. This service providing process, which is also known as aspect weaving, is *usually* done in an oblivious fashion, i.e., the service provider (aspect) is impelled toward the consumers without them being aware of aspect's existence. Recent work has pointed out that obliviousness is neither an essential nor a desirable property of aspects [32]. Nevertheless, aspects need to explicitly specify the conditions, locations, and implications of the intended interactions.

This description of the term "requirements aspect" is very generic and thus it is not surprising that the term is used to describe rather different concepts: a collaboration in requirements for software components [14], an extension in a use case diagram [20], a softgoal in a goal model [36], an instance of terminological interference in viewpoints-based requirements models [25], a non-functional requirement (NFR) in a software requirements specification [17], and more.

The purpose of this paper is to try to clarify these different views by providing a taxonomy for requirements aspects. We therefore do not try to give one concise, closed definition. Instead, we will show the different features and characteristics a requirements aspect must or can have, thereby classifying the different kinds of requirements aspects as they are used today.

3   A Feature Diagram for Requirements Aspects

This section presents the results of applying domain analysis to existing approaches that tackle requirements aspects. Domain analysis is concerned with analyzing and modeling the variabilities and commonalities of systems or concepts in a given domain, thereby developing and maintaining an information infrastructure to support reuse [11].

We document our domain analysis results – a taxonomy of requirements aspects – using feature diagrams [21]. Essentially, a feature diagram is a hierarchy

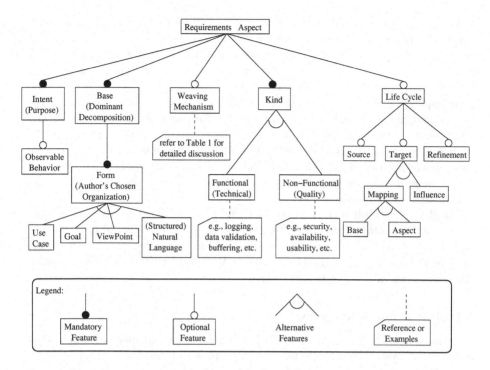

Fig. 1. A feature diagram for asymmetric requirements aspects

of common and variable features characterizing the set of instances of a concept [9]. In our case, the features provide a taxonomy and representation of design choices for approaches dealing with aspects at the requirements level.

We do not aim for this taxonomy to be normative and immune from change. In fact, the relatively new area of early aspects has already experienced many overloaded terms, and many of the terms we use in our taxonomy are often used differently in descriptions of other approaches. Consequently, we provide minute examinations of the terms and concepts as we use them. Furthermore, we expect the taxonomy to evolve as our understanding of requirements aspects matures. Our main goal is to show the vast range of available choices as represented by the current approaches, from a reuse perspective.

Figure 1 depicts a feature diagram we use as a basis for our discussion on requirements aspects. We deliberately restrict the diagrammatic notations in Fig. 1 to conforming with those originally proposed in [21], with reference and annotated examples provided to illustrate specific concepts. In particular, only three types of lines (edges) connecting boxes (nodes) are presented: mandatory, optional, and alternative (XOR-choice). This is because the notations in [21] are free of ambiguities, whereas later modified feature diagram variants are neither precise nor ambiguity-free [33]. While we will clarify the diagram semantics on the fly, we refer the interested reader to [21,9,33] for detailed discussion on feature modeling.

In Fig. 1, the features (denoted by the boxes) of the concept *requirements aspect* are described, which is located at the top of the feature diagram. The boxes directly connected to *requirements aspect* are the direct sub-features of a requirements aspect. The little circles at the edges connecting the features define the semantics of the edge. A filled circle means mandatory. Thus, every requirement aspect has an *intent* or *purpose* of existence, is of a certain *kind*, and cuts across multiple *base* modules according to the *dominant decomposition*. Optionally (denoted by the outlined circle at the edge), a requirements aspect provides *life cycle* information, and defines some *weaving mechanism*. Alternative features means an exclusive-or choice. For example, analysts organize requirements using one and only one base form in a particular RE stage like use cases, goals, viewpoints, and so forth.

We elaborate sub-features presented in Fig. 1 in the following sub-sections, and apply the taxonomy to compare different requirements aspects approaches. As long as we organize the discussion by (sub-)features, "aspects" emerge and cross-cut this dominant decomposition structure. We therefore discuss these crosscutting properties in a separate sub-section.

3.1   Intent and Life Cycle

An aspect represents some concern, which only matters to specific stakeholders of a software system. A requirements aspect represents stakeholder interest in the problem domain, including high-level concerns like user satisfaction and happiness, system qualities like security and efficiency, software capabilities like fault tolerance and persistent storage, overall considerations like development time and return on investment, and many others. Each requirements aspect, therefore, needs to have an intent to help justify its very existence with particular stakeholder interest.

In many cases, the intent is further formulated and elaborated through observable behaviors to reflect what the stakeholder has in mind to expect the software to do or bring about. For example, to ensure security, the software system shall disable user accounts after the wrong password is entered three times. These observable behaviors are what make the intent operationalizable and measurable. Naturally, test cases can be derived to check whether the resulting software meets the intent, addresses the stakeholder concern, and guarantees the desired behavior.

Test cases present an instance of the *life cycle* feature, which supports traceability of requirements aspects throughout the software development life cycle. Requirements traceability is defined by Gotel and Finkelstein [13] as the ability to describe and follow the life of a requirement in both a forwards and backwards direction, i.e., from its origins, through its development and specification, to its subsequent deployment and use, and through all periods of on-going refinement and iteration in any of these phases.

Tracing a requirements aspect backwards to its origins helps uncover its intent and the source of stakeholder interest: whether the aspect is a concern relating to business, technology, organization, process, etc. From the standpoint of aspect-oriented program analysis and evolution, this source information about requirements aspects provides a baseline to validate code aspects against stakeholder relevance: are they merely refactored based on particular implementations or originally required by specific stakeholders?

Tracing a requirements aspect forwards to its subsequent development involves systematic decision making. An aspect identified at the requirements level can be designed as a coherent module conforming with the author's chosen dominant organization structure. For example, synchronization can be mapped to a single class in an object-oriented implementation. Alternatively, a requirements aspect can be mapped to an architectural-, code-, or test-level aspect, following the aspect-oriented software development paradigm. This preserves the concern's crosscutting nature throughout the software development life cycle. Other than being modularized definitively in design and implementation, a requirements aspect can be recorded as a tentative issue to influence ensuing development and decision making.

This tentative tracing strategy allows requirements aspects to be refined so that nobody is forced to make premature design decisions. Refinement supports iterations of analysis and interactions with stakeholders. The goal is to elaborate requirements and architecture in parallel within the system context,[1] better determine what crosscuts what, and tease out the implications of the identified crosscuttings.

3.2   Base and Weaving

Traditional waterfall development process produces artificially frozen requirements documents for use in the next step in the development life cycle. Alternatively, this process creates systems with constrained architectures that restrict users and handicap developers by resisting inevitable and desirable changes in requirements. It would be imprudent to assume that one could fully understand and document system requirements up-front. In practice, key requirements are not fully understood until the architecture is baselined at the conclusion of the refinement and elaboration phase.

The Twin Peaks model presented by Bashar Nuseibeh [27] vividly depicts this iterative and progressive process, and strongly emphasizes the concurrent interplay between requirements and architecture: candidate architecture can constrain designers from meeting particular requirements, and the choice of requirements can influence the architecture that designers select or develop [27]. Although the Twin Peaks model develops requirements and architectural specifications concurrently, it continues to separate problem structure and specification from solution structure and specification, in an iterative process that produces progressively more detailed requirements and design specifications, as Fig. 2 suggests.

---

[1] We will discuss the Twin Peaks model of weaving together requirements and architecture [27] in more detail in the next sub-section.

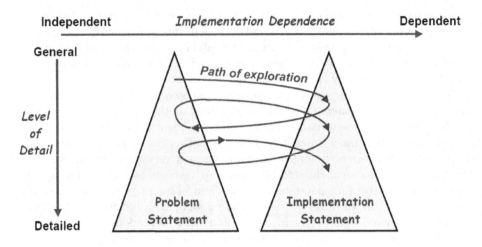

Fig. 2. The Twin Peaks model (*Adpated from [27]*)

The Twin Peaks model further suggests an agenda "from early aspects to late requirements", because identifying aspects too early is counterproductive [28]. Following this school of thought, we can safely assume an asymmetric, base-aspect separation approach to tackling requirements aspects. That is, progressively exploring crosscutting aspects is built upon a relatively well-structured set of requirements of the author's chosen base organization, with the form varies over a wide range: such as (structured) natural languages, use cases, viewpoints, goal models, etc. [26].

On the contrary, a symmetric approach does not separate base from aspects. There is no core system, and only one type of concern development process exists to create designs that realize crosscutting and non-crosscutting concerns [16]. Requirements are decomposed in a uniform fashion, which makes it possible to project any particular set of requirements on a range of other requirements [23], hence supporting a multi-dimensional separation of concerns [34].

In an asymmetric approach, parallel concern development processes coexist: one that creates and expands the base model and another that creates aspects that crosscut the base. An early identification of requirements aspects improves the base structure's modularity since scattered and tangled stakeholder interests are clarified. A requirements aspect does not exist in isolation. It needs to be progressive, as suggested by the Twin Peaks model in Fig. 2, and interact with base requirements in order to provide some service according to its intent. This service providing process is specified by certain weaving mechanisms.

It should be noted that, depending on how requirements aspects are modeled and traced in the software life cycle, one may not define a specific weaving mechanism for every requirements aspect. That is why weaving mechanism is an optional feature shown in Fig. 1. Nevertheless, requirements approaches that support early aspects analysis unexceptionally treat weaving as a crucial component.

Table 1. Comparison and classification of asymmetric requirements aspects approaches

Base Form	Requirements Aspects	Advices	Join Points	Pointcuts	Weaving	Sample Approach
use case	extensions	extension behaviors	extension points	list of extension points	extension composition	[20]
goal model	softgoals	advising tasks	goals and tasks	contribution links	composing algorithm	[36]
multi–stakeholder description	terminological interferences	vocabulary mappings	conflicts and correspondences	requirements discordances	reconciling concepts	[24,25]
viewpoint	concerns	stakeholder requirements	viewpoints	contribution table	resolving conflicts	[30,31]
problem frame	security	vulnerabilities	functional requirements	threat descriptions	composition process	[15]
natural language	non–functional terms	occurrences	requirements statements	indicator terms	information retrieval	[17]

We use AspectJ-like terminologies to compare and classify existing aspect-oriented requirements analysis approaches according to their base forms. To define the terms used in the comparison, we follow the metaphor that every requirements aspect acts as a service provider to some base modules.[2]

- **Advice** defines the body or the content of the service that a specific requirements aspect provides. It describes *what* the service is about.
- **Join points** are points in the base which a requirements aspect interacts with. They describe *where* the service is provided.
- **Pointcut** represents a set of join points. It describes the *situational patterns* of the service that an aspect provides.
- **Weaving** is the process of coordinating service providers (requirements aspects) and consumers (base requirements). It describes *when* and *how* the service takes place.

In addition, the mandatory feature "intent" of a requirements aspect describes *why* the service is needed in the first place. We interpret the above concepts from a requirements engineering perspective, as part of the primary contribution of this paper. Table 1 summarizes the comparison of requirements aspects approaches based on our proposed taxonomy and terminologies. We classify the asymmetric approaches according to their base forms, and provide sample references for each category. This examination and classification were performed

---

[2] The following interpretations of the concepts may depart from the traditional explanations developed from the aspect-oriented programming perspective, which can be found in [1], for example.

independently by the first author and the third author following a pre-defined artifact analysis protocol [8], and the differences were reconciled.

Note that the comparison presented in Table 1 is not intended to be exhaustive or complete by any means. What we desire is a way of framing our surveyed representative approaches under the umbrella of our conceptual framework, so that Table 1 both exemplifies the taxonomy's use and substantiates its value. One of our future research areas is to extend the comparison results in Table 1 to cover all the features presented in Fig. 1.

3.3 Kind

Aspects at the requirements level can be classified according to their kind, i.e., the matter they concern. Requirements standards and textbooks typically classify requirements into *functional* requirements on one hand, and *non-functional* requirements or attributes on the other hand. In this classification, requirements given in terms of required operations or data are considered to be functional, while quality requirements, such as performance, security, reliability, maintainability, are classified as non-functional.

A functional requirement can pertain to a function or to data. In mathematical terms, given any element, say x, in the domain, a function assigns exactly one element in the co-domain to x. Thus, a widespread function that a system shall perform, such as logging and tracking memory usage, is a functional requirements aspect. A functional aspect can also describe the data item or data structure that shall be part of a system's state, e.g., data integrity for multicast overlay networks. Besides, functional aspects can address crosscutting architectural and technical concerns like buffering and caching, as the Twin Peaks model in Fig. 2 shows.

Non-functional requirements address system qualities. They are typically broad in scope in that they have impacts on multiple requirements modules. Sample non-functional aspects include: performance in terms of time (points in time, reaction time, time intervals), speed, volume, throughput, or rates (volume per time unit), and properties of product management, such as availability, testability, interoperability, portability, etc. Security – one of the most mentioned non-functional requirements aspects – will be further discussed in section 4.

Note that there exist many requirements classification frameworks other than the functional versus non-functional one. For example, the satisfaction of requirements can be hard or soft, the representation of requirements can be operational, quantitative, qualitative, or declarative, and so forth. Discussion of specific schemes to classify requirements into different kinds is beyond the scope of this paper. What we want to emphasize here is that requirements aspects give rise to a separate dimension for stakeholders to concentrate on requirements crosscutting properties. And we have used the *de facto* classification scheme to show that both functional and non-functional requirements can be considered as aspects, provided that the concerns they address cut across other concerns of the base requirements structure.

3.4   Crosscutting Properties

In explaining and elaborating the proposed taxonomy, we use the feature diagram shown in Fig.1 as a baseline to present diverse characteristics a requirements aspect must or can have. As we choose features to organize our discussion, "aspects" that crosscut more than one feature emerge. We now discuss some of these crosscutting properties as follows:

- *Constraints*. A constraint is a limitation of possibilities. For example, a common constraint to the identification and modularization of aspects is the amount of time available for early requirements engineering activities.
- *Dependencies*. Determining a particular feature may rely on other features. For example, weaving mechanism highly depends on requirements base forms and related aspect concepts, as manifested in Table 1.
- *Trade-offs*. Trade-offs involve determining the optimum balance among certain factors. A trade-off analysis is a systematic examination of the advantages and disadvantages of the alternatives. For example, choosing between mapping and influence as target for an identified requirements aspect in the software life cycle invokes detailed trade-off analyses.
- *Rationale*. A rationale records an underlying reason or an explanation of controlling principles of opinion, choice, or practice. For example, the rationale of using natural language as the base form is to facilitate the contractual process for requirements procurement.
- *Consistency*. Maintaining consistency helps achieve harmony of features to one another and as a whole. For example, resolving conflicts is crucial for viewpoint-based frameworks to weave requirements aspects, as indicated in Table 1.

The above is only a partial list of interplays between features shown in the taxonomy. Nevertheless, it illustrates the necessity and importance of understanding these interplays for effectively managing requirements aspects.

4   A Reified Requirements Aspect – Security

To further explore the usefulness of the taxonomy, we study one of the most discussed requirements aspects in the literature – security, which tends to be stated as a crosscutting concern that impacts many requirement-level concerns and artifacts.

Security requirements are concerned with how assets are to be protected from harm [22]. An asset is something in the context of the system, tangible or not, that is to be protected [18]. A threat is the potential for abuse of an asset that will cause harm in the context of the problem. A vulnerability is a weakness in the system that an attack exploits. Security requirements are constraints on functional requirements intended to reduce the scope of vulnerabilities. Thus, security requirements stipulate the elimination of vulnerabilities that an attacker can exploit to carry out threats on assets, thereby causing harm [15].

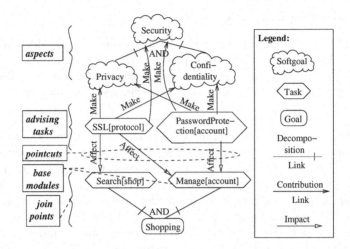

Fig. 3. Security aspects in requirements goal models (*Adpated from [25]*)

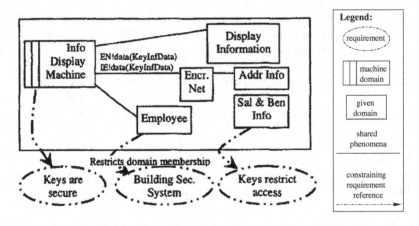

Fig. 4. Security aspects in problem frames (*Adpated from [15]*)

In many practices, the security needs of a given system are often not de-termined until well into the implementation, resulting in late and expensive attempts to shoehorn security into the work in progress [15]. This leads to the situation that security requirements are often stated in terms of *how* (e.g., the system shall use cryptography), and not in terms of *what* problems to be solved in the first place, leaving it unclear how the security requirements affect other stakeholder concerns.

Treating security as a requirements aspect helps first determine what crosscuts what, and then tease out the implications of this crosscutting. We demonstrate the applicability and competence of the taxonomy described in section 3 by delineating sample aspect approaches that deal with security requirements. The

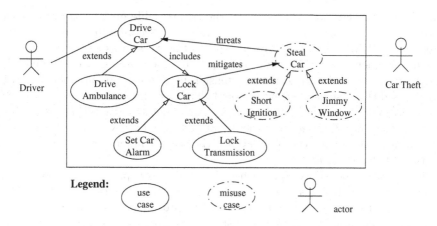

Fig. 5. Security aspects in (mis)use cases

discussions are structured by the base forms of the authors' chosen organizations: goal models, problem frames, and use cases. A more detailed investigation that aims to cover all features in Fig. 1 is currently under planning.

The context of Fig. 3 are goal models developed for a media shop to investigate requirements for new on-line services [25]. In Fig. 3, security is expressed as a softgoal to suggest that intended software is expected to satisfy the security requirements within acceptable limits, rather than absolutely [7]. As Table 1 indicates, softgoals in a goal model are requirements aspects, and concrete tasks such as SSL[protocol] are advices which are to be weaved into proper join points (hard goals and functional tasks). Composing algorithms are defined in [36] to guide the weaving procedure.

Figure 4 illustrates the work on deriving security requirements from crosscutting threat descriptions [15]. Problem frames are used as requirements base form to provide a shape of a solution for various problem classes [19]. In Fig. 4, functional requirements, such as "salary and benefits information shall be available to each managerial employee for perusal", are represented by problem frames and give vulnerabilities. Threat descriptions like "releasing salary information to unauthorized individuals could damage the company's reputation" help determine which functional requirements are exposed to specific vulnerabilities. Vulnerabilities are then ameliorated by security requirements, which are expressed as frames' constraints like "keys restrict access" and "restricts domain membership". Details of the composition process of weaving threat descriptions into problem frames are discussed in [15].

A misuse case is a use case from the point of view of an actor hostile to the system under design. Its goal is not a system function, but a threat posed by that hostile actor. One of the applications of misuse cases is to elicit security requirements [2]. Figure 5 shows a scenario in which malign agents and misuse cases are explicitly modeled. This helps to focus attention on the struggle against exposed threats. For example, in Fig. 5, the car theft's intention is to break into the car and to short the ignition, thus stealing the car, possible mitigating approaches are to set the car alarm, or lock the transmission. According to Jacobson [20], extensions in UML share much of the spirit of aspects in aspect-oriented software development: they both allow developers to slice a system over all life cycle models. It is important to keep the extension mechanism nonintrusive, i.e., aspects extend the base use case with more behavior without having to change the base. The goal is to achieve modular design and code by structuring them from a base and let the system grow without cluttering the base with statements that have nothing to do with the base, even if the statements are important for the additional behavior [20].

Discussion of the above approaches shows that our proposed taxonomy of requirements aspects indeed serves as an umbrella for a variety of ideas. The non-functional security requirements intend to protect assets from harm. They cut across many author's chosen base structures: goal models, problem frames, and use cases. They are modularly represented, successively refined, and systematically composed with functional requirements in order to guide development throughout the entire software life cycle.

5   Related Work

The early aspects Web portal [12] remains one of the most comprehensive resources for investigating current challenges and exploring future directions on aspect-oriented requirements engineering and architecture design. Two early aspects landscape reports are available in the Web portal.

In [4], the authors lay out a conceptual landscape for how the concept of early aspects pertains to domain analysis, requirements engineering, and architectural design. The report distills all the concepts special to each, and provides a conceptually unified view of early aspects in general. An extensive survey of aspect-oriented requirements engineering approaches is provided. An aspect at the requirements level is defined as a broadly-scoped property, represented by a single requirement or a coherent set of requirements (e.g., security requirements), that affects multiple other requirements in the system so that: 1). it may constrain the specified behavior of the affected requirements; 2). it may influence that affected requirements in order to alter their specified behavior [4]. Our taxonomy of requirements aspects enhances this view with emphasis on the intent behind this constraining and influence. Besides the behavioral view, our proposed taxonomy also captures requirements aspects' structural and life cycle properties.

The authors of [6] provide a survey of contemporary aspect-oriented analysis and design approaches, considering their origins, aims, and contributions. A very general description is given for requirements aspects: "if some requirements are not effectively modularized, ... such requirements are termed crosscutting (or aspectual) requirements" [6]. In order to compare existing aspect-oriented analysis and design approaches, the authors define some metrics: traceability, composability, evolvability, and scalability. While our taxonomy clearly fine-tunes the description about requirements aspects provided in this survey, the comparison criteria characterized in [6] supplement our work in quality issues of requirements aspects approaches.

Requirements aspects often recur in the literature. For instance, security is the most prevalent requirements aspect discussed in nearly all aspect-oriented requirements engineering approaches. Orthogonal to the taxonomy proposed in this paper, catalogue or ontology-based approaches attempt to collate, from a wide range of sources, verifiable information in specific domains. Along this line, the most relevant work to requirements aspects is the non-functional requirements catalogue devised by Chung and his colleagues [7]. Non-functional requirements are hard to be allocated into independent modules, therefore have huge potential to become candidate early aspects [25]. One of the main motivations of catalogue or ontology building is the possibility of knowledge sharing and reuse: as soon as a particular domain is fixed (e.g., security of a media shop as shown in Fig. 3), it seems reasonable to expect a large part of domain knowledge to be the same for a variety of applications (e.g., security of information display in Fig. 4 and of car antitheft in Fig. 5), so that the high costs of knowledge acquisition can be better justified. Non-functional requirements or requirements aspects catalogue building could benefit from our work since the taxonomy helps filter out feature nuggets one needs to consider when cataloguing requirements aspects.

The idea of using feature diagrams to depict a concept has become popular in software engineering, since feature modeling overcomes the drawback of presenting domain knowledge in a flat and coarse form. Recent work has been carried out in understanding both familiar and relatively new concepts. For example, the notion of components is investigated by Voelter [35], and a feature-based survey of model transformation approaches is provided by Czarnecki and Helsen [10]. These pieces of work greatly inspired us to explore the notion of requirements aspects. The taxonomy proposed in this paper is, to the best of our knowledge, the first attempt to characterize the concept of requirements aspects using feature diagrams in order to efficaciously serve the early aspects community.

6   Summary and Future Directions

Maintaining a clear separation of concerns throughout the software life cycle has long been a goal of the software community. Aspects provide the mechanism that enables the source code to be structured to facilitate the representation of multiple perceptions and to alleviate tangling and scattering concerns. Many of these concerns often arise in the problem domain [28], and, therefore, it is important to identify and represent concerns that arise during the early phases of software development, and to determine how these concerns interact. The Twin Peaks model [27] suggests that at the stage when requirements need to be mapped onto elements of a software solution, identifying aspects may become much more worthwhile.

In this paper, we have presented a preliminary attempt to structure the requirements aspects domain with a taxonomy, characterizing mandatory, optional, and alternative features of a requirements aspect as it is used today in the literature. We then use the taxonomy to compare and classify existing requirements engineering approaches that handle aspects. We have also studied crosscutting security requirements to exemplify the taxonomy's use, substantiate its value, and demonstrate its applicability and usefulness.

The work reported here can be continued in many directions. Obviously, the literature study we based the taxonomy could be expanded, either within the published work or by consulting researchers and practitioners in the community. Also of interest would be extending the taxonomy to cope with symmetric, multi-dimensional concern separation, approaches. Moreover, the future research agenda includes investigating the taxonomy's applicability to handle architectural-, code-, and test-level aspects. Furthermore, it is necessary to establish comparison criteria and metrics in order to conduct a more critical examination that is intended to clarify what is better and/or worse in every considered approach. Finally, experience from practical applications will have to be evaluated with respect to the taxonomy's usefulness: should it be modified, simplified, or extended with additional features?

The area of early aspects continues to be a subject of intense research. The time is ripe for consolidating early aspects knowledge into a set of polished best practices and patterns. We hope the proposed generic, feature-based taxonomy of requirements aspects can be an important contribution to existing knowledge, advance the current state of the art, and serve as a basis for more rigorous investigations in this area.

Acknowledgement. We would like to thank Awais Rashid for helpful remarks, and Krzysztof Czarnecki for help with feature modeling. Financial support was provided by NSERC.

References

1. Aspect-oriented software development community wiki (Last accessed on april 16, 2007), http://www.aosd.net/wiki/
2. Alexander, I.: Initial industrial experience of misuse cases in trade-off analysis. In: Intl. RE Conf., pp. 61–68 (2002)
3. Araújo, J., Whittle, J., Kim, D.-K.: Modeling and composing scenario-based requirements with aspects. In: Intl. RE Conf., pp. 58–67 (2004)
4. Araújo, J., Baniassad, E., Clements, P.C., Moreira, A., Rashid, A., Tekinerdoğan, B.: Early aspects: the current landscape. Technical Report COMP-001-2005, Lancaster Univ. (2005)
5. Baniassad, E., Clements, P.C., Araújo, J., Moreira, A., Rashid, A., Tekinerdoğan, B.: Discovering early aspects. IEEE Software 23(1), 61–70 (2006)
6. Chitchyan, R., Rashid, A., Sawyer, P., Garcia, A., Alarcon, M., Bakker, J., Tekinerdoğan, B., Clarke, S., Jackson, A.: Survey of aspect-oriented analysis and design approaches. AOSD-Europe-ULANC-9, AOSD Europe (2005)

7. Chung, L., Nixon, B.A., Yu, E., Mylopoulos, J.: Non-Functional Requirements in Software Engineering. Kluwer Academic Publishers, Dordrecht (2000)
8. Course Website – Empirical Research Methods in Software Engineering (last accessed on april 16, 2007), http://www.cs.toronto.edu/~sme/CSC2130
9. Czarnecki, K., Eisenecker, U.W.: Generative Programming: Methods, Tools, and Applications. Addison-Wesley, Reading (2000)
10. Czarnecki, K., Helsen, S.: Feature-based survey of model transformation approaches. IBM Systems Journal 45(3), 621–645 (2006)
11. P.-Díaz, R.: Domain analysis: an introduction. ACM SIGSOFT Softw. Eng. Notes 15(2), 47–54 (1990)
12. Early aspects portal (Last accessed on april 16, 2007), http://www.early-aspects.net/
13. Gotel, O., Finkelstein, A.: An analysis of the requirements traceability problem. In: Intl. Conf. on RE, pp. 94–101 (1994)
14. Grundy, J.: Aspect-oriented requirements engineering for component-based software systems. In: Intl. Symp. on RE, pp. 84–91 (1999)
15. Haley, C.B., Laney, R.C., Nuseibeh, B.: Deriving security requirements from cross-cutting threat descriptions. In: Intl. Conf. on AOSD, pp. 112–121 (2004)
16. Harrison, W.H., Ossher, H.L., Tarr, P.L.: Asymmetrically vs. symmetrically organized paradigms for software composition. RC22685, IBM Thomas J. Watson Research Center (2002)
17. Cleland-Huang, J., Settimi, R., Zou, X., Solc, P.: The detection and classification of non-functional requirements with application to early aspects. In: Intl. RE Conf., pp. 39–48 (2006)
18. ISO/ICE: information technology – security techniques – evaluation criteria for IT security. Geneva Switzerland: ISO/IEC (1999)
19. Jackson, M.: Problem Frames. Addison Wesley, Reading (2001)
20. Jacobson, I.: Use cases and aspects – working seamlessly together. Journal of Object Technology 2(4), 7–28 (2003)
21. Kang, K.C., Cohen, S.G., Hess, J.A., Novak, W.E., Peterson, A.S.: Feature-oriented domain analysis (FODA) feasibility study. Technical Report CMU/SEI-90-TR-21, Software Engineering Institute, Carnegie Mellon Univ (1990)
22. Moffett, J.D., Nuseibeh, B.: A framework for security requirements engineering. YCS368, Dept. of Computer Science, Univ. of York (2003)
23. Moreira, A., Araújo, J., Rashid, A.: A concern-oriented requirements engineering model. In: Pastor, Ó., Falcão e Cunha, J. (eds.) CAiSE 2005. LNCS, vol. 3520, pp. 293–308. Springer, Heidelberg (2005)
24. Niu, N., Easterbrook, S.: Analysis of early aspects in requirements goal models: a concept-driven approach. In: Trans. on AOSD (to appear, 2007)
25. Niu, N., Easterbrook, S.: Discovering aspects in requirements with repertory grid. In: Early Aspects Wkshp at ICSE, pp. 35–41 (2006)
26. Nuseibeh, B., Easterbrook, S.M.: Requirements Engineering: A Roadmap. In: The Future of Software Engineering, IEEE Computer Society Press, Los Alamitos (2000)
27. Nuseibeh, B.: Weaving together requirements and architectures. IEEE Computer 34(3), 115–117 (2001)
28. Nuseibeh, B.: Crosscutting requirements. In: Intl. Conf. on AOSD, pp. 3–4 (2004)
29. Ramesh, B., Jarke, M.: Toward reference models for requirements traceability. IEEE Trans. Softw. Eng. 27(1), 58–93 (2001)
30. Rashid, A., Sawyer, P., Moreira, A., Araújo, J.: Early aspects: a model for aspect-oriented requirements engineering. In: Intl. RE Conf., pp. 199–202 (2002)

31. Rashid, A., Moreira, A., Araújo, J.: Modularisation and composition of aspectual requirements. In: Intl. Conf. on AOSD, pp. 11–20 (2003)
32. Rashid, A., Moreira, A.: Domain models are not aspect free. In: Intl. Conf. on MoDELS/UML, pp. 155–169 (2006)
33. Schobbens, P.-Y., Heymans, P., Trigaux, J.-C.: Feature diagrams: a survey and a formal semantics. In: Intl. RE Conf., pp. 139–148 (2006)
34. Tarr, P.L., Ossher, H., Harrison, W.H., Sutton, S.M.: N degrees of separation: multi-dimensional separation of concerns. In: ICSE, pp. 107–119 (1999)
35. Voelter, M.: A taxonomy of components. Journal of Object Technology 2(4), 119–125 (2003)
36. Yu, Y., do Prado Leite, J.C.S., Mylopoulos, J.: From goals to aspects: discovering aspects from requirements goal models. In: Intl. RE Conf., pp. 38–47 (2004)

Flexible and Expressive Composition Rules with Aspect-oriented Use Case Maps (AoUCM)

Gunter Mussbacher[1], Daniel Amyot[1], Jon Whittle[2], and Michael Weiss[3]

[1] SITE, University of Ottawa, 800 King Edward, Ottawa, ON, K1N 6N5, Canada
{gunterm, damyot}@site.uottawa.ca
[2] Information & Software Engineering, George Mason University,
Fairfax, VA 22030, USA
jwhittle@gmu.edu
[3] School of Computer Science, Carleton University, 1125 Colonel By Drive, Ottawa,
ON, K1S 5B6, Canada
weiss@scs.carleton.ca

Abstract. Technologies based on aspect-orientation and multi-dimensional separation of concerns have given software engineers tools to better encapsulate concerns throughout the software lifecycle. Separated concerns must be composed, even during early lifecycle phases, to obtain an overall system understanding. Concern composition languages therefore must be expressive, scalable, and intuitive. Otherwise, gains achieved by concern separation are offset by the complexity of the composition rules. This paper focuses on a composition language for the requirements modeling phase and, in particular, on composition of concerns described with use cases or scenarios. We propose that existing composition techniques (such as before and after advices from AOP) are insufficient for requirements model composition because they do not support all composition rules frequently required for use cases or scenarios. Furthermore, composition rules for a modeling language should be visual and use the same notation as the modeling language. This paper presents Aspect-oriented Use Case Maps (AoUCM) and evaluates its flexible, expressive, and exhaustive composition technique. Moreover, the composition rules are expressed in the same notation already used for UCMs. The usefulness and necessity of our composition rules are demonstrated through examples modeled with the jUCMNav tool.

Keywords: Aspect-oriented Requirements Engineering, Aspect Composition, Use Case Maps, Scenario Notations, User Requirements Notation.

1 Introduction

Aspects have been accepted into the array of software engineering techniques because of their ability to encapsulate concerns which are notoriously difficult to modularize with the chosen dominant modularization technique alone (e.g. with object-oriented concepts). At any stage of the software development lifecycle, however, separate concerns must be composed together in order to gain a greater understanding of the overall system. Existing approaches for concern

A. Moreira and J. Grundy (Eds.): Early Aspects 2007 Workshop, LNCS 4765, pp. 19–38, 2007.

composition at the requirements level do not allow general composition rules to be expressed, but are largely based on the composition rules of aspect-oriented programming (AOP) or ad-hoc extensions of them (i.e. the insertion of behavior before, after, or around a specific location in the base model). More complex composition rules, however, are necessary to model systems in practice [27].

Aspect-oriented Use Case Maps (AoUCM) [17,18] are a modeling technique for early aspects and model concerns expressed as use cases or scenarios at an abstraction level suitable for requirements models (i.e. a level where interactions between model entities are important, but details of messages and data are not yet relevant). AoUCM are an extension of the Use Case Maps (UCMs) [23] modeling language. This paper a) introduces a case study of an Online Newspaper Management System in order to illustrate frequently required composition rules for scenario-based models, and b) provides a qualitative evaluation of the general concern composition technique of AoUCM based on the following properties for the composition of aspect-oriented requirements models:

Oblivious. A composition technique should allow concerns to be defined without changes to other concerns. This is a crucial point of aspect-orientation as a concern must not be polluted by non-concern-specific information.

Exhaustive. Models may be composed in many different, complex, and unexpected ways. A composition technique must be exhaustive in that it should provide the means to express all desired compositions. Considering frequently required composition rules for scenario-based approaches, composition rules should therefore cover not just sequences and alternatives (i.e. before/after/around) but make use of all constructs of the modeling language (e.g. concurrency, loops, and interleaving).

Scalable. A composition technique should scale to large industrial models. In most cases, this means that composition rules have to be parameterized in some way in order to cope with large numbers of similar compositions.

Familiar. In order to ease adoption of the composition technique, the composition language should be a language that is already familiar to requirements engineers. If the chosen language is a visual language, then the composition rules should also be visual in order to avoid switching between modeling paradigms (e.g. by using graphical and purely textual representations at the same time).

Formal. The composition technique should be as formal as possible without becoming a barrier in practice.

At the right abstraction level. For a composition technique to be effective for requirements models, the employed technique should be at the right abstraction level where message or data details of interactions are not yet relevant.

Note that if the modeling language used for the system is also chosen as the language for the composition technique, the composition properties *exhaustive* and *familiar* are already addressed.

In the remainder of this paper, Sect. 2 gives an overview of Use Case Maps and aspect-oriented Use Case Maps. Section 3 shows how complex compositions can be modeled with aspect-oriented Use Case Maps and presents an example system as an illustration for such compositions. Section 4 gives a comparison of scenario-based modeling techniques for aspect-oriented requirements. Section 5 concludes the paper and identifies future work.

2 Background

2.1 Use Case Maps

Use Case Maps (UCMs) [23] are a visual scenario notation that is being standardized by the International Telecommunication Union (ITU) as part of the *User Requirements Notation* (URN) [24]. Within URN, UCMs are complemented by a language for goal modeling and the description of nonfunctional requirements (GRL – the Goal-oriented Requirement Language [22]). URN is the first standardization effort to address links between goal and scenario models explicitly in a graphical way.

UCMs are ideally suited for the description of functional requirements and, if desired, high-level design. Paths describe the causal flow of behavior of a system (e.g. one or many use cases). By superimposing paths over components, the architectural structure of a system can be modeled. In general, components describe any kind of structural entity at any abstraction level (e.g. classes or packages but also systems, actors, sub-systems, objects, aspects, hardware). UCMs focus on the interaction between architectural entities without going into the details of message exchange and communication infrastructures. As many scenarios and use cases are integrated into one combined UCM model of a system, it is possible to use UCM specifications as a base for further analysis. Undesired interactions between scenarios can be detected, performance implications can be analyzed, testing efforts can be driven based on the UCM model, and various architectural alternatives can be analyzed. Over the last decade, UCMs have successfully been used for service-oriented, concurrent, distributed, and reactive systems such as telecommunications systems, agent systems, e-commerce systems, operating systems, and health information systems. UCMs have also been used for business process modeling. For further information, the reader is referred to the UCM Virtual Library [21].

The basic elements of the UCM notation are shown in Fig. 1. A *map* contains any number of *paths* and structural elements (*components*). *Responsibilities* describe required actions or steps to fulfill a scenario. Paths express causal sequences. *OR-forks* (possibly including guarding *conditions*) and *OR-joins* are used to show alternatives, while *AND-forks* and *AND-joins* depict concurrency. Loops can be modeled implicitly with OR-joins and OR-forks. UCM models can be decomposed using *stubs* which contain sub-maps called *plug-ins*. Plug-in maps are reusable units of behavior and structure. *Plug-in bindings* define the continuation of a path on a plug-in by connecting in-paths and out-paths of a

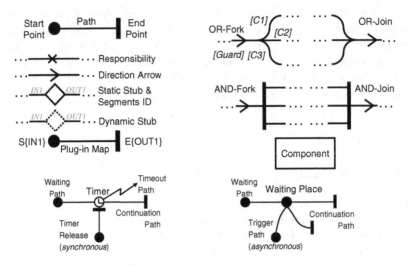

Fig. 1. Basic Elements of UCM Notation

stub with start and end points of its plug-ins, respectively. A stub may be *static* which means that it can have at most one plug-in, whereas a *dynamic* stub may have many plug-ins which may be selected at runtime. A *selection policy* decides which plug-ins of a dynamic stub to choose at runtime. Map elements which reside inside a component are said to be *bound* to the component. Components have various types and characteristics (not discussed in this paper) and can contain sub-components.

Other notational elements of UCMs are *timers* and *waiting places*. A timer may have a *timeout path* which is indicated by a zigzag line. A waiting place denotes a location on the path where the scenario stops until a condition is satisfied. If an endpoint is connected to a waiting place or a timer, the stopped scenario continues when this end point is reached (synchronous interaction). Asynchronous, in-passing triggering of waiting places and timers is also possible. A more complete coverage of the notation elements is available in [1,7,9,23].

The Eclipse-based jUCMNav [19] is an editing tool for UCMs developed at the University of Ottawa and Carleton University. The tool makes it possible to create, maintain, analyze, and transform UCM models. It is a true URN tool that offers GRL modeling in addition to UCM modeling.

2.2 Aspect-oriented Use Case Maps

A shortcoming of object-oriented software engineering is that units of interest to the requirements engineer (i.e. *concerns*) cannot readily be encapsulated with object-oriented units [11]. This leads to concern *scattering* (parts of a concern are scattered over many classes) and concern *tangling* (one class contains parts of many different concerns). This effect is due to the tyranny of the dominant decomposition [20], as a chosen modularization technique (e.g. objects) inevitably will cause unwanted side-effects in the model to which the technique is applied (e.g. scattering and tangling). In the mid 1990s, *aspect-oriented programming* (AOP) [14] emerged to address these shortcomings based on a more general philosophy called *multi-dimensional separation of concerns* (MDSOC) [11,20]. Many concerns exist for which aspects provide a better encapsulation than objects (e.g. authorization/authentication, caching, concurrency management, debugging, distribution, logging, testing, transaction management, or even use cases [13]). A defining characteristic of these concerns is that they *crosscut* other concerns multiple times (i.e. each concern needs to be merged with many other concerns).

Aspects identify locations in a model (called *joinpoints*) through parameterized expressions (called *pointcuts*). Joinpoints are defined in a *joinpoint model* that clearly defines all possible locations in the modeling or programming language. Aspects specify *advice* (behavior and possibly structure) which will be inserted into the locations specified by pointcuts. Note that we are using AspectJ terms [5], but that the concepts also apply to other flavors of AOP and aspect-oriented modeling in general.

Aspect-oriented Use Case Maps (AoUCM) [17,18] extend UCMs with the concepts of aspect, advice map, pointcut stub, and pointcut map in order to enable the modeling of concerns. These concepts, however, do not require new notational elements as they are just specializations of already existing concepts. The concrete syntax of UCMs does not need to be altered, allowing the requirements engineer to continue using UCMs as before.

A prerequisite for the extension of the UCM modeling language is the existence of a *joinpoint model* for AoUCM. For AoUCM, any path element is deemed to be a joinpoint, except for purely visual elements such as direction arrows. This allows an aspect to add behavior and structure not only relative to responsibilities (i.e. functionality) but also relative to causal flow constructs such as alternatives, concurrency, and loops.

In the context of AoUCM, an *aspect* is simply an organizational construct that contains all the UCMs required to describe a concern. In particular, it contains any number of specialized maps called advice maps and pointcut maps. These types of maps are used to specify crosscutting behavior. Note that the dashed arrows in Fig. 2 and most following figures are not part of the UCM notation but have been added to the figures to clearly indicate plug-in bindings for the UCM model (the jUCMNav tool manages plug-in bindings much more concisely).

An *advice map* is syntactically the same as a traditional UCM as it describes behavior and structure in the same way as UCMs do. As the name suggests, an advice map specifies the advice (or behavior and structure) of a concern that needs to be added to the base model. The differentiating factor between an advice map (see Advice Map in Fig. 2) and a traditional map (see Base Model in Fig. 2) is that advice maps contain one or more pointcut stubs. A *pointcut stub* is a placeholder for pointcut expressions which in turn identify joinpoints in the AoUCM model. Pointcut stubs are structurally the same as dynamic stubs but have a slightly different semantic meaning (indicated by the P in the dynamic stub symbol). While dynamic stubs contain plug-in maps that further describe

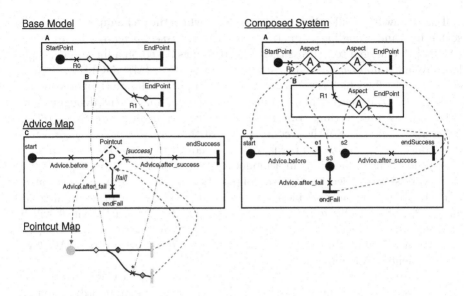

Fig. 2. Basic Elements of AoUCM Notation

the structure and behavior of a system, pointcut stubs contain zero or more pointcut maps. This is the only semantic change to traditional UCMs required in order to model concerns with AoUCM.

A *pointcut map* visually defines a pointcut expression. For example, the pointcut map in Fig. 2 matches against all maps that contain an OR-fork followed by a responsibility on at least one branch. The wildcard "*" indicates that any responsibility will be matched. The usage of wildcards ensures that more than one location in the base model can be identified by one single composition rule. In addition to "*", logical operators such as "and", "or", and "not" can also be used. Start and end points without labels are not included in the match but only denote the beginning and end of the partial map to be matched (therefore they are shown in gray in Fig. 2). Note that a pointcut map is structurally the same as a traditional UCM. Although not shown here, a pointcut map can contain UCM components (e.g. component A and B from the base model). In fact, any behavioral or structural UCM modeling element can be used on a pointcut map, allowing a wide array of partial maps to be matched. More examples of pointcut maps are available in [17,18].

By modeling advice and pointcut expressions on separate maps, each can be reused independently from the other. For example, an advice map can be used in another UCM model because new pointcut expressions specific to the UCM model can be plugged into the pointcut stub as desired. Similarly, the same pointcut map can be used for different aspects.

The relative locations of pointcut stubs and advice indicate where advice needs to be inserted into the base model. *Composition rules* are therefore defined

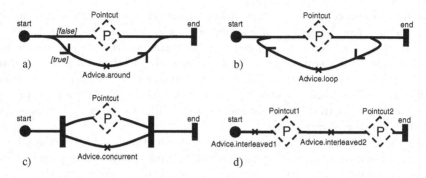

Fig. 3. More Examples of Composition Rules

in a visual way. Figure 2 shows that Advice.before must be inserted before the joinpoint identified by the expression in the pointcut stub. Advice.after_returning and Advice.after_throwing are inserted after the identified joinpoint in the success case and fail case, respectively. In addition to the composition rules before and after, advice maps can also easily model the composition rule around (see Fig. 3.a) as well as loops (see Fig. 3.b), concurrency (see Fig. 3.c), and interleaving (see Fig. 3.d). Figure 3 shows very clearly the separation of pointcut expression and composition rule. For each advice map in Fig. 3 (except obviously Fig. 3.d), the pointcut expression may be the same as each pointcut stub may contain the same pointcut map. The composition rules, however, are specified on the advice map and differ in each case. The pointcut stubs in Fig. 3.d reference two different locations of a scenario in order to interleave the advice of the aspectual scenario with the referenced scenario.

Since advice maps are structurally the same as standard UCMs, it is possible to define aspects on other aspects. Pointcut maps are simply also matched against advice maps in addition to standard UCMs.

The small diamonds in Fig. 2 identify the insertion points in the base model and the long-dash-dot-dotted lines without arrowheads show the mapping of the pointcut expression to the base model (i.e. the mapping shows how the pointcut expression matches the base model). Any AoUCM tool must retain the mappings and insertion points in order to navigate and reason about the AoUCM model in an aspect-oriented way. For example, the notational element for an insertion point could be the small diamond, and double-clicking on the small diamond could present a list of all mapped (i.e. matching) pointcut expression to the requirements engineer. Selecting one of them could take the requirements engineer to the advice map where the relevant portion of the map could be highlighted.

Furthermore, visualizing the composed system with standard UCMs is also quite straightforward for AoUCM models as shown in Fig. 2. The visualization is based on the insertion of *aspect stubs* that are placed at the insertion points identified by the small diamonds in the base model. An aspect stub contains plug-in maps that describe the relevant path segment of the advice map according to the composition rules defined on advice maps. A stub is ideally suited to describe the result of composition rules. If more than one concern needs to add advice to the same location in the base model, a dynamic stub can be used instead of a static stub. The dynamic stub will then contain a plug-in map for each added advice. At the least, the dynamic stub indicates potential conflicts in the composed system. Even if concerns do not add advice to the same locations but to different locations on the same UCM, stubs are essential to reduce the complexity of maps.

In order to visualize the composed system with standard UCMs, the advice map is first transformed into a standard UCM with several paths by removing the pointcut stub. Each of these paths corresponds to an advice. On the advice map, each advice is connected to the pointcut map through a plug-in binding (see dashed arrows in Fig. 2; for example, Advice.before is connected with the start point on the pointcut map by the left-most plug-in binding of the pointcut stub). Furthermore, each plug-in binding unambiguously identifies one insertion point (e.g. the plug-in binding that points to the start point in Fig. 2 identifies the left-most insertion point on the pointcut map and consequently the left-most insertion point in the base model). This establishes which advice must be inserted at which insertion point in the base model. When an aspect stub is added to the base model at a particular insertion point, the path with the correct advice can now be plugged into the aspect stub. For more details on the visualization of the composed system and the techniques used to carry out composition of AoUCM see [18].

3   Composition of Aspect-oriented Use Case Maps

While Mussbacher et al. [17,18] introduced the principles of AoUCM (as summarized in Sect. 2.2), this section describes with the help of an example how compositions that are much more complex can be modeled exhaustively with AoUCM. This is useful since Whittle et al. [27] have shown that complex composition rules are necessary in practice.

As explained in Sect. 2.1, the UCM modeling notation contains modeling elements to describe basic causal flow constructs such as sequence, alternatives, concurrency, and loops. Most scenario-based modeling and programming languages have the same constructs. Therefore, we claim that it is useful and necessary for AoUCM (and other aspect-oriented modeling languages) to compose concerns at a minimum in sequence (before and after), as alternatives (around), in parallel, and in loops. Typical aspect-oriented modeling techniques based on scenarios and programming languages only cover the first two compositions but not the last two. In addition, two concerns modeled as scenarios are often arbitrarily interleaved with each other. Therefore, we claim that an exhaustive composition technique should provide the means to model interleaved concerns separately without loosing the overall flow of each individual concern and without loosing the concern's context within the system. Finally, any combination of these compositions may occur and is only restricted by the expressiveness of the modeling language itself. We claim that an exhaustive composition technique must be able to deal with such compositions and should only be restricted by the syntax of the modeling language in use.

In order to motivate and substantiate our claim of being able to model exhaustively complex compositions with AoUCM, we present an example system, first as a traditional UCM model (see Sect. 3.1) and then refactored using AoUCM (see Sect. 3.2). The example system is based on a management system supporting the various workflows involved in producing an online newspaper. The UCM model describes selected workflow scenarios for one of the actors, the reporter. The example system, although simple, already requires the use of complex composition rules.

3.1   UCM Model of the Online Newspaper Management System

The following use cases are described in the UCM model in Fig. 4, consisting of one root map at the left and three plug-in maps bound to the stubs in the root map as indicated.

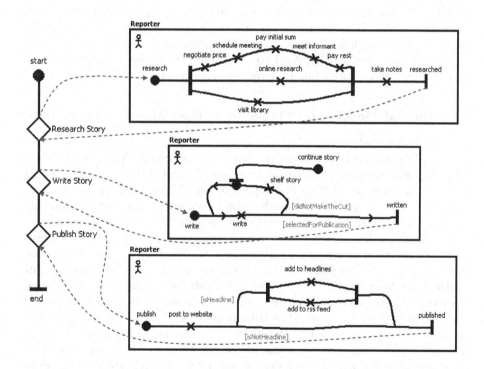

Fig. 4. Traditional UCM Model of Online Newspaper System

Research Story. The reporter meets with informants, researches the story online and in the library, and takes notes after doing so.

Write Story. The reporter writes the story after researching it. The story is shelved if it does not make the cut for publication but may be continued at a later point.

Publish Story. After writing the story, it is published at the newspaper's website. If the story is very important, it is also added to the headline section of the website and to the RSS feed.

These three use cases are sufficiently separated in the UCM model. Various concerns, however, are described within each of these use cases.

Research Story contains three responsibilities – negotiate price, pay initial sum, and pay rest – that are related to paying the informant. As this may not apply to all informants or company policy may not allow for it at some point, these three responsibilities should be factored out into the **Pay Informant** scenario. This is an example for interleaved scenarios. Note that it is not possible to model each of the two interleaved scenarios on a separate map with traditional UCMs without breaking up one of the scenarios into several disjoint paths or loosing its contextual information.

Write Story also contains two concerns: writing and shelving a story. This is an example of two concerns that may occur in a loop where one concern is enabling another which in turn enables the first one. **Shelf Story** should be factored out.

Finally, Publish Story addresses the concern related to RSS feeds in addition to the standard publishing process. As RSS technology may change or may be replaced by other technology, **Add to RSS Feed** should be factored out. This is an example of a composition that requires concurrency.

3.2 AoUCM Model of the Online Newspaper Management System

The aspect-oriented version of the example system captures the following six concerns in separate maps: Research Story, Pay Informant, Write Story, Shelf Story, Publish Story, and Publish To RSS Feed. Not all of these are crosscutting concerns but each one of them is encapsulated in its own aspect in the AoUCM model in order to increase modularity. For each concern, the composition rule and, if applicable, the crosscutting type are indicated in parentheses.

Fig. 5 shows the various advice maps, pointcut stubs, and pointcut maps necessary to describe the system. **Research Story** (Fig. 5.a, no composition rule) does not need a pointcut stub and map because it is the base map in this model. Note, however, that Write Story or Publish Story could have been chosen just as likely as the base map because there is only a simple sequence relationship between these three concerns. **Pay Informant** (Fig. 5.b, composition rule and crosscutting type: interleaving) describes the three responsibilities related to this concern and identifies two pointcuts on the Research Story map. Note how the use of several pointcut stubs enables the reader to understand the context under which the behavior for Pay Informant is executing. At the same time, the causal relationships between the three responsibilities related to the Pay Informant concern are clearly expressed on one map.

Write Story (Fig. 5.c, composition rule: after) indicates that its behavior occurs after Research Story by reusing the Research Story map as a pointcut map. The Research Story map is plugged into the pointcut stub on the Write Story map. **Shelf Story** (Fig. 5.d, composition rule: loop) identifies a pointcut on the Write

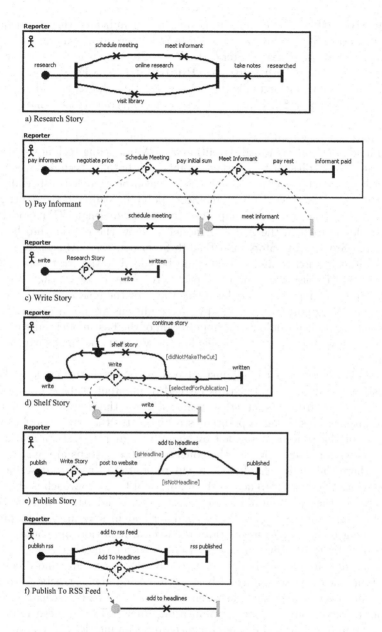

Fig. 5. AoUCM Model of Online Newspaper System

Story map and describes the loop behavior between these two scenarios. The map shows that the reporter can choose to continue writing the story. In this case, the loop is executed again.

Publish Story (Fig. 5.e, composition rule: after) indicates that its behavior occurs after Write Story by reusing the Write Story map as a pointcut map. Similarly to the reuse of Research Story, the Write Story map is plugged into the pointcut stub on the Publish Story map. **Publish To RSS Feed** (Fig. 5.f, composition rule: concurrent) extends the behavior of Publish Story by identifying a pointcut on the Publish Story map and describing the concurrent behavior to be added.

The approach taken for the model in Fig. 5 deliberately focuses on aspect-oriented modeling and disregards traditional UCM modeling techniques such as root maps and conditions for starting points. With these techniques some of the causal relationships between concerns can also be modeled (especially, the relationships described by the Research Story pointcut stub and the Write Story pointcut stub). The same root map used for the traditional UCM model (see Fig. 4) could be used in the AoUCM model to show the relationship between the Research Story, Write Story, and Publish Story concerns. Alternatively, conditions such as researched and written could be added to the start points of the Write Story and Publish Story maps, respectively. Note, however, that only simple sequential ordering can be modeled this way. For the relationships expressed with the remaining pointcut stubs in Fig. 5, conditions are not appropriate and the root map approach would result in pollution of the base model. Furthermore, our experience with large UCM models has shown that root maps can become very complex.

One could also argue that Fig. 5 just advocates good structuring methods and that existing UCMs with static stubs instead of pointcut stubs could be used. While this is true from a syntactical point of view, there are conceptual and practical implications. Using a pointcut stub indicates that this model element is not part of the concern described by the advice map whereas a static stub describes behavior that is part of the concern. Pointcut stubs are only used to indicate where the advice should occur, but they are not used to describe concern behavior. The key difference to the traditional UCM approach is that each scenario would then be polluted by other concerns. In addition, the traditional approach often results in concerns being described in several disjoint plug-in maps, making it difficult to understand the overall behavior and context. This occurs especially when scenarios are interleaved with each other.

The examples in Fig. 5 show that, even in simple systems, more complex composition rules beyond the usual before/after/around constructs are needed to model all causal relationships between concerns expressed as scenarios or use cases. Shelf Story requires a loop composition, Publish To RSS Feed requires a concurrent composition, and Pay Informant requires an interleaving composition. Each composition rule is useful since they allow the requirements engineer to keep all concerns separate from each other in the AoUCM model.

The number of composition rules, however, is not restricted to sequence, alternatives, concurrency, loops, and interleaving. Any number of combinations can be described visually with the AoUCM notation. The composition technique is therefore only limited by the modeling notation itself. Any causal relationship

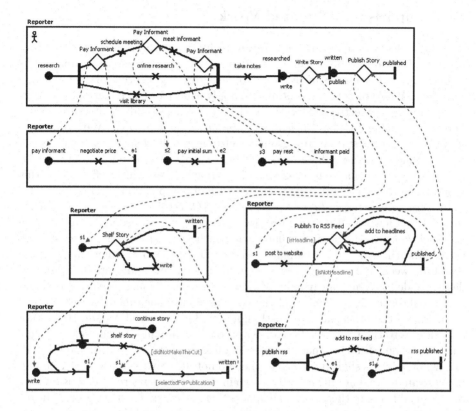

Fig. 6. Composed System

between scenarios or use cases that can be modeled with the UCM notation can also be used in a composition rule. Composition rules have the same expressiveness as the modeling notation and are therefore *exhaustive*.

The composed system is shown in Fig. 6. It is very similar to the traditional UCM model, the difference being that concerns are now encapsulated in stubs instead of described with responsibilities directly on the maps of a base scenario. In all cases, stubs are added directly to the map identified by the pointcut map. Note that the top-down approach with a root map in the traditional UCM model has been replaced by a more peer-oriented approach.

Fig. 6 is the result of merging all defined concerns into a composed system. This is not always the case as the inclusion of a concern in the composed system is optional, making it easier to select a set of scenarios or use cases for a particular system version.

The current algorithm for merging all advice maps into the composed system simply adds stubs to the appropriate locations on the base maps [18]. This approach clearly identifies concerns added to the base behavior but may result in more complicated maps in some cases. We leave the investigation of other heuristics for merging advice maps with the base model as future work (see Sect. 5).

4   Comparison of Related Work

Initially, aspects were an implementation technique with an ever-growing number of tools for major programming languages [2]. Now, the aspect-community is focusing on earlier phases in the software development lifecycle. *Aspect-oriented modeling* (AOM) or *early aspects* aims to apply aspect-oriented concepts in order to manage more effectively concerns at the requirements and architecture stages. Many approaches to *aspect-oriented requirements engineering* (AORE) are described in a recent survey [10], grouped into viewpoint, goal, scenario/use case, concern, and component-based approaches. As AoUCM are more closely related to the group of scenario/use case-based approaches, we will briefly review this group in more detail with respect to their use of composition techniques.

In *Aspect-Oriented Software Development (AOSD) with Use Cases* [13], Jacobson and Ng view a well-written use case as a concern. Jacobson and Ng describe how such concerns can be encapsulated with the help of aspect-oriented techniques throughout the software development lifecycle. In doing so, the fundamental mismatch between units of interest in requirements models and units of interest in design models is significantly reduced. The focus of the book, however, is on structural analysis/design models and the composition of such models. Behavioural modeling on the other hand is mostly ignored. Jacobson and Ng add the notion of *pointcuts* to the traditional use case approach. Pointcuts in one use case reference extension points in other use cases in a textual way. The traditional usage of extension points is slightly altered as they do not directly reference the extending use case anymore, but only identify a step in the use case where an extension may occur. In addition to the traditional *application use cases*, Jacobson and Ng introduce new kinds of use cases, the *infrastructure use case* and the *perform transaction use case*. The former describes scenarios required to address non-functional requirements. The latter is a generic description of all possible types of interactions an actor may have with the system. Infrastructure use cases reference pointcuts in the perform transaction use case which is eventually mapped to application use cases. This effectively weaves aspect behaviour described by infrastructure use cases into application use cases. The composition of concerns, however, is limited to extension use cases during use case modeling and to AspectJ-like constructs (before/after/around) in later phases.

In *Scenario Modeling with Aspects* [25], Whittle and Araújo use UML sequence diagrams to describe non-aspectual scenarios and sequence-diagram-like *interaction pattern specifications* (IPS) to describe aspectual scenarios. IPS define roles for classifiers, messages, and parameters which can be bound to elements in other sequence diagrams in order to create a composed system, which is then translated into state machines for validation. Alternatively, the sequence diagrams and IPS are first both translated into state machine representations (finite state machines and *state machine pattern specifications* (SMPS), respectively) and then composed together at the state machine level [4] with the same binding technique. SMPS are state machines that also define roles. In both cases, the binding is specified textually and identifies explicitly elements to be bound. On one hand, this allows for a very flexible composition that is as expressive as the modeling language itself. On the other hand however, explicit bindings do not scale as well as parameterized bindings since each binding must be specified individually.

The *Aspectual Use Case Driven Approach* is the third major research direction discussed for scenario/use-case based approaches in [10]. Moreira *et al.* [3,16] propose to add extensions to UML use case and sequence diagrams in order to visualize how crosscutting non-functional requirements are linked to functional requirements expressed by use case diagrams or sequence diagrams. Non-functional requirements are captured with the help of templates. [15] builds on this work, extending the set of use case relationships to include "constrain", "collaborate", and "damage" relationships and making use of *activity pattern specifications* (APS). The new relationships describe how one use case impacts another (restricting it, contributing positively to it, or contributing negatively to it). APS extend UML activity diagrams by allowing the specification of roles similar to IPS [25] and SMPS [4]. APS are used to describe use cases in more detail. Various activity diagrams are composed by composition rules which are similar to the binding in [4,25].

Barros and Gomes [6] apply aspect-orientation to UML activity diagrams. The approach is based on an additional composition operation called *activity addition* which allows the fusing of stereotyped nodes in one activity diagram with nodes in another. Stereotyping is effectively used as a pointcut expression, identifying explicitly nodes in another activity diagram for behavior merging.

Whittle *et al.* [27] suggest a composition technique based on graph transformation formalisms that could be applied to any UML model even though their research's focus is on UML state diagrams. Graph transformation rules (i.e. composition rules) are described with state diagrams containing pattern variables. These variables are matched against elements in other state diagrams. The matching criteria are based on the UML metamodel for state diagrams. Once a match is found, the match is transformed into a new composed state diagram according to the graph transformation rule. Similarly, Whittle *et al.* [26] use graph transformations to compose sequence diagrams.

In the UCM community, the applicability of UCMs to model aspects was identified very early on by Buhr [8] but received little attention since then with the exception of de Bruin and van Vliet [12]. The approach suggested by de Bruin and van Vliet, however, pollutes each map (*not oblivious*) and *does not scale* very well as it requires the addition of "Pre" and "Post" stubs for each location on a UCM that requires a change. These stubs allow the current behaviour and structure to be refined with additional pre/post-processing in a top-down approach, thus limiting composition rules to after and before (*not exhaustive*).

As illustrated in Sect. 3, aspect-oriented scenarios or use cases can be modeled with AoUCM without any new notational concepts *(familiar)*. All elements of a concern can be modeled visually and without polluting the base model with concern-specific information *(oblivious)*. Our experience with standard UCM models and aspect-oriented UCM models indicates that AoUCM is at least as scalable as standard UCM models. Parameterized pointcut expressions further improve *scalability*. Given the abstract nature of UCMs, concerns can be modeled at the *right level of abstraction* for requirements models where often message and data details of interactions are not yet relevant. The composition rules described with AoUCM are also *exhaustive* because the same notations are used to describe the system itself and the composition rules.

Graph transformation-based approaches [26,27] to composition of aspect-oriented models also address most of the properties discussed in the previous paragraph when applied to requirements models at the right abstraction level. In addition, graph transformation-based approaches have a *formal* foundation which is an advantage over the *semi-formal* nature of the composition rules in AoUCM. Specifications for graph transformation rules, however, may become too complex, possibly requiring training in formal methods. While graph transformations are very powerful and can be applied to any language defined by a metamodel, they do require the modeler to learn a new pattern language for matching joinpoints (*not familiar*).

In general, approaches based on AspectJ-like composition rules are not exhaustive for requirements models since only a fixed and limited set of rules – namely before, after, and around – can be used, leading to scalability issues as large models must be broken down before the rules can be applied [27]. Approaches based on MDSOC are also not exhaustive because a predefined merge algorithm is used and not all compositions can be easily expressed. Overriding of default settings is possible but very low-level and not graphical [27]. Neither of these composition approaches satisfies all properties identified in Sect. 1, in particular complex composition rules cannot be expressed.

The remaining scenario/use case-based approaches to AORE mentioned in this paper successfully address only some but not all of the properties listed in Table 1. Jacobson and Ng [13] add the new concept of pointcut to use case modeling and change the meaning of extension points (*not familiar*). Concurrency, loops, and interleaving are not addressed (*not exhaustive*). Extension points are also still added directly to the base model causing the base model to be polluted with concern-specific information (*not oblivious*).

Moreira *et al.* [3,15,16] require several extensions to UML diagrams in order to visualize aspects (*not familiar*) and does not address concurrency, loops, and interleaving (*not exhaustive*). Barros and Gomes [6] also do not explicitly address concurrency, loops, and interleaving (*not exhaustive*).

Compared to the rigor and *formal* foundation of graph transformations, all other composition techniques qualify at the most as semi-formal notations. Most approaches are problematic in terms of *scalability* because composition rules identify targets of the composition only explicitly: Moreira *et al.* [3,15,16] represent composition rules in an explicit and textual way without allowing parameterized expressions. Whittle and Araújo [4,25] use textual and non-parameterized binding rules. Barros and Gomes [6] also use a textual representation of pointcuts and also explicitly link nodes in UML activity diagrams, not allowing parameterized expressions. Jacobson and Ng [13], however, address scalability to a certain degree by modeling perform transaction use cases that capture generic interactions between an actor and the system.

In terms of *abstraction levels*, AoUCM are at a higher level of abstraction than the work by Whittle and Araújo [4,25] which is at the message/state machine level. Moreira et al. [3,15,16] make use of some models that are at the same and some models that are at a lower level of abstraction than AoUCM. All other approaches are at the same abstraction level as AoUCM.

Table 1. Comparing Composition Techniques of Scenario-Based Approaches to AORE

O ... Oblivious, E ... Exhaustive, S ... Scalable
Fa ... Familiar, Fo ... Formal, AL ... Abstraction Level

	O	E	S	Fa	Fo	AL
Jacobson and Ng [13] (AOSD with Use Cases)		X			1)	X
Whittle and Araújo [4,25] (Scenario Modeling with Aspects)	X	X		X	1)	
Moreira et al. [3,15,16] (Aspectual Use Case Driv. Appr.)	X				1)	
Barros and Gomes [6] (UML Activity Diagram)	X			X	1)	X
Whittle et al. [26,27] (Graph Transformation)	X	X	X		X	X
de Bruin and van Vliet [12] (Quality-Driven Sw. Arch. Comp.)				X	1)	X
Aspect-oriented Use Case Maps (AoUCM) [17,18]	X	X	X	X	1)	X

1)   Only qualifies as a semi-formal composition technique compared to graph transformations.

5   Conclusion

This paper evaluates AoUCM for the specification of complex composition rules for aspect-oriented requirements models based on scenarios or use cases. Several required properties of such a composition technique were identified in Sect. 1 and were listed again in Table 1. Of all discussed techniques, AoUCM and graph transformation-based approaches satisfy most the desired properties. While AoUCM is a familiar but semi-formal notation, graph transformation-based approaches are more formal but may require special training.

Future work could try to reduce the complexity of maps in the composed system. The composed system in Fig. 6 can be generated automatically with the lowest level maps in Fig. 6 corresponding to advice maps and all other maps corresponding to composed maps. Heuristics for a better visualization of the composed system should be investigated. For example, root maps could be used for some composition rules. Composition rules involving concurrency and loops

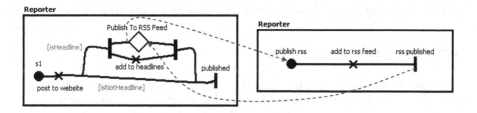

Fig. 7. Different Visualization of Publish Story in Composed System

could show concurrency and loops at the level of composed maps and not at the level of advice maps (see Fig. 7 for an example). This raises an interesting question of what portion of the advice map should remain in the advice map level of the composed system and what should be visible at the composed map level. Another avenue to explore with respect to visualization is the flattening of maps in the composed model. For example in Fig. 6, the following three pairs of maps could each be flattened into one map: Research Story and Pay Informant, Write Story and Shelf Story, and Publish Story and Publish To RSS Feed. Combined with a root map approach for simple sequences, the result could be the original UCM model from Fig. 4. In any case, heuristics would have to include criteria to identify advice maps for which a visualization method other than the standard one should be used.

A combination of the rigor of graph transformation and the intuitive nature of AoUCM may be promising. AoUCM could serve as a front-end for graph transformation-based approaches if advice maps and pointcut maps could be automatically translated into pattern descriptions suitable for the graph transformation-based approach. The notions of pattern variable from graph transformation-based approaches and pointcut stub from AoUCM seem to be sufficiently similar in order to do so.

UCMs have been used for feature interaction detection [21]. This research could be applied to aspects as it allows properties such as pre-conditions and post-conditions of individual aspects to be defined which can then be checked in the composed system.

Jacobson and Ng [13] have shown that use cases can be encapsulated with the help of aspects not just in requirements models but also in (detailed) design models and the implementation because the aspect compiler can reliably merge use cases. This allows for clear traceability links to be established between requirements models, design models, and the implementation. Future work could investigate programming constructs that best support composition rules such as loops, concurrency, and interleaving and how to represent them in (detailed) design models.

A more detailed usability study is also required to shed further light on the advantages and disadvantages of the discussed approaches.

The Goal-oriented Requirement Language (GRL) [22], which is the complement of UCMs in the User Requirements Notation (URN), is another area for future work. Aspect concepts could be added to GRL and complex composition rules for GRL could be investigated. If successful, URN would combine aspect-oriented, goal-oriented, and scenario-based modeling techniques in one framework.

Acknowledgments

This research was supported by the Natural Sciences and Engineering Research Council of Canada, through its programs of Discovery Grants and Postgraduate Scholarships, and by the Ontario Research Network on e-Commerce.

References

1. Amyot, D.: Introduction to the User Requirements Notation: Learning by Example. Computer Networks 42(3), 285–301 (2003)
2. AOSD Community Wiki (accessed January 2007), `http://aosd.net/wiki/index.php?title=Research_Projects` and `http://aosd.net/wiki/index.php?title=Tools_for_Developers`
3. Araújo, J., Moreira, A.: An Aspectual Use Case Driven Approach. VIII Jornadas de Ingeniería de Software y Bases de Datos (JISBD 2003), Alicante, Spain (November 2003)
4. Araújo, J., Whittle, J., Kim, D.: Modeling and Composing Scenario-Based Requirements with Aspects. In: RE 2004. Proceedings of the 12th IEEE International Requirements Engineering Conference, Kyoto, Japan, pp. 58–67. IEEE CS Press, Los Alamitos (2004)
5. AspectJ web site (accessed January 2007), `http://www.eclipse.org/aspectj/`
6. Barros, J.-P., Gomes, L.: Toward the Support for Crosscutting Concerns in Activity Diagrams: a Graphical Approach. In: Workshop on Aspect-Oriented Modelling (held with UML 2003), San Francisco, California, USA (October 2003)
7. Buhr, R.J.A., Casselman, R.S.: Use Case Maps for Object-Oriented Systems. Prentice-Hall, Englewood Cliffs (1996)
8. Buhr, R.J.A.: A Possible Design Notation for Aspect Oriented Programming. In: Jul, E. (ed.) ECOOP 1998. LNCS, vol. 1445, Springer, Heidelberg (1998)
9. Buhr, R.J.A.: Use Case Maps as Architectural Entities for Complex Systems. IEEE Transactions on Software Engineering 24(12), 1131–1155 (1998)
10. Chitchyan, R., et al.: Survey of Analysis and Design Approaches. AOSD-Europe Report ULANC-9 (May 2005) (acc. January 2007), `http://www.aosd-europe.net/deliverables/d11.pdf`
11. Clarke, S., Baniassad, E.: Aspect-Oriented Analysis and Design: The Theme Approach. Addison Wesley, Reading (2005)
12. de Bruin, H., van Vliet, H.: Quality-Driven Software Architecture Composition. Journal of Systems and Software 66(3), 269–284 (2003)
13. Jacobson, I., Ng, P.-W.: Aspect-Oriented Software Development with Use Cases. Addison-Wesley, Reading (2005)
14. Kiczales, G., Lamping, J., Mendhekar, A., Maeda, C., Lopes, C., Loingtier, J.-M., Irwin, J.: Aspect-Oriented Programming. In: Aksit, M., Matsuoka, S. (eds.) ECOOP 1997. LNCS, vol. 1241, pp. 220–242. Springer, Heidelberg (1997)
15. Moreira, A., Araújo, J.: Handling Unanticipated Requirements Change with Aspects. In: Proceedings of the 16th International Conference on Software Engineering and Knowledge Engineering (SEKE), Banff, Canada (June 2004)
16. Moreira, A., Araújo, J., Brito, I.: Crosscutting Quality Attributes for Requirements Engineering. In: SEKE. Proceedings of the 14th International Conference on Software Engineering and Knowledge Engineering, Ischia, Italy, pp. 167–174. ACM Press, New York (2002)
17. Mussbacher, G., Amyot, D., Weiss, M.: Visualizing Aspect-Oriented Requirements Scenarios with Use Case Maps. In: International Workshop on Requirements Engineering Visualization (REV 2006), Minneapolis, USA (September 2006)
18. Mussbacher, G., Amyot, D., Weiss M.: Visualizing Early Aspects with Use Case Maps. To appear in Transactions on Aspect-Oriented Software Development

19. Roy, J.-F., Kealey, J., Amyot, D.: Towards Integrated Tool Support for the User Requirements Notation. In: Gotzhein, R., Reed, R. (eds.) SAM 2006. LNCS, vol. 4320, pp. 198–215. Springer, Heidelberg (2006), http://www.softwareengineering.ca/jucmnav

20. Tarr, P., Ossher, H., Harrison, W., Sutton, S.M.: N degrees of separation: Multidimensional separation of concerns. In: Proceedings of the 21st Intl. Conference on Software Engineering (ICSE 99), IEEE, Los Angeles, ACM press, pp 107–119 (May 1999)

21. UCM Virtual Library (accessed January 2007), http://jucmnav.softwareengineering.ca/twiki/bin/view/UCM/UCMVirtualLibrary

22. URN - Goal-oriented Requirement Language (GRL), ITU-T Draft Recommendation Z.151. Geneva, Switzerland (September 2003) (accessed January 2007), http://www.UseCaseMaps.org/urn

23. URN - Use Case Map Notation (UCM), ITU-T Draft Recommendation Z.152. Geneva, Switzerland (September 2003) (accessed January 2007), http://www.UseCaseMaps.org/urn

24. User Requirements Notation (URN) - Language Requirements and Framework, ITU-T Recommendation Z.150. Geneva, Switzerland (February 2003) (accessed January 2007), http://www.itu.int/ITU-T/publications/recs.html

25. Whittle, J., Araújo, J.: Scenario Modelling with Aspects. IEE Proceedings - Software 151(4), 157–172 (2004)

26. Whittle, J., Araújo, J., Moreira, A.: Composing Aspect Models with Graph Transformations. In: Early Aspects at ICSE: Workshop in Aspect-Oriented Requirements Engineering and Architecture Design, Shanghai, China (May 2006)

27. Whittle, J., Araújo, J., Moreira, A., Rabbi, R.: Graphical Composition of State-Dependent Use Case Behavioral Models. ISE Department Technical Report, George Mason University, ISE-TR-07-01 (accessed January 2007), http://ise.gmu.edu/techrep/2007

Improving Functional Testing Through Aspects: A Case Study

Paolo Salvaneschi

University of Bergamo, Faculty of Engineering
and Salvaneschi & Partners
paolo.salvaneschi@unibg.it

Abstract. It is shown how the aspect-oriented approach may help the design of a functional test plan of a product not specified using aspect-orientation. The method derives, from the available documentation, a hierarchy of functions (base functional model) and identifies the crosscutting relevant functions (for instance a user process involving more elements of the base models or a state-transition model for an application object). Specific testing techniques are chosen for the base functions (e.g. combinatorial approaches) and for the crosscutting functions (e.g. a control flow model and path coverage approach). We present and discuss the application of the method to the on going test of a large health care application: prescription and administration of pharmacological drugs (both for protocol based therapies for oncology and non protocol based ones) in a hospital.

Keywords: Aspect oriented functional testing, Aspect oriented requirements, Experience report.

1 Introduction

The issue of functional requirements identification has been thoroughly addressed by traditional requirements engineering. The result of this phase is a specification document providing a list of functions to be implemented.

Aspect-Oriented requirements engineering approaches improve the traditional requirements engineering explicitly recognizing the importance of clearly addressing both functional and non-functional crosscutting concerns, in addition to non-crosscutting ones.

The specification document (both based on a non-aspect oriented or an aspect oriented analysis) is the basis for deriving a functional test plan (a set of test cases designed using only the specification of a program and not its design or implementation structure), which is the most widely used verification approach [15]. For testing purposes, in many cases the information included in the document is complemented by the observation of the implemented product (for example a form may include a number of details abstracted in the initial specification).

The functional test plan usually assumes [15] that the specification is a hierarchy of functions to be tested through some testing strategy. In this approach each function is

A. Moreira and J. Grundy (Eds.): Early Aspects 2007 Workshop, LNCS 4765, pp. 39–54, 2007.

tested in isolation. A limitation of the approach is that functional aspects that are paths through many functions are not explicitly tested, even if they are very important for the application. For example in an e-catalog application developed for supporting the procurement process of a large retail company, it is reasonable to test every function (for example every form and every equivalence class of the form input data). This strategy only considers a functional hierarchy and doesn't explicitly test the authorization process flowing through the forms or the possible state changes of a product in the catalog caused by the execution of forms. Both these aspects are important for the application and their test should be added to the test of forms. A partial solution of this problem is the use case based testing technique. A use case is a specific use of the application, flowing through many functions [18] (See section 4 to compare our approach with the use case base testing).

The availability of aspect-oriented requirements influences the functional testing strategy. A good strategy should take into account both the functional hierarchy and the important functional crosscutting concerns that have been identified.

Even if the specification document doesn't make use of the AOSD approaches, the identification of the most critical crosscutting functions is useful for improving the test quality. This is the specific issue we are dealing with in this paper.

Note that we focus on functional aspects and we do not consider the non-functional ones. This is in general true, even if, in the case study, we tested some additional aspects related to the safety characteristic of the software product.

In section 2 we describe a process of functional testing improvement through the discovery and the exploitation of functional crosscutting concerns. The artifacts delivered by the process are also described. The process is supported, for the specific application area of Information Systems, by a classification of crosscutting functions that are common in this area.

Section 3 demonstrates the application of the process to the on going test of a large health care application: the management of medicinal drugs (both for protocol based therapies for oncology and non protocol based ones) in a hospital.

Section 4 compares the method with the existing approaches.

Section 5 discusses the scope and the advantages of the method. It is also discussed the level of guideline and support it provides.

Finally, section 6 comments the limitations and the possible improvements and draws some conclusions.

2   Improving Functional Testing Through Aspects

The class of software products we are referring to is composed of Information Systems applications in industry or public administration. In the majority of cases, these systems are composed of form-based interactive components, batch procedures and data structures hosted in a relational database.

The initial assumption of the method is the availability of a specification document of the software product to be tested. In many real cases this document provides an abstract view of system functions that is not sufficient for designing a set of test cases (a test plan). In this case the implementation itself (for instance the forms) is used as additional specification. It is also assumed the availability of people knowing the application domain. This will help the discovery of existing crosscutting functions. Finally we assume that the specification task didn't use the concept of aspect orientation.

This set of assumptions is important because it identifies a large set of presently developed applications.

Functional testing is mostly used for validating this type of applications.

As stated in [15] "functional testing, or more precisely, functional test case design, attempts to answer the question "What test cases shall I use to exercise my program?" considering only the specification of a program and not its design or implementation structure".

A methodology for functional test design [15] systematically helps by decomposing the functional test design activity into elementary steps. Complex functions are decomposed for generating a hierarchy of elementary functions to be tested through some testing strategy.

According to this methodology, the functional testing process includes the following steps:

1. Write a hierarchy of functions;
2. Apply a risk analysis for ranking the functions (most critical classes of functions will be tested more thoroughly);
3. Define testing techniques (for example equivalence partitioning of input) and coverage criteria [15];
4. Establish the testing strategy according to the risk ranking (define techniques and coverage criteria for each class of functions);
5. Write the list of test cases (the test plan);
6. Execute the test cases and report the results.

The process doesn't include the consideration of crosscutting functions. Basing a testing plan on just a hierarchical decomposition misses important aspects to be tested. For example a critical business process crosscutting a number of functions, or constraints affecting the change of state of an application entity through the execution of different functions, will not be specifically considered in this testing strategy.

A better strategy should also include test cases for validating the correct flow of control and information through the functions supporting the business process and the correct state changes of the application entity.

If we improve the testing process using the concepts of aspect orientation we provide a new useful tool for verifying a large class of applications. Moreover, as we will see in the following, a side effect of the process is the delivery of models of the important crosscutting functions. This provides an additional benefit because it improves the quality of the requirements document and delivers an additional support for the evolution of the system.

The new process improves the standard process above mentioned, adding the discovery, modeling and testing the important crosscutting functional requirements. It is composed of the following steps:

1. Derive, from the available documentation, a hierarchy of functions (base functional model);
2. Identify the crosscutting relevant functions. The discovery process uses the domain knowledge and can take advantage of the classification showed in fig. 1. The result of the step is a list of functions and a short description for each of them.

Classes of crosscutting functions for Information Systems	
Important Business processes	Important business processes that are not confined in a function of the base model but flow through a number of them. Example of relevance criteria are: – Most relevant for the success of the application; – Most difficult or complex; – To be executed in critical conditions (for example emergency or stress conditions).
States / transitions of application objects	State and transitions of application objects (data structures) that change their state through the execution of more than one function of the base model.
Common services	Functional aspects, visible to users, that provide common services to many functions of the base model. Examples are: – History or version management. The data base maintains an historical record of the data structures changes or maintains multiple versions of the data structures. Many functions are involved in the management; – Logging. The user actions are logged for certification and further analysis.
Internal common services	Aspects that are critical for the correct behavior of functions but are working in background and provide technical support to many functions of the base model. They are not directly visible to users. They are not necessarily defined in the specification document and their identification may require some knowledge of the internal design of the software product. Examples are: – Transaction management in case of multiple data structures. In this case the transaction management is programmed in the developed code and not simply delegated to the RDBMS system. Many functions are involved in the management; – Long transactions management. A transaction may remain open for long time across functions.

Fig. 1. Classification of crosscutting functions for the application area "Information Systems"

3. Apply a risk analysis for ranking both crosscutting and non crosscutting functions;
4. Choose the testing techniques suitable for the base functions (e.g. combinatorial approaches);
5. Choose the testing techniques for the crosscutting functions (e.g. a control flow model and path coverage approach);
6. Establish the testing strategy according to the risk ranking (define techniques and coverage criteria for each base or crosscutting function);
7. If required by the testing strategy, model the crosscutting functions;
8. Write the test plan;
9. Execute and report the results.

Step 1 doesn't change the standard functional testing process.

In step 2 we identify the most critical crosscutting functions through the following process:

– Study the base functional model and the available documentation.
– Organize meetings with the domain experts and, through the knowledge from documentation and experts, identify the existence of crosscutting functions.
   The classification of fig 1 provides help for this task. The table includes types of crosscutting functions that are frequent patterns of Information Systems.
– For each crosscutting function, mark the related functions in the hierarchy and annotate a short story of the function.

Step 3 applies a risk analysis for ranking both crosscutting and non-crosscutting functions. For example functions that may lead, in case of misbehaviors, to significant economical losses are ranked with very high risk level; important business processes are ranked with high level and the remaining functions are ranked with medium level.

The delivered artifacts (new with respect to a standard test plan) are a hierarchical functional model (base model) and a list of aspect-based functions.

Each function has an associated risk level and a description (or a link to existing descriptions and screenshots). Each aspect-based function is related to the crosscutted functions of the base model.

In step 4 and 5 we select, for each level, the more suitable testing techniques.

The testing techniques may vary according to crosscutting or non-crosscutting functions. For instance, a widely used technique for testing a form-based function is the quantization of the input space (through the definition of equivalence classes; see [15] for details of the technique) and the application of some combinatorial testing technique (for example one-wise or two-wise combinatorial coverage [15]).

Crosscutting functions will be tested through different techniques. For example a business process could be modeled describing the control flow through the process steps. In this case a structural testing technique may be applied (for example one can generate a test case set with full decisions covering or with full paths and level one of loops deepness covering [15]).

The testing strategy (step 6) assigns the specific technique and coverage criterion to each function (both crosscutting and non crosscutting) according to the risk ranking.

If required by the testing strategy, the crosscutting functions are modeled through a formal language (for example a Petri Net or a Finite State Automaton) for supporting the definition of the test cases set through a well-founded coverage criterion (step 7). This may be required also for non-crosscutting function, even if, for the class of systems we are dealing with, it is less usual. On the contrary, this modeling need is useful for the crosscutting functions. Examples may be the model of an important business processes trough a Petri Net or the model of a transaction through multiple data structures using a Finite State Automaton.

The delivered artifact (new with respect to a standard test plan) is a set of models related to the aspect-based functions.

Finally in step 8 and 9 the test cases are written and executed and the results are reported.

Note that the crosscutting test cases are added to the non-crosscutting ones. For example, if a crosscutting function implements a business process making use of a number of interaction forms, we will implement in the test plan both the test cases for each form (as in a standard test plan) and the test cases checking the correct flow of control and data through the forms.

The new test plan extends the standard one, obviously with the drawback of a higher cost.

3 The Case Study

We present and discuss the application of the method to the on going test of a large health care software system for prescription and administration of pharmacological drugs (both for protocol based therapies for oncology and non protocol based ones) in a hospital.

The aim of the system is to fully support the prescription, preparation and administration of pharmacological drugs in a hospital of north Italy (1400 beds and 4000 employees). It will involve many organizational units of the hospital: doctors, clinical units and the central chemist's shop.

The system is composed of a central Oracle based DBMS and a number of components developed in the Java Jsp environment with Tomcat application server. It is currently in the testing and pre-delivery phase.

We will present an example of the delivered artifacts taken from the part of the test plan related to the protocol based therapies for oncology.

3.1 The Base Functional Model

Fig 2 shows the base functional model for protocol-based functions. Each function is named through the managed data entity.

The components written in italics are leafs of the hierarchy. Each of them is an interaction screen or a set of screens.

The risk level has been identified through a couple of indexes each ranked Low, Medium, High. The "effects severity" index defines the level of threat for a patient in case of software misbehavior while the second index classifies the complexity level of

	Protocol based therapy Base functions	Effects severity	Complexity level
TP 1	Search		
TP 1.1	*Patients*	M	H
TP 1.2	*Clinical Episodes*	M	H
TP 1.3	*Present Patients*	M	M
TP 2	Patient		
TP 2.1	*Personal data*	M	M
TP 2.2	*List of clinical episodes*	M	M
TP 3	Therapy treatment		
TP 3.1	*Active therapies*	M	M
TP 3.2	*History of therapies*	M	M
TP 3.3	*History of pharmacological drugs administrations*	M	M
TP 3.4	*Drugs delivery*	M	M
TP 3.5	*New protocol-based therapy*	M	H
TP 4	Clinical Unit working plans		
TP 4.1	*Patients with active therapy cycles*	M	M
TP 4.2	*Working plan*	M	H
TP 4.3	*Drug sets composition*	M	H
TP 4.4	*Drugs administration*	M	H
TP 4.5	*Additional therapies*	M	M
TP 5	Utilities		
TP 5.1	*List of drug components*	M	M
TP 5.2	*New drug components*	M	M
TP 5.3	*List of protocols*	M	M
TP 5.4	*New protocol*	M	H
TP 5.5	*Administration means*	M	M
TP 5.6	*Measuring units*	M	M
TP 5.7	*Pharmacological implementation*	M	M
TP 5.8	*Drugs dosages*	M	M
TP 5.9	*Unit handbook*	M	M
TP 5.10	*Time planning*	M	M
TP 6	Working plans for chemist's shop		
TP 6.1	*Supervisor list*	M	H
TP 6.2	*Chemist's list*	M	H
TP 6.3	*Historical data*	M	M

Fig. 2. Software system for prescription and administration of pharmacological drugs: protocol based therapies for oncology. Base functional model. The function name is the name of the managed data entity.

the function (a function composed by many screens and fields is classified "High"). The final risk index for each function is the maximum of the two values.

3.2 Deriving and Modeling Aspects

Fig 3 shows the crosscutting (aspect-based) functions for protocol-based therapies. Each function involves the execution of more functions of the base model (see fig. 2). The crosscutted functions of the base model are written under the function name.

The functions have been derived from the available documentation and a set of meetings with experts in the application domain who contributed to the specification of the system and know the application from the users' point of view.

The classification of fig. 1 provided guidance for the discovery and was used as a list of possible types of functions (patterns) to be identified. In fact the first three functions of fig. 3 belong to the class of "important business processes", while the last two are in the class "states / transitions of application objects".

	Protocol based therapy Crosscutting functions	Effects severity	Complexity level
TP 7.1	*Select patient and clinical episode* (TP 1.1, TP 1.2, TP 2.1, TP 2.2)	M	H
TP 7.2	*Set a new cycle of a therapy* (sub functions of TP 3.5)	M	H
TP 7.3	*Drugs sets set up, composition and administration* (TP 4.2, 3 4 TP 6.1, 2)	M	H
TP 8.1	*States management for a therapy cycle* (TP 3.5, TP4.3, TP4.4, TP 6.2, TP 6.1)	M	H
TP 8.2	*States management for a drug* (TP 1.1, TP 1.2, TP 2.1, TP 2.2)	M	H

Fig. 3. Software system for prescription and administration of pharmacological drugs: protocol based therapies for oncology. Crosscutting functions.

Note that the available documentation doesn't explicitly model the identified aspects.

As we will see in the following, these aspects are not just important for testing purposes. They are also very significant pieces of knowledge to be identified during the specification phase.

Moreover the availability of a modular and clear statement of them will be very useful during the future evolutionary life of the system.

We are not saying that these aspects were not considered during the specification phase and the following phases of design and implementation. People involved in the specification and development know them. Information about them is available from documentation. However, the aspects were not accurately described and modularized and their knowledge will progressively vanish during the evolution.

Aspect-based functions from TP 7.1 to 7.3 are critical business processes flowing through the screens of the application.

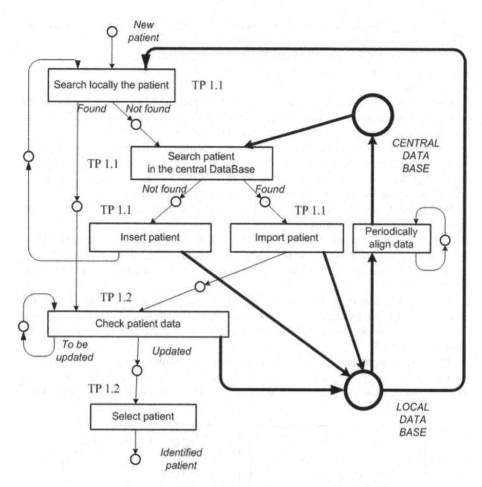

Fig. 4. Software system for prescription and administration of pharmacological drugs: protocol based therapies for oncology. Crosscutting functions: first part of the model for the function TP7.1 - *Select patient and clinical episode.*

For example the function "Select patient and clinical episode" is the process followed by a doctor to identify both the patient he/she has to deal with and the clinical episode of the patient itself (the therapy is composed of more than one episodes spanning through a time period).

This is the fundamental process required before starting any therapy. During the selection of the patient many different situations must be managed. For instance a patient must be registered locally to the system even if his registration is not yet completed in the central database of the hospital (for example the patient is coming from the emergency management unit).

During the first identification of the aspect we wrote a short description, we annotated the different cases and took all the relevant screenshots.

We also ranked the aspect-based function to a High complexity level and we decided to write a Petri Net based model of the function.

Fig 4 shows the first part the Petri Net based model that is related to the selection of the patient. The Place-Transition Petri Net models the flow of control between many functions.

Each transition (rectangle) models a function (or part of) belonging to the list of the crosscutted functions. Each transition is annotated with the function name of the base model. The oriented arcs and the places model the flow of control.

An arc label (for example "found") defines the condition required for producing a token (a synthetic notation that modifies the standard firing rule of a transition). Additional rules for modifying the standard firing rule (for example input conditions) may be associated to a rectangle (the rules are not reported in the figure).

We added to the net the model of the existing databases and the read / write operations on them (bold arrows).

This is our own notation, but we assume that these oriented arcs and operations don't change the behavior of the net (they don't influence the firing rules) and don't affect the structural testing techniques we will use for testing the possible behaviors of the net.

TP 7.2 *"Set a new cycle of a therapy"* is a special case. It is confined in the function TP 3.5, but this function is very complex and composed of many screens. For this reason we decided to model the aspect crosscutting the sub functions that are composing TP 3.5.

TP 8.2 is an aspect related to the states of the object "drug".

The states (see fig. 5) are part of a state machine and the execution of functions of the base model causes the state changes according to the drug state-transition model.

Drug states	Therapy Cycle states
To be confirmed	Prescribed
Added	Confirmed
To be prepared	In composition
Added – To be prepared	In administration
To be composed	Cancelled
To be administered	Suspended
In administration	Closed with anomalies
Not administered	Completed
Administered	
Cancelled	
Suspended	
Interrupted	

Fig. 5. Software system for prescription and administration of pharmacological drugs: protocol based therapies for oncology. States of the objects "Drug" and "Therapy Cycle". The execution of functions of the base model causes the state changes according to the state machines for drugs and therapy cycles.

The state machine crosscuts the base model functions TP 3.5, TP4.3, TP4.4, TP 6.2 and TP 6.1.

TP 8.1 is a model of the same type and was developed for specifying states and possible changes of a therapy cycle.

A protocol based therapy involves more drugs administration events called "cycles". The executions of the base model functions TP 1.1, TP 1.2, TP 2.1, TP 2.2 cause the state change of the therapy cycle state-transition model

Aspect-based functions TP 8.1 and TP 8.2 are not business processes. They are constraints working across functions (see the base model) the user may execute.

The test plan also includes the non-functional aspect-based functions TP 9.1 to 9.3 (see fig 6) that are related to safety requirements. Each of them collects a path of computation and data management related to an aspect critical for the patient health.

	Protocol based therapy Crosscutting functions	Effects severity	Complexity level
TP 9.1	Dosage management for the specific patient (TP 3.5, TP 4.2)	VH	M
TP 9.2	Drugs sequences management (TP 3.5, TP 4.4)	VH	M
TP 9.3	Drug-patient association (TP 4.3, TP 4.4)	VH	M

Fig. 6. Software system for prescription and administration of pharmacological drugs: protocol based therapies for oncology. Safety related crosscutting functions.

For example the functional aspect "Dosage management for the specific patient" deals with the quantities definition of the pharmacological drugs of a therapy for a specific patient. The quantities depend both on the oncological protocol and the anthropometric values of the patient.

The aspect is computationally simple but is spread into multiple functions. Despite his simplicity, it is one of the most critical aspects for the level of patient threat in case of software misbehavior.

3.3 Testing Base Model and Aspect-Based Models

The testing strategy was defined as follows. The test cases for each base function were generated through the definition of equivalence classes of input and the application of different combinatorial testing technique depending on the risk level. We also added negative and special test cases.

Aspect-based functions from TP 7.1 to 7.3 were tested using a structural testing technique over the Petri Nets. Each path, at level one of loops deepness covering, generated a test case. The test cases also verified the correct reading and writing of the databases.

The functions TP 8.1 and TP 8.2 were tested covering all the possible transitions between states.

Functions from TP 9.1 to TP 9.3 were tested through specific sets of test cases for verifying both the detail of the computation and the management of the data in the DBMS.

4 Related Works

Our methodology is related to early application of the AOSD concepts, even if our main focus in not on developing aspect based requirements. We focus on using requirements (both aspect-based and non aspect-based functional requirements) for deriving and improving the functional test. A side effect is the discovery, modularization and modeling of functional aspects not explicitly modeled.

From this point of view we don't suggest new methods for supporting an aspect oriented requirement phase (see [1] for an overview of the existing Aspect-Oriented Requirements Engineering Approaches). Rather we extend the scope of the aspect-oriented requirements to the important and related area of functional testing.

Part of our classification of aspect-based functions is based on the identification of important business cases flowing through more than one function of the base functional model. This technique for identifying aspects is similar to the use case and scenario-based AO approaches proposed by Aspect-Oriented Software Development with Use Cases [2], Scenario Modeling with Aspects approach [3], and Aspectual Use Case Driven Approach [4]. Business processes may be considered as use cases.

A difference with the use case based approaches is that we complement them with the use of other classes of possible aspect-based functions (see fig. 1).

Petri nets [5] have been used for many modeling applications. In [6] it is shown the use of a kind of Aspect-oriented Petri nets for security evaluation of software systems.

AOSD testing concentrated the research efforts in the problem of testing programs developed using an aspect-oriented technology.

Alexander et al. [7] identify the key issues and the challenges related to the testing of AOP programs. They introduce a fault model for them. The basic idea is that different types of faults may arise from the integration of different aspects woven into the final code. Each type of faults is related to specific constructs of AOP languages and requires different test criteria. The approach is oriented toward the unit and integration test.

Our approach share a similar concept, but at specification level and is oriented toward the functional testing. Different aspects of the specification document may generate different fault classes. Fig 1 is a first classification of functional aspects, for the specific class of information systems, which may lead to different fault types. The classification is not based on specification language constructs, as in the Alexander's model, but on typical requirements (patterns) of a software application area. In particular, referring to the approach of the Alexander's fault model, our classification assumes that a fault resides in the base functional model or in a functional aspect and doesn't explore faults coming from interactions between functional aspects or between base model and functional aspects.

Silveira et al. [8] include a survey of the proposed approaches for testing AOP programs. They also raise the question of the relation between Aspect Oriented and functional test, but the authors do not suggest possible approaches.

In fact proposals for different test strategies of AOP programs are available. Zhao [9] proposes a data-flow-based unit testing approach by combining the unit testing and data flow testing techniques. Zhou et al. [10] define an algorithm based on control flow analysis for selecting relevant test cases. Xu et al. [11] present a state-based approach to incremental testing of aspect-oriented programs. Zhao et al. [12] propose an AspectJ program testing method based on a fault model with the help of a dependency model and an interaction model. Finally Zhao et al. [13] propose a different approach suggesting testing the woven code simply using OOP testing methods. In all this cases the proposed method are oriented toward the unit and integration test.

An interesting approach is proposed by Xu et al. [14]. They are concerned with testing an entire system based on system's specification and present an approach for generating system test requirements from aspect-oriented use cases [2]. Aspect-oriented use case diagrams and descriptions are transformed into aspect-oriented Petri nets, an application of Predicate/Transition Nets. This formalization of use cases makes it possible to generate use case sequences (test cases) with respect to various coverage criteria.

In our approach use cases are just one possible source of functional aspects to be tested. See the following discussion for this issue. We also use multiple types of models for representing functional aspects and for deriving test cases, included Petri Nets. Finally our aim is to extend the aspect orientation to the functional testing of software products not originally specified using aspects.

Concerning testing in general, the books of testing, at the section "Functional Testing" describes a set of techniques that are well suited for testing a hierarchy of functions and doesn't deal with functional aspects. See [15] and [16], for a survey of the state of the art.

A special consideration must be devoted to the comparison of our approach with the use case based testing one. Use cases are generally exploited in acceptance testing to verify the system behavior against typical uses. See [17] and [18] as application examples.

Use case based testing is a helpful and well known technique. We extended the idea along the following direction: important use cases (or business processes, as we prefer to call them) are just one of the possible interesting aspects to be identified for improving the functional testing.

State changes of business objects, common services or internal common services are examples of other important classes of aspects that are not use cases. If these aspects (they crosscuts more functions of the functional hierarchy available to the user) are important for a specific application, their identification, modelling and test is important for the quality of a test plan.

Only if we use the concept of "aspect", we are able to correctly classify the concept of "use case" and discover other very important aspects to be considered in a functional test plan.

From this point of view the "aspect based testing" is a more general approach that includes as a subset the "use case based testing".

Moreover use case based testing is normally adopted in isolation (see for example [17] and [18]. Our approach integrates the functional testing based on a hierarchy of functions with modeling and testing different types of crosscutting functions, including use cases.

5 Discussion

The paper shows a process and the deliverables of a functional testing strategy that improves the traditional approach through the discovery and the exploitation of functional aspects.

What is the scope of the method?

The case study is a specific information system, but it is an example of a wide class of Information Systems. We applied the method to other types of Information Systems: two examples are the e-catalog application for a large retail company and the information system for real estate management of a local authority.

Despite the different application areas, the three systems share the architectural style "repository" [19]. They include a set of form-based interactive components, batch procedures and data structures hosted in a relational database.

In all the cases we found that:

–   Testing the hierarchy of functions is necessary but doesn't capture important functional characteristics of the software product that involves many functions.

–   These characteristics may be classified as recurrent patterns. We found in all the cases the presence of crosscutting functions belonging to the list of fig. 1.

Our research needs to be extended and consolidated, but we think that the method has potentially a broad scope of applicability.

What are the advantages?

Testing functional aspects add value to the approach based on testing each function in isolation. See for example the case study above. The test plan based on the hierarchical functional model doesn't capture important and critical processes to be verified. This fact doesn't depend on the amount of testing effort spent for testing the hierarchy. For example, the verification of important business processes or state changes of objects through the functions is only possible if the crosscutting nature of such functions is captured and modeled in a modularized way.

During the testing activity shortly presented in the case study, we also discovered that the system stakeholders strongly appreciated the side effect of the availability of explicit models for aspect-based functions. Their opinion is that these models will be a major artifact for supporting the future evolution of the product.

Does the method provides a robust support or is based on "ad hoc" solutions?

A first point is how the method supports the identification of the crosscutting paths through the hierarchy of functions.

We think that the best way for giving support to this step of the method is the identification and description of crosscutting functions patterns and related testing patterns for specific classes of software products. The classification of fig. 1 is a first step towards the availability of this support. See also the above comments related to the scope of the method.

Through patterns, we can support the identification of typical classes of crosscutting functions. It is more difficult to support the choice of specific functions of a class, because this highly depends on the specific application.

A second point is how the method can provide support for the classification of the criticality of a particular function. We think that we can add suggestions to the identified pattern and provide guidelines, but the criticality classification of a specific function is strongly related to the specific application.

6 Conclusion

The methodology has to be further assessed through the verification of other software products. Moreover, the classification of types of crosscutting functions of information systems (see fig. 1) is now a draft version. It has to be improved through the classification of more patterns in the considered class of software products and a richer set of examples and suggestions. In our opinion, this is a very important point. If we are able, for a specific and significant class of software applications, to derive patterns of crosscutting functions classes, these can be play, for functional testing, the same important role of design patterns for the design phase.

Moreover the methodology is now related only to functional requirements testing. A significant improvement will be to integrate in the test plan not only the verification of the functional specifications, but also the non-functional ones.

The approach has been used for testing a large health care software application. The results are encouraging both for the quality of the testing plan and for the improvement of the requirement document.

More application and research are required, but this methodology may give a significant contribution both to the improvement of functional testing and to the delivery of better support for software products evolution. The methodology may also contribute to the diffusion and acceptance of the aspect-oriented approaches in the early phases of software development in a large class of software applications.

Acknowledgements. I would like to thank the anonymous reviewers for their helpful comments and the colleagues that provided comments and suggestions during the Vancouver Early Aspect workshop.

References

1. AOSD-Europe, Survey of Aspect-Oriented Analysis and Design Approaches (2005), www.aosd-europe.net
2. Jacobson, I., Ng, P.-W.: Aspect-Oriented Software Development with Use Cases. Addison Wesley Professional, Reading (2005)
3. Whittle, J., Araujo, J., Kim, D.-K.: Modeling and Validating Interaction Aspects in UML. In: AOSD Modeling With UML Workshop (located with UML 2003), San Francisco (2003)
4. Moreira, A., Araujo, J., Brito, I.: Crosscutting Quality Attributes for Requirements Engineering. In: Software Engineering and Knowledge Engineering Conference (SEKE), Ischia, Italy (2002)
5. Peterson, J.L.: Petri Net Theory and the Modeling of Systems. Prentice-Hall, Englewood Cliffs (1981)
6. Nygard, K., Xu, D.: A Threat-Driven Approach to Modeling and Verifying Secure Software. In: ASE 2005, Long Beach, California, USA (2005)
7. Alexander, R.T., Bieman, J.M.: Towards the systematic testing of aspect-oriented programs. In: Proc. 27th Annual IEEE International Computer Software and Applications Conference (COMPSAC 2003), Dallas, Texas (2003)

8. Silveira, F.F., de Resende, A.M.P.: The testing activity on the Aspect-Oriented Paradigm. In: Proc. of the First Workshop on Testing Aspect-Oriented Programs (WTAOP 2005), Chicago (2005)

9. Zhao, J.: Data-flow-based unit testing of aspect-oriented programs. In: Proc. of the 27th Annual IEEE International Computer Software and Applications Conference (COMPSAC 2003) (2003)

10. Zhou, Y., Richardson, D., Ziv, H.: Towards a practical approach to test aspect-oriented software. In: Proc. of the 2004 Workshop on Testing Component-Based Systems (TECOS) (2004)

11. Xu, D., Xu, W.: State-Based Incremental Testing of Aspect-Oriented Programs. In: AOSD 2006, Bonn (2006)

12. Zhao, C., Alexander, R.T.: Testing AspectJ Programs using Fault-Based Testing. In: Proc. of the Third Workshop on Testing Aspect-Oriented Programs (WTAOP'07), Vancouver (2007)

13. Zhao, C., Alexander, R.T.: Testing Aspect-Oriented Programs as Object-Oriented Programs. In: Proc. of the Third Workshop on Testing Aspect-Oriented Programs (WTAOP 2007) Vancouver (2007)

14. Xu, D., He, X.: Generation of Test Requirements from Aspectual Use Cases. In: Proc. of the Third Workshop on Testing Aspect-Oriented Programs (WTAOP 2007), Vancouver (2007)

15. Pezzè, M., Young, M.: Software Testing and Analysis: Process, Principles, and Techniques. Wiley, Chichester (2007)

16. Harrold, M.J.: Testing: A Roadmap, The Future of Software Engineering. In: Finkelstein, A. (ed.), ACM Press, New York (2000)

17. Bertolino A., Gnesi S.: Use Case-based Testing of Product Lines. In: Proc of ESEC/FSE 2003, Helsinki, Finland (2003)

18. Roubtsov, S., Heck, P.: Use Case-Based Acceptance Testing of a Large Industrial System: Approach and Experience Report. In: Proc of Testing: Academic and Industrial Conference - Practice And Research Techniques TAIC PART 2006 (2006)

19. Shaw, M., Garlan, D.: Software Architecture. Perspectives on an emerging discipline. Prentice Hall, Englewood Cliffs (1996)

DERAF: A High-Level Aspects Framework for Distributed Embedded Real-Time Systems Design

Edison Pignaton de Freitas[1], Marco Aurélio Wehrmeister[1], Elias Teodoro Silva Jr.[1], Fabiano Costa Carvalho[1], Carlos Eduardo Pereira[1,2], and Flávio Rech Wagner[1]

[1] Computer Science Institute – Federal University of Rio Grande do Sul (UFRGS)
Caixa Postal 15.064 – 91.501-970 – Porto Alegre – RS – Brazil
[2] Electrical Engineering Department, Federal University of Rio Grande do Sul, Brazil
{epfreitas, mawehrmeister, etsilvajr, fccarvalho,
flavio}@inf.ufrgs.br, cpereira@ece.ufrgs.br

Abstract. Distributed Embedded Real-time Systems (DERTS) have several requirements directly related to characteristics that are difficult to handle when a pure object-oriented method is used for their development. These requirements are called Non-Functional Requirements (NFR) and refer to orthogonal properties, conditions, and restrictions that are spread out over the system. Pure object-oriented methods do not address successfully those concerns, so new technologies, like aspect orientation, are being applied in order to fulfill this gap. This work presents a proposal to use aspect orientation in the analysis and design of DERTS. To support our proposal, we created DERAF (Distributed Embedded Real-time Aspects Framework), an extensible high-level framework (i.e. implementation-independent) to handle NFR of DERTS. DERAF is used together with RT-UML in the design phase, aiming to separate the handling of non-functional from functional requirements in the Model Driven Design of DERTS. A qualitative assessment of DERAF separation of concerns is also presented.

Keywords: Requirements Specification, Distributed Real-time Embedded Systems, Aspect-Orientation applied to DERTS, Separation of DERT Concerns.

1 Introduction

The increasing complexity of Distributed Embedded Real-Time Systems (DERTS) requires new development techniques in order to support system evolution and maintainability, and the reuse of previously developed artifacts. An important concern involved in DERTS design is how to deal with Non-Functional Requirements (NFR), which have crosscutting concerns, that means, some NFRs may affect very distinct parts of the system under development. If not properly handled, NFRs are responsible for tangled code and loss of cohesion. In the literature, it is possible to find several references addressing this separation of concerns where the crosscutting concerns are identified as NFRs, as in [1], [4] and [6]. In order to promote a separation of concerns, guidelines to handle NFRs separately from the functional ones have been proposed, using concepts such as subject-oriented programming [2] and aspect-oriented

A. Moreira and J. Grundy (Eds.): Early Aspects 2007 Workshop, LNCS 4765, pp. 55–74, 2007.

programming [3]. Both approaches address the problem at the implementation level. Some other approaches propose to take NFR into account as soon as possible that means, in the early phases of the specification and design, as in the Early-Aspects [4] approach.

Real-time systems have a very important NFR which is the concern about timing aspects, such as deadlines, maximum jitter, worst case execution time, tolerated delays, and other. The complexity related to the non-functional analysis of these systems increases when they become distributed and embedded. To deal with some of these NFR, some proposals suggest the use of aspects, as in [5] and [6] Aspects can help to deal with crosscutting NFRs into DERTS design, modularizing their handling. Besides the modularization capability, more abstract aspects are easier to reuse because they define the handling of a concern at high-level and also how it can be applied (or how it affects) the system without implementation or platform constraints.

This work presents the Distributed Embedded Real-time Aspects Framework (DERAF), which provides an extensible set of aspects to deal with NFRs of DERTS at a high-level of abstraction. On other words, DERAF is a set of implementation-independent aspects to handle NFRs during the creation of DERTS RT-UML [10][11] models at design phase. In this initial version, DERAF handles the following NFRs (see Section 2): timing, precision, performance, distribution, and embedded behavior. DERAF was created to be an extensible framework, such that it can be extended to include support to other important aspects (e.g. fault-tolerance). However, these new aspects must follow the high-level nature of the framework and also the implementation-independence. It is important to highlight that, in spite of the high-level of abstraction, aspects within DERAF must be implementable. On other words, the realization of each aspect must be possible, avoiding unfeasible aspects.

The remaining of this paper is organized as follows. Section 2 outlines a brief discussion on NFRs within DERTS domain. The following section presents an aspects framework to handle the identified NFRs. Section 4 presents the transition from requirements to design of DERTS using the DERAF. A case study and a qualitative assessment of final design are presented in Section 5. Finally, the related work is presented in section 6, and final remarks and future work in Section 7.

2 DERTS Non-functional Requirements

In order to deal with NFRs in early design phases of DERTS, it is firstly necessary to define and understand the main concepts involved in the system context. The need of this information motivates the classification of these concepts in terms of non-functional concerns, which can affect the behavior and structure of the DERTS being designed. Fig. 1 presents some key requirements related to DERTS development, which are mainly based on the study presented in [14], on the IEEE glossary [15] and on the SEI glossary [16].

The real-time concern is captured by the requirements stated in the *Time* classification, which is divided in *Timing* and *Precision* requirements. The first one is concerned with the specification of temporal limits for system activities execution, such as established deadlines and periodic activations. Requirements classified as

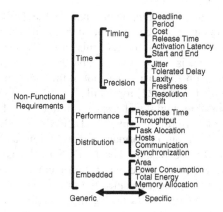

Fig. 1. NFR classification for DERTS

Precision denote constraints that affect the temporal behavior of the system in a "fine-grained" way, determining whether a system has hard or soft time constraints. An example of this is the *Freshness* requirement, which denotes the time interval within which the value of a sampled data is considered updated. Another key requirement in this classification is the *Jitter*, which directly affects the system predictability, because large variance degrades system determinism.

The *Performance* requirements are tightly related to those presented in the *Time* classification. However, these requirements have also an important relation with those concentrated in the *Distribution* classification, so we decided to put them in a distinct classification. They represent requirements usually employed to express a global need of performance, like the end-to-end response time for a certain activity performed by the system and the required throughput rate.

The goal of *Distribution* classification is to identify key requirements related to the distribution of DERTS activities, which usually execute concurrently. For instance, these concerns address problems such as task allocation over the system nodes, as well as the communication needs and constraints.

Concerns related to embedded systems generally present requirements related to memory usage, energy consumption, and required hardware area size. The *Embedded* classification has concerns that deal with monitoring and controlling these three issues.

3 DERAF: High-Level Framework to Deal with Non-functional Concerns

As already mentioned, the idea behind this work is to allow the handling of NFRs from earlier stages of DERTS design. To support this idea, an aspects framework named DERAF (Distributed Embedded Real-time Aspects Framework) has been created to deal with common NFRs of DERTS presented in the previous section. The goal of DERAF is to provide a modularized way to handle NFRs, improving the reuse of aspects in different DERTS projects. The goal of this section is to present the

DERAF framework and how its components handle the NFRs in a high level of abstraction. It is important to notice that the internal mechanisms of the aspects included in the framework are not the focus of this paper. This is a theme more related to the implementation, what is not a concern that this paper supposes to deal with. Further more, a discussion on AO concepts is out of the scope of this paper. Interested readers should refer to [3], [7] and [22] for details.

DERAF is an extensible high-level aspects framework based on the aspect orientation conceptual model proposed in [22]. DERAF provides a set of aspects to facilitate the handling of timing, performance, distribution, and embedded NFRs at the modeling phase of DERTS design. The DERTS model is described using RT-UML and shows DERAF aspects affecting system elements. The main idea behind DERAF is to provide aspects which enhance the modeled system by adding specific behavior and structure to handle NFRs during the modeling phase, without binding the DERTS model to a specific implementation technology. To reach this implementation independence, details about how to implement the aspect adaptations were abstracted. This means that the designer selects aspects to use in DERTS design, based on how the aspect improves the system elements, and then defines which elements will be affected by selected aspects. The set of aspects available in DERAF is depicted in Fig. 2.

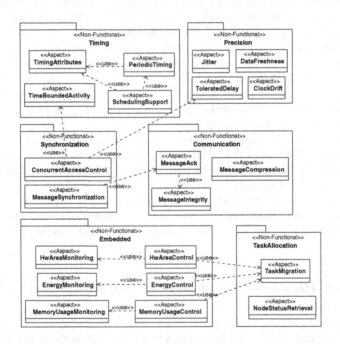

Fig. 2. DERAF aspects set to handle DERTS NFR

Each concern can be handled by one or more aspect, thus a brief description of the behavior/structural adaptations provided by the available aspect is necessary:

- **TimingAttributes:** adds timing attributes to active objects[1] (e.g. deadline, priority, WCET, start/end time, and so on), and also the corresponding initialization of these attributes;
- **PeriodicTiming:** adds a periodic activation mechanism to active objects. This improvement requires the addition of an attribute representing the activation period and a way to control the execution frequency according to this period;
- **SchedulingSupport:** inserts a scheduling mechanism to control the execution of active objects. Additionally, this aspect handles the inclusion of active objects into the scheduling list, as well as the execution of the feasibility test to verify if the scheduling list is schedulable;
- **TimeBoundedActivity:** temporally limits the execution of an activity[2], that is, adds the mechanism to restrict the maximum execution time for an activity (e.g. limits the time which a shared resource can be locked by an active object). The time counting begins immediately before the starting of the activity and must provide a wait to interrupt and stop this execution if the time limit is reached;
- **Jitter:** measures the start/end of an activity, calculates the variation of this metrics and, if the tolerated variance was overran, corrective actions must be taken;
- **ToleratedDelay:** temporally limits the beginning of an activity execution (e.g. limits the time which an active object can wait to acquire a lock on a shared resource). This aspect adds a time counting mechanism, starting it immediately before the beginning of an activity execution and, if the maximum tolerated time is reached, corrective actions must take place;
- **DataFreshness:** associates timestamps to data, verifying their validity before using them. Every time after that "validity controlled data" are written, the timestamp must be updated. Analogously, before reading them, the timestamps must be checked and, if the validity is expired, some corrective actions must take place (e.g. read the sensor again and update the value and timestamp);
- **ClockDrift:** measure the time at which an activity starts and compares it with the expected beginning of this activity; if the accumulated difference exceeds the maximum tolerated clock drift, then some corrective actions are taken;
- **ConcurrentAccessControl:** adds a control mechanism to the concurrent access of shared resources. Every time that an active object needs to access a shared resource, it requests a lock to the control mechanism and after its use, the active object must notify the mechanism that the lock on the shared resource can be released;
- **MessageSynchronization:** adds a waiting mechanism which pauses the execution until the arrival of an acknowledge message, after a message has been sent. The waiting mechanism can be implemented either as a busy wait or by blocking the active object execution and calling the scheduler. This decision is made only at aspect implementation level, allowing the implementation independence of this aspect;
- **MessageAck:** adds a message delivery guarantee mechanism. This aspect has two facets: (i) at sender side, after a message is sent, the mechanism must be notified

---

[1] Active object is an object that owns a thread and executes its behavior concurrently with other active objects [10][11].

[2] The term "activity" used in this paper follows the activity specification presented in the UML meta-model [10], meaning a set of ordered actions.

that a message was sent and an acknowledge message must arrive; (ii) at receiver side, after delivering a message, an acknowledge message must be sent;

- **MessageIntegrity:** verifies the integrity of a received message. This aspect has also two facets: (i) at sender side, before sending the message, a checker algorithm (e.g. parity, CRC, etc) must generate a check information that will be appended to the message; (ii) at receiver side, after receiving the message, the checker algorithm must generate the check information from the received message and compare it with the check information received within the message;

- **MessageCompression:** adds a compression mechanism to improve the bandwidth usage. At sender side, the message is compressed before sending it, and, at receiver side, the message is decompressed before delivering it;

- **EnergyMonitoring:** inserts an energy monitoring mechanism to measure the energy consumption of an activity. Before the activity execution, the current energy level is measured, and, after the end of the execution, the energy level is measured again and the difference is calculated and stored;

- **EnergyControl:** adds a mechanism which implements an energy control policy that performs control actions depending on the remaining energy level, such as to eliminate unnecessary tasks, migrate active objects, loose temporal requirements, decrease system frequency, shutdown unnecessary hardware, among others.

- **MemoryUsageMonitoring:** inserts a mechanism to provide information on the total memory used by system objects. Before every memory allocation, the amount of requested memory must be added to the total used memory, as well as, after every memory release, the total of released memory must be subtracted from the total used memory;

- **MemoryUsageControl:** performs memory control based on the selected policy, such as memory compression, migration of active objects, releasing of unused objects, among other control policies;

- **HwAreaMonitoring:** provides a mechanism to monitor the use of FPGA area. If the DERTS use reconfiguration techniques, then, depending on the reconfiguration policy, the previous used FPGA area must be subtracted from the total used area and the new reconfigured area added to this total, before each FPGA reconfiguration;

- **HwAreaControl:** verifies if the requested hardware reconfiguration is possible and, if so, allows the reconfiguration;

- **TaskMigration:** provides a mechanism to migrate active objects from node to node or from software to hardware or the opposite. It is used by the aspects that control embedded concerns (EnergyControl, MemoryUsageControl, and HwAreaControl), which are responsible for the decision on migration;

- **NodeStatusRetrieval:** inserts a mechanism to retrieve information about processing load, message send/receive rate, and/or the node availability (i.e. "I'm alive" message). Before/after every execution start/end of an active object, the processing load is calculated. Before/after every sent/received message, the message rate is computed. Additionally, the node availability message is sent at every "n" messages or periodically with an interval of "n" time units.

As stated previously, the goal of DERAF is to provide high-level aspects to be used at the modeling phase of DERTS design to handle NFRs. In the following phases (e.g. implementation), these aspects must be realized through either application or platform[3] code. Therefore, to proceed with the DERTS design process, the implementation of DERAF aspects must be provided, thus binding each aspect with an implementation technology. The high-level semantics of "how" and "where" each aspect affects system elements are defined and must be preserved, such that every implementation must follow these semantics in order to allow the reuse of previously developed aspects implementation. The idea is to build a library of aspects implementations which could be easily reused in further designs, thus reducing the design effort.

Sometimes, it is also interesting to evaluate the impact of the aspects implementation into the original DERTS at the modeling phase. Therefore, it is necessary to provide models to describe how each aspect implementation affects the original specification. On other words, it is necessary to provide an aspects model weaving, like the ideas presented in 7. In spite of its importance, a detailed discussion about both implementations (models and code), as well as model weaving are out of the scope of this paper, which proposes a (very) high-level aspect framework to be used at the modeling phase.

Finally, it is important to highlight that DERAF does not provide aspects to handle all NFRs present in a DERTS design. Fault-tolerance is an important NFR that still does not have support in the initial version of DERAF. However, DERAF was intended as an extensible framework, and the support to fault-tolerance is possible and can be easily incorporated in a further version of the framework.

4 From Requirements to Design

As stated in the previous section, DERAF was created to handle NFRs at earlier stages in DERTS design. To support its use, the FRIDA (From Requirements to Design using Aspects) methodology [17] was adapted in order to map NFRs from the analysis phase into DERAF aspects that handle them. FRIDA provides a consistent method to separate non-functional from functional requirements at early phases of system development, representing a relevant contribution to the system analysis and to the mapping of requirements into design elements. Additionally, we propose to use RT-UML models (i.e. UML [10] models annotated with the real-time profile [11]) to specify DERTS, in order to use a standard and widely accepted representation of real-time features.

FRIDA focuses on the fault tolerance domain, with a vocabulary and tools designed to support the analysis of fault tolerant systems. In the initial proposal, real-time concerns were not considered, thus to fit FRIDA into the DERTS domain, the first step was to consider the concerns presented in Section 2 to adapt FRIDA tools. An important tool used to identify and specify NFRs is the check-list, which is a form with several fields that intends to capture information about NFRs present in the system description. A sample check-list is showed in case study of the next section (see Fig. 4). The first column lists the non-functional requirements, inferring questions organized by Generic Requirement (time, performance, distribution, and

---

[3] According [12], platform is a set of previously developed and tested hardware and software components that can be configured and reuse.

embedded) and by the respective sub-classification. The second column means relevance of the requirement, while the third column gives its priority (i.e. importance within system context) and the fourth column gives information about restrictions, conditions, and/or a description of the requirement.

The next step is to fill a template for each identified NFR using the information provided by the tools previously presented. This template presents a summary of the information necessary to specify a NFR. The organization of the template for NFRs is presented in Fig. 3. The first column identifies information items while the second one describes the meaning of each item.

As can be observed in the template shown in Fig. 3, the specification of the NFRs details how given functional requirements of the system are affected, by way of the specification of use cases, a description of the concern, and context items. Additionally, functional requirements are also specified by means of a specific template (similar to the NFR one) that gives information about system use cases.

An important step that follows the specification of the NFRs is the reasoning about the relative importance among the different requirements present in the system. It represents an important task in order to avoid undesired conflicts in design phase. To perform this task, the field "priority" of the NFR template is used. Based on the value of the priority, a requirement can be changed in order to avoid the conflict with another with a higher priority. For instance, if a distribution requirement degrades the requirement of performance with a greater priority, the first is changed in order to reduce to an accepted level, or eliminate the negative impacts. In cases in which there is a great difference between the priorities of two requirements and changes in the requirements do not solve the conflict, the one with the lowest priority can even be removed from the scope of the system. However, it is a drastic situation that must be exhaustively discussed with the stakeholders.

	Item	Description
Identifi-cation	**Identifier**	An identification that will allow the traceability of concern over the whole project.
	Name	Crosscutting concern's name.
	Author	The responsible for the concern identification and definition.
Specification	**Classification**	Class to which the concern belongs.
	Description	Description of how the concern affects system functionality.
	Affected Use Cases	List of the use cases affected by the concern.
	Context	Determines when the concern is expected to affect a use case.
	Scope	(Global/Partial) The requirement is global if it affects the whole system, and it is partial if affects only a part of the system.
Decision/ Evolution	**Priority**	A number used to decide the relative importance among non-functional concerns.
	Status	A requirement can have one of the following status: 0 - identified; 1 - analysed; 2 - specified; 3 - approved; 4 - cancelled; 5 - finished;

Fig. 3. NFR Specification Template

At the end of the requirement analysis, a use case diagram is composed by use cases representing functional and non-functional requirements. NFRs are represented by use cases annotated with the <<non-functional>> stereotype. These "non-functional" use cases are linked with the conventional use cases representing functional requirements that are affected by NFRs.

Finally, an important task of the requirement analysis is the decision on how the system will handle the specified requirements. To describe this, a mapping table is created to indicate the classes handling functional requirements and the aspects handling non-functional ones, based on the information captured in the analysis phase. An example of the mapping table showing information on the case study is shown in Fig. 7, which is organized as follows: non-functional requirements are set in the top row; functional requirements are set in the first column from the left side. Aspects that handle a specific NFR are set in the bottom row in the corresponding column, while classes that handle a FR are set in the column at the right side of the table, in the corresponding row. Cells relating FR that are affected by NFR are marked with an "X". It is important to highlight that, as well as some FRs can be handled by more than one class, NFRs can also be handled by more than one aspect. On other words, a requirement can be handled by at least one class and/or aspect. The use of the presented mapping table provides the traceability from requirements to design elements and vice versa. More details about the FRIDA adaptation to DERTS domain were presented in [18].

5 Case Study: Wheelchair Automation

To illustrate the adapted FRIDA methodology and the use of DERAF, this section presents a case study that consists in the design of a distributed real-time embedded automation and control system for an "intelligent" wheelchair to support people with special needs. Hard-real time requirements must be accomplished for safety reasons. The whole automation design includes functions like movement control, collision detection, automatic movement, scheduled movement (e.g. convey patient to room 11 at 10:00 am), and so on. Due to space constraints, this paper will focus on the movement control subsystem, which is composed by one conventional lever joystick, rotation angle and speed sensors, and two motors (i.e. one for each wheel). The movement control was designed to be distributed in two different nodes: one responsible for sensing and other to control the wheel motors.

The first step is to use the check-list to assess the NFRs that are important and appear in the wheelchair distributed automation. Fig. 4 shows the check-list for the timing NFRs (sub-division of time), which has questions concerning the time constraints and temporal expected behavior of DERTS activities.

After the NFR identification and assessment, the templates must be filled. Fig. 5 shows the template related to the periodicity (i.e. the period NFR, included in the timing NFR classification) of DERTS activities, which was elicited from the check-list shown in Fig 4. This template shows the initial assessment of the periodicity NFR, regarding the activities performed by the wheelchair automation system.

	R.	P.	R./C./D.
Time			
Timing			
Is there any periodic activity or data sampling?	X	8	Joystick sensing, Movement Control and sensing
Is there any sporadic activities?			
Is there any aperiodic activity?	X	7	Alarm
Is there any restriction in relation to the latency to start an execution of a system activity?	X	9	Deal with maximum latency overrun
Is there any specific instant to start or finish an execution of a system activity?			

Fig. 4. Check-list to Time/Timing NFR

	Item	Wheelchair System
Identifi-cation	**Identifier**	NFR-1
	Name	Periodicity
	Author	Edison
Specification	**Classification**	Time/Timing/Period
	Description	The system has some activities that must be executed in regular periods of time: (1) data acquisition from joystick; (2) angle and speed acquisition from movement sensors; and (3) the control of wheelchair movement.
	Affected Use Cases	(1) Joystick Sensing; (2) Movement Sensing; (3) Movement Control
	Context	When the system needs to update the data collected from (1) the joystick position and (2) the angle and speed sensors, as well as (3) during the wheelchair movement control
	Scope	Global
Decision/ Evolution	**Priority**	8
	Status	5

Fig. 5. Template for Periodicity

After the requirements specification, a use case diagram is created to describe graphically the functional and non-functional requirements. The notation used in this work is not standardized by the OMG. It follows ideas taken mainly from [21] and [7]. In Fig. 6, it can be seen how the non-functional requirements affect the desired system functionality, represented with the same syntax of a use case with a stereotype applied over it (<<non-functional>>), indicating that this is a crosscutting concern. We chose to show only the general NFR (i.e. the periodicity is represented within the timing general NFR) to simplify the representation of the crosscutting relation in the use case diagram. In order to represent how those non-functional requirements crosscut system functions, an arrow goes from the element representing the non-functional requirements till the affected use case. This arrow is noted with the stereotype <<crosscut>>. As shown in Fig 6, the timing, distribution, and embedded NFRs (see Section 2) affect the functionality related to sensing and controlling the movement control subsystem. The NFR effect certainly implies a decentralized handling in the final system (thus making harder the reuse and maintainability).

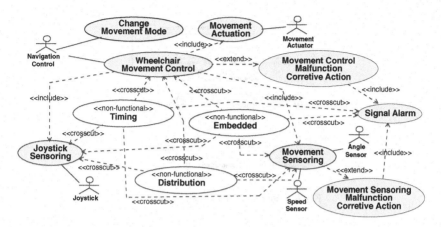

Fig. 6. Wheelchair movement control FRs and NFRs

		Non-Functional Requirements				Classes responsible for handling FRs
		Deadline	Periodicity	Tolerated Delay	...	
Functional Requirements	Joystick Sensing	X	X	X		JoystickDriver JoystickInformation
	Movement Control	X	X			MovementController MovementActuator
	Alarm	X				Alarm
	...	...		...	...	...
Aspects responsible for handling NFRs		Timing Attributes	Periodic Timing	Tolerated Delay	...	

Fig. 7. Mapping table

Following the methodology, the mapping from requirements to classes and aspects must be described using the mapping table. Fig. 7 shows the mapping table fragment describing three NFRs with the aspects handling them and also three FRs with their related classes.

After the requirements mapping, the functional requirements must be described using RT-UML diagrams. The structure of DERTS is described using the class diagram, and the behavior using interaction diagrams. Fig. 8 shows the class diagram for the movement control, which shows classes annotated with the <<SAschedRes>> representing classes of active objects, and with <<SAresource>> representing classes whose objects are accessed concurrently by active classes. Fig. 9 shows the movement controller active object behavior. As can be seen, this active object represents a periodic task, which is activated every 20 milliseconds (message *run* is annotated with the <<SAtrigger>> stereotype).

Concluding the DERTS functional specification, the modeler must describe where (i.e. which modeled element) the selected DERAF aspects will insert adaptations, in order to handle the NFRs that crosscut the system. The elements where an aspect introduces modifications are named *join point* [22]. This work follows the ideas

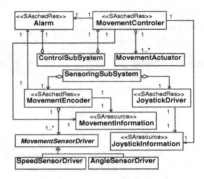

Fig. 8. Functional Specification: Structure

proposed by [23], which uses the Join Point Designation Diagram (JPDD) to describe the join point selection at modeling level. The use of high-level join point descriptions improves their reuse, allowing that the same join point may be used with different introduced adaptations. JPDD can be modeled using interaction, activity and statechart diagram capturing, respectively, control flow, data flow, and state models. For this initial proposal, we use only the interaction JPDD to capture control flow join points.

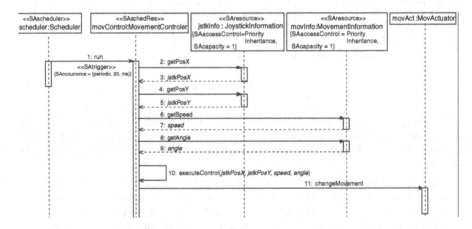

Fig. 9. Functional Specification: Behavior

For illustration purposes, two very simple aspects were chosen to show how to specify JPDDs and how they adapt the functional specification. The chosen DERAF aspects are *TimingAttributes* and *PeriodicActivation*, which handle the *timing* NFRs (see Section 2). Fig. 10 shows the JPDD that selects structural and behavioral elements. The stereotype <<JPDD>> indicates that the diagram represents a join point selection. The <<JoinPoint>> stereotype indicates the element that will be selected when the JPDD is evaluated. For details on the elements naming pattern and wildcards, please refer to [23]. In Fig. 10a, all classes that are annotated with <<SAschedRes>> are selected by the *ActiveObjectClass* JPDD, while in Fig. 10b all messages sent from the scheduler to active objects that are annotated with <<SAtrigger>> are selected by the *PeriodicActivation* JPDD. Summarizing, *ActiveObjectClass* selects all classes of active objects (e.g. *JoystickDriver*, *MovementControl*, *MovementEncoder* of Fig. 8), and *PeriodicActivation* selects the activation message which starts the execution of an active object (e.g. *run* message of Fig. 9).

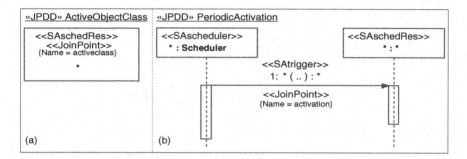

Fig. 10. Join point selection: (a) Class (b) Message

The next step is to link the joint point selection with the aspect. The linking of join points with adaptations is called *pointcut*. Fig. 11 shows one part of Aspects Crosscuting Overview Diagram (ACOD) describing *TimingAttributes* and *PeriodicTiming* aspects. The aspects are represented as classes annotated with the <<Aspect>> stereotype, the pointcuts are represented as attributes annotated with the <<Pointcut>> stereotype, and the adaptations represented as operations annotated with the <<StructuralAdaptation>> or <<Behavioral Adaptation>> stereotype. As stated before, a pointcut links join points with adaptations. Behavioral adaptations can have a relative position where the adaptation is applied. For instance, in the *PeriodicTiming* aspect, the frequency control will be added after the execution of the behavior triggered by the *run* message, e.g. "<<Pointcut>> pcFreqCtrl (PeriodicAtivation.activation, FrequencyControl, AFTER)". Another important feature is the setup of the time properties of active objects. As can be seen in Fig. 11, the *TimingAttributes* aspects define the deadline, priority, and worst case of each active object. These attributes are inserted into all active object classes by using the *ActiveObjectClass* JPDD with structural adaptations, and their values are passed as parameters (see [7]) to the structural adaptation through the <<Crosscut>> stereotyped association.

The final step in the modeling phase is to generate the Aspect Crosscuting Overview Diagram (ACOD), which shows all used aspects improving all functional classes of DERTS design. The idea is that the ACOD can be generated automatically by a tool that evaluates all JPDDs to discover the classes affected by the selected DERAF aspects. At the moment, the ACOD must be specified manually.

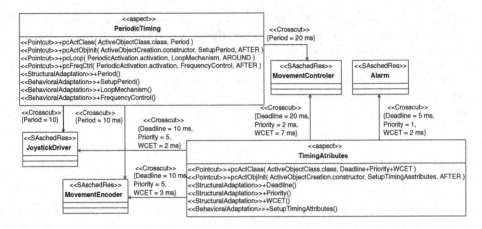

Fig. 11. Linking JPDD with aspects and adaptation

5.1 Qualitative Assessment

In order to assess how useful is to apply aspects in the modeling of a DERTS, a set of metrics specific to AO development was applied to the case study presented in the previous section. Those metrics are reported in [19] and are based on the Childamber and Kemerer (C&K) Metrics Suíte [20]. According [19], a set of metrics is not enough to determine the quality of a system. It is also required to know how those metrics interact to provide meaningful information about how well designed the system is, thus [19] presents an assessment framework (i.e. a set of metrics integrated in a quality model) to infer the quality of the system by measuring its reusability and maintainability. To provide a qualitative assessment of the DERAF use, a subset of the metric and concepts related to system design of that assessment framework was used. Accordingly to the proposal presented in [19], the subset of metrics that we used in the wheelchair case study evaluation is applicable to a system in both design and implementation levels. The implementation related metrics were not used due to the focus of this paper, which does not cover the implementation phase. Additionally, it is important to highlight that this paper concentrates on "reusability" instead of "reusability and maintainability" as in the assessment framework.

5.1.1 The Metrics Suite

As proposed in [19], the metrics suite captures information about the design in terms of fundamental attributes such as separation of concerns, coupling, cohesion, and size. For each attribute there is a set of specific metrics, as follows:

1) **Separation of Concerns Metrics:** They refer to the ability to identify, encapsulate, and manipulate those parts of the system that are relevant to a particular concern. Two metrics compose this attribute:

   i) *Concern Diffusion over Components (CDC):* it counts the number of primary components (aspects or classes) whose main purpose is to contribute to the handling of a certain concern;

ii)*Concern Diffusion over Operations (CDO):* it counts the number of primary operations (methods in classes or advices and methods in aspects) whose main purpose is to contribute to the handling of a concern.

2) **Coupling Metrics:** They identify the strength of interconnections between the components in a system. Two metrics compose this attribute:

i) *Coupling between Components (CBC):* it is the amount of components (class or aspect) which are coupled to a component;

ii)*Depth of Inheritance Tree (DIT):* it is defined as the hierarchy level, describing how far down are the components (classes or aspects) from the root of the inheritance hierarchy.

3) **Cohesion Metric:** It is the closeness measure for the relationship of a component with its internal components. It is translated by the following metric:

i) *Lack of cohesion in Operations (LCOO):* measures the amount of methods and advices that do not access the same instance attribute.

4) **Size Metrics:** They measure the size of the system and are inferred by two metrics:

i) *Vocabulary Size (VS):* it counts the number of system components, i.e. the number of classes and aspects into the system;

ii)*Number of Attributes (NOA):* it counts the internal vocabulary of each component, i.e. the number of attributes of each class or aspect.

5.1.2 The Quality Model

In order to achieve an interpretation of the metrics aiming at the assessment of system reusability quality, the relationship among metrics must be defined. One or more metrics compose internal attributes, which, in turn, compose intermediate qualities (named factors) that compose system qualities [19].

The attributes that classify the metrics presented above are considered the internal attributes of the system. There are four internal attributes: Separation of Concerns, Coupling, Cohesion, and Size. The combination of all those internal attributes gives the understandability factor, which indicates the difficulty level for studying and understanding a system design. The relationship among coupling, cohesion, and separation of concerns gives another factor: flexibility. This factor indicates the difficulty level for performing drastic changes to one system's component without requiring changing others. Finally, by composing these two factors it is possible to assess the reusability quality of the system.

Fig. 12 shows the relationship among metrics, attributes, and factors to infer the system quality, representing a subset of the quality model presented in [19]. In our

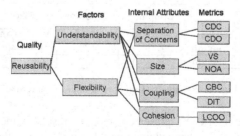

Fig. 12. The Quality Model

quality model we remove the implementation related metrics due to our focus on design and modeling of DERTS.

5.1.3 Applying Metrics to the Case Study

As stated above, the application of the described metrics to a system design can provide useful information about its quality related to the reusability. In order to verify the improvement of this system quality, a comparison between the presented AO design and an OO design of the control system of the automated wheelchair system is provided. The complete OO design are shown in [24].

The application of separation of concerns metrics shows how effective was the use of aspects to model elements to handle time, distribution, and embedded concerns. The values presented in Fig. 13 show that all those three non-functional concerns were better separated in the AO design if compared to the OO version. The scattering problem had already a significant decrease in this case study. It is important to notice that in larger systems, i.e. with more active classes (those stereotyped with <<SAschedRes>>), the advantage of the use of aspects could be much larger. This can be noticed by the decrease of CDC and CDO in the handling of the Time concern, which had a decrease of 50% in the first metric and 65% in the second. The same occurs with distributed and embedded concerns.

Concern	Time		Distribution		Embedded	
Metric	CDC	CDO	CDC	CDO	CDC	CDO
OO Design	10	23	8	17	7	8
AO Design	5	8	4	7	2	3

Fig. 13. Results for Separation of Concerns Metrics

The application of coupling, cohesion, and size metrics also resulted in some advantage when aspects are used, but not so clear as for the results shown in the separation of concerns. Fig. 14 shows the resulting values.

Analyzing coupling results, it can be seen that values for both versions of the design were almost the same. A slight advantage for the AO version is presented by the decrease of the CBC. The DIT metric did not change, showing that the use of aspects did not modify the inheritance tree of the proposed design. The almost the same result in coupling for both versions shows that the previous OO design was concerned about the modularization.

Internal Attributes	Coupling		Cohesion	Size	
Metrics	CBC	DIT	LCOO	VS	NOA
OO Design	39	1	174	18	48
AO Design	35	1	132	23	25

Fig. 14. Results for Coupling, Cohesion, and Size

The cohesion metric LCOO presented a better result in the AO version. This increase of the cohesion can be explained mainly by the use of the *PeriodicTime* and *TimeAttribute* aspects that concentrate the attributes related to time handling (e.g.

period and deadline). Grouping all time properties into these aspects, it was possible to eliminate from the application classes all *get* and *set* methods that were required to handle those properties.

In the size metrics, we found a single drawback in the AO design version. The VS metric was 27% larger in the AO version due to the small size of the wheelchair control system. Even this result shows a disadvantage in the use of aspects, in larger and more complex system the AO design could show better results. On the other hand, the NOA metric had a decrease of 48% in the AO design, showing that a significant reduction in the internal vocabulary of system components can be obtained due to the move of several NFR related attributes to aspects.

Following the quality model presented in the previous section, the reusability can be assessed by grouping these metric results (i.e. the internal attributes) into factors. The understandability factor is influenced by all internal attributes measured. The separation of concerns directly affects the understandability of a system, because the more localized are the concerns, the easier is to find and understand them. The cohesion and coupling affect the understandability, because it is difficult to understand a system component that requires an understanding of many others at the same time. The size of the design affects the effort needed to understand the proposed system solution. For the flexibility factor, the key attributes are coupling, cohesion, and separation of concerns. A component is flexible if it is independent or almost independent of the rest of the system, meaning that it represents a specialized part of the system which has a specific and well defined mission. These characteristics are translated in low coupling and high cohesion (i.e. it has a low dependence on other parts of the system) and a good separation of concerns (i.e. the component is responsible for a well defined mission).

Understandability is very important to the reuse quality of a system, thus it is supposed that the designer has a good understanding of a component before its reuse. In the same way, flexibility plays a remarkable role in the reuse quality, because it defines the difficulty to take a component from a system and plug it into another one without many adaptations. The results presented for the case study show that the AO design version has a better understandability and flexibility if compared with the OO design version, since the majority of the metrics presented better results in the AO version. Therefore, it is possible to state that the AO design has a better reusability if compared to the OO version.

6 Related Work

Although aspect-orientation (AO) is a relatively new concept, there are some proposals to use it in DERTS design, especially to handle real-time requirements. However, most approaches propose the use of aspects in the implementation phase, such as the approach presented in [6]. In that work, aspects were extracted from real-time Java code of a sentient traffic simulator, to non-functional concerns such as threads, memory management, and asynchrony. The paper compares of the pros and cons of the object-oriented and aspect-oriented implementation of a simulator. In the approach proposed in this paper, AO concepts are applied at higher abstraction levels using a top-down approach instead of re-factoring an existing source code in a bottom-up approach.

In [5], a set of tools named VEST (Virginia Embedded System Toolkit) use aspects to compose a new DERTS based on a component library. Those aspects check the possibility of composing components with the information taken from system models. Results presented in the paper indicate a reduction in design time when using VEST. This work uses the concept of aspects to check and test dependencies among library components. We propose a different approach in which aspects are used to directly deal with NFRs from the analysis phase. Additionally, in our work aspects play an important role during the design of crosscutting concerns.

AODM (Aspect-Oriented Design Model) [7] is an UML extension to deal with AO design concepts. It reproduces constructs of the AspectJ [8] AO language using UML's standard extension mechanism that is stereotypes and tagged values. Additionally, AODM also proposes a weaving mechanism to apply the aspects' improvements within the system model. AODM was proposed to be used in the general computing system domain, which does not have too stringent NFRs as the embedded real-time domain. Our work proposes to deal with DERAF's supported NFR at a high-level of abstraction, providing traceability to these NFRs from earlier stages of design. Additionally, the proposed approach is not limited to a specific programming language due to the abstract nature of DERAF aspects.

In [26], it is described a proposal to separate functional and non-functional requirements in the system structure. This is done by the use of stereotypes to represent aspects in class diagrams and text-based annotations representing logical conditions related to the non-functional requirements. One shortcoming of this work is that it uses too much text-based tags in diagrams. Our proposal, instead, uses model elements to represent the non-functional dimension of the system. It is important to highlight that in our proposal we also support a link between the mentioned model elements and the information contained in the analysis phase, what is not addressed in this mentioned related work.

ACCORD [25] also introduces the aspect concept in the development of DERTS. It proposes the development based on aspects and components. They divide the system in several components that will compose a library to be reused. The non-functional concerns that crosscut those components are encapsulated in aspects, making easier the reuse of components stored in the library. However, this work does not handle the earlier phases of system development (i.e. analysis), as our proposal does.

Another relevant proposal in DERTS development is [27]. This approach proposes a platform-independent component modeling language to address DERTS non-functional requirements (i.e. QoS), in systems that are based on a middleware component solution. It represents an important contribution to the domain of DERTS development, however, as it does not use the aspect-oriented paradigm to handle the non-functional dimension, all the problems found in the object-oriented development are still present. Our approach differs from that mainly because it uses aspects and also because it works with the requirements in the early phases of development.

7 Final Remarks and Future Work

This paper proposes the use of AO to deal with non-functional concerns that crosscut since earlier modeling and design phases, such as requirements and analysis of DERTS project. To support our proposal, a high-level aspects framework named DERAF has been developed, which comprises a set of aspects to deal with time, distribution, and embedded NFRs. DERAF is used to map NFRs from requirements elicitation and analysis to design elements in the modeling phase, using a methodology adapted from FRIDA. To illustrate the use of DERAF in DERTS design, a wheelchair movement control system was presented as case study. It has been shown how to use DERAF aspects to model the handling of non-functional concerns using RT-UML. This work follows the language independent AO model presented in [22] and the graphical notations presented in [23] to query model elements that will be affected by aspects.

Regarding the qualitative assessment of the AO and DERAF utilization, we can state that the separation of concerns from early phases of development allows a better understanding of system complexity and also a better base to build the system structure. Another advantage is the improvement of the reusability of system components, because the non-functional handling is not intermixed in functional elements. However, AO does not improve all evaluated metrics. The vocabulary size (VS) metric, in the AO version of the control system, increases 27% mainly due to the small system size. We believe that in larger systems this metric will certainly show better results in the AO version. Additionally, the use of RT-UML is advantageous because it enables the application of knowledge from the real-time community, which is materialized as the real-time profile.

As future works, we intend to implement DERAF aspects in order to allow their use in implementation phase of DERTS development. In addition, we plan to use the DERAF implementation to generate DERTS source code automatically (as complete as possible, that is, not only code skeletons) from RT-UML using DERAF aspects. New features of the UML 2.0 are been studied in order to improve the proposed model, as well as other standard UML profiles (besides RT-UML) are under analysis.

References

1. Chung, L., Nixon, B.A.: Dealing with Non-Functional Requirements: Three Experimental Studies of a Process-Oriented Approach. In: Proc. of 17th International Conference on Software Engineering, pp. 25–37. ACM Press, New York (1995)
2. Ossler, H., Tarr, P.: Using subject-oriented programming to overcome common problems in object-oriented software development/evolution. In: Proc. of 21st Int. Conf. on Software Engineering, pp. 687–688. IEEE Computer Society Press, Los Alamitos (1999)
3. Kiczales, G., et al.: Aspect-Oriented Programming. In: Aksit, M., Matsuoka, S. (eds.) ECOOP 1997. LNCS, vol. 1241, pp. 220–240. Springer, Heidelberg (1997)
4. Rashid, A., Sawyer, P., Moreira, A., Araujo, J.: Early Aspects: A Model for Aspect-Oriented Requirements Engineering. In: Proc. of IEEE Int. Conf. on Requirements Engineering, pp. 199–202 (2002)
5. Stankovic, J.A., et al.: VEST: An Aspect-Based Composition Tool for Real-Time System. In: Proc. of 9th IEEE Real-Time and Embedded Technology and Applications Symposium, RTAS, pp. 58–59 (2003)
6. Tsang, S.L., Clarke, S., Baniassad, E.: An Evaluation of Aspect-Oriented Programming for Java-based Real-Time Systems Development. In: Proc. of the 7th Int. Symp. on Object-Oriented Real-Time Distributed Computing, IEEE Computer Society, Los Alamitos (2004)
7. Stein, D., Hanenberg, S., Unland, R.: A UML-based Aspect-Oriented Design Notation for AspectJ. In: Proc. of Int. Conference on Aspect-Oriented Software Development, pp. 106–112. ACM Press, New York (2002)

8. Aspect J, v.1.5.2 (September 2006), www.aspectj.org
9. France, R., Ray, I., Georg, G., Ghosh, S.: An Aspect-Oriented Approach to Early Design Modeling. IEE Software 151, 173–186 (2004)
10. Object Management Group.: Unified Modeling Language: Superstructure, v.2.0 (September 2006), www.omg.org/cgibin/doc?formal/05 -07-04
11. Object Management Group.: UML profile for Schedulability, Performance and Time, v.1.1 (September2006), www. omg.org/cgi-bin/doc?formal/2005-01-02
12. Burns, A., et al.: The Meaning and Role of Value in Scheduling Flexible Real-Time Systems. Journal of Systems Architecture: the EUROMICRO Journal 46(4), 305–325 (2000)
13. Keutzer, K., Malik, S., Newton, R., Rabaey, J., Sangiovanni-Vicentelli, A.: System Level Design: Orthogonalization of Concerns and Platform-Based Design. IEEE Transactions on Computer-Aided Design of Integrated Circuits and Systems 19(12), 1523–1543 (2000)
14. Burns, A., Wellings, A.: Real-time systems and programming languages, 2nd edn. Addison-Wesley, Reading (1997)
15. Institute of Electrical and Electronics Engineering.: IEEE Standard Glossary(September 2006), http://standards.ieee.org/catalog/olis/ arch_se.html
16. Carnegie Mellon Software Engineering Institute.: Online Technical Terms Glossary (September 2006), http://www.sei.cmu.edu/str/ indexes/glossary/
17. Bertagnolli, S.C., Lisbôa, M.L.B.: The FRIDA Model. In: Cardelli, L. (ed.) ECOOP 2003. LNCS, vol. 2743, Springer, Heidelberg (2003)
18. Freitas, E.P., Wehrmeister, M.A., Pereira, C.E., Wagner, F.R., Silva Jr., E.T., Carvalho, F.C.: Using Aspects to Model Distributed Real-Time Embedded Systems. In: Proc. of Workshop on Aspect-oriented Software Development, Florianopolis, Brazil (2006)
19. Sant'anna, C.N., et al.: On the Reuse and Maintenance of Aspect-Oriented Software: An Assessment Framework. In: Proc of Simpósio Brasileiro de Engenharia de Software, Manaus, Brazil, pp. 19–34 (2003)
20. Chidamber, S.R., Kemerer, C.F.: A Metrics Suite for Object-Oriented Design. IEEE Transaction on Software Engineering 20(6), 476–493 (1994)
21. Araújo, J., et al.: Aspect-Oriented Requirements with UML. In: Proc. of Workshop on Aspect-oriented Modeling with UML, UML 2002, Germany (2002)
22. Schauerhuber, A., et al.: Towards a Common Reference Architecture for Aspect-Oriented Modeling. In: Proc. of International Workshop on Aspect-Oriented Modeling AOSM (2006)
23. Stein, D., Hanenberg, S., Unland, R.: Expressing Different Conceptual Models of Join Point Selections in Aspect-Oriented Design. In: Proc. of 5th Int. Conf. on Aspect-Oriented Software Development, pp. 15–26. ACM Press, New York (2006)
24. Wehrmeister, M.A, Becker, L.B., Wagner, F.R., Pereira, C.E.: On Object-Oriented Platform-based Design Process for Embedded Real-Time Systems. In: Proc. of the 8th IEEE Int. Symp. on Object-Oriented Real-Time Distributed Computing, pp. 125–128. IEEE Computer Society, Los Alamitos (2005)
25. Tesanovic, A., Nyström, D., Hansson, J., Norström, C.: Aspects and Components in Real-Time System Development: Towards Reconfigurable and Reusable Software. Journal of Embedded Computing 1(1) (2005)
26. Zhang, L., Liu, R.: Aspect-Oriented Real-Time System Modeling Method Based on UML. In: Proc. 11th. IEEE Real Time and Embedded Technology and Applications Symposium, RTAS (2005)
27. Schmidt, C.D., et al.: A Platform-Independent Component Modeling Language for Distributed Real-time and Embedded Systems. In: Proc. 11th. IEEE Real Time and Embedded Technology and Applications Symposium, RTAS (2005)

On the Symbiosis of Aspect-Oriented Requirements and Architectural Descriptions

Lyrene F. Silva[1], Thais V. Batista[2], Alessandro Garcia[3], Ana Luisa Medeiros[2], and Leonardo Minora[4]

[1] State University of Rio Grande do Norte (UERN) – Natal/RN - Brazil
[2] Federal University of Rio Grande do Norte (UFRN) – Natal/RN – Brazil
[3] Lancaster University - Lancaster – United Kingdom
[4] Federal Center of Technological Education of Rio Grande do Norte (CEFET-RN) – Brazil
lyrene@gmail.com, thais@ufrnet.br, garciaa@comp.lancs.ac.uk,
analuisafdm@gmail.com, minora@cefetrn.br

Abstract. With iterative development increasingly becoming the de facto-practice in mainstream software processes, distinct early lifecycle artifacts need to be synchronized in order to leverage their correspondences. Requirements engineering and software architecture models have been recently enriched with aspect-oriented (AO) abstractions and composition mechanisms. In this context, this paper proposes a symbiotic relation between early AO development phases by specifying mapping rules between a requirements model, AOV-graph, and an architecture description language, AspectualACME. AOV-graph and AspectualACME are, respectively, symmetric AO extensions to the V-graph goals model and the ACME language, with features to modularize crosscutting concerns. The meta-models of these modeling languages offer abstractions that are recurrently supported in other requirements models and architectural approaches. Hence, this paper also discusses how the proposed suite of mapping rules can be exploited in other similar approaches. The evaluation of the mappings is carried out in the context of a case study called Health Watcher.

Keywords: Requirements, architecture, ADLs, models mapping.

1 Introduction

Aspect-oriented software development (AOSD) [6] has emerged as a contemporary modularization approach to promote improved separation of crosscutting concerns. Innovative AOSD techniques have been defined and targeted at different development phases in order to foster superior changeability and smooth inter-phase transitions across the software lifecycle. However, such benefits will be hampered if aspect-oriented (AO) artifacts produced in distinct development phases are not symbiotically integrated. Phase-to-phase symbiosis implies that elements of the different artifacts are associated in such a way that it is possible to quickly propagate changes between them and navigate from requirements to architecture and vice-versa.

Requirements engineering and software architecture are two fundamental early development phases that have been recently enhanced with AO abstractions and

A. Moreira and J. Grundy (Eds.): Early Aspects 2007 Workshop, LNCS 4765, pp. 75–93, 2007.

composition mechanisms [2]. The mapping from requirements models to architectural specifications is essential for supporting multiple stakeholders with the correct understanding of artifacts' correspondences. The presence of such a mapping support minimizes the gap between these two development phases and their models. This in turn reduces the effort of generating initial AO candidate architectures as they can be more smoothly derived from the requirements model. In addition, with iterative, incremental software development increasingly growing as the de facto practice in mainstream software development, the symbiosis of AO requirements and architecture design also facilitates: (i) horizontal traceability of requirements to architecture models, and (ii) forward and backward change propagation.

In this context, this paper defines a suite of mapping rules from an AO requirements model to an AO Architecture Description Language (ADL). The mapping support focuses on the syntax of AOV-graph [23], an extension of the V-graph goal model [27], and AspectualACME [2], an extension of the ACME [10] ADL. Although these two approaches have been developed in an independent way, they share a list of underlying principles. First, any element (requirement or component) can crosscut any other crosscutting or non-crosscutting element. Second, they are symmetric AO languages and, as a consequence, non-crosscutting and crosscutting elements are represented by the same abstraction; there is no separate abstraction for aspects and the distinction of crosscutting concerns is established based in the way that they interact (or compose) with the rest of the system. Finally, a special relationship or connector extends the base modeling languages as a way to support the composition of concerns that are tangled and spread in the system.

Furthermore, both AO approaches extend *representative* models on requirements and architecture stages. V-graph is a type of goal model that provides representations to functional (goals and tasks) and non-functional requirements (softgoals), as well as captures multiple forms of relationships between them. Goal models make explicit the inherent complexity of these relationships and expose how some concerns crosscut each other. ACME is a general-purpose ADL that provides a simple structural framework for representing architectures, together with a liberal annotation mechanism that supports the definition of semantic descriptions. ADLs are the conventional forms to show how architecture design copes with both functional and non-functional concerns.

This paper is structured as follows. Section 2 describes the main concepts of aspect-oriented requirement modeling, AOV-graph, aspect-oriented architectural modeling and AspectualACME. Section 3 defines how to map the crosscutting support of AOV-graph to AspectualACME. Section 4 presents a case study that evaluates the mapping proposed. Section 5 contains a comparison with related work. Section 6 presents our final remarks and future works.

2 Basic Concepts

Section 2.1 discusses the concepts of aspect-oriented requirements and AOV-graph [23]. Section 2.2 presents the concepts of aspect-oriented software architecture and AspectualACME. The Health Watcher system is used to illustrate the concepts of AOV-graph and AspectualACME in Sections 2.1 and 2.2, as well as to discuss the mapping between the requirements and architecture models in Section 3. Health Watcher's goals are to collect and control the complaints and notifications, and provide important information to the citizen about the health system; see [24] for detailed information.

2.1 Aspect-Oriented Requirements Models and AOV-graph

With the growing popularity of AOSD, several aspect-oriented requirements modeling languages have been created, namely Theme/Doc [1] and a RDL - Requirements Description Language [3]. In addition, there have emerged some aspect-oriented extensions to conventional use cases [12][26], to requirements sentences [17][20], to the original V-graph model [23], and other conventional goal models [7].

AOV-graph firstly exposed the importance of the interactions between requirements (goals, softgoals and tasks) in order to define how concerns are crosscutting, in opposition to [1][3][7][17][20][26] that define first-order elements to represent crosscutting concerns. This extension to the V-graph model was defined in the context of an aspect-oriented strategy to requirements modeling, specified in [23]. This strategy defines mechanisms to separate, compose, and visualize crosscutting concerns during the requirements definition. The separation and modeling of crosscutting concerns is achieved by using an aspect-oriented requirements modeling language (AORML) [23]. AORML is a general purpose language that defines a new type of relationship named *crosscutting relationship*. This new relationship must be inserted in requirements modeling languages such as scenarios, lexicon, goal models, in order to avoid the tangling and scattering of crosscutting concerns in requirements models.

The crosscutting relationship is inspired on the traditional elements of AOSD, materialized by AspectJ (pointcut, advice and intertype declaration) and other non-programming aspect-oriented languages, and with a proper semantics to the requirements level. As illustrated in Fig. 1(b), crosscutting relationships are described by: (i) *source* – the source of the relationship; (ii) *pointcut* – the target of the relationship, i.e., the points affected by a crosscutting concern; (iii) *advice* – element of the source point that crosscuts the target points. In this case, the advice types are *before*, *around* and *after* and they can indicate, respectively, pre-condition, decomposition and post-condition, although they can assume other semantic depending on the type of the requirements model; and (iv) *intertype declaration* – define new element types, also crosscutting, that emerge with the integration of the features in the source and the target of the crosscutting relationship. There are two types of intertype declarations: *element* – when the new type refers to instances of existing element types in the requirement model, for example, instances of tasks, goals and softgoals (illustrated in Fig. 1 with a task named *[DB] setting*); and *attribute* – when the new types refer to non-existing attributes in the requirement model, such as *resources* and *costs* in the use cases model or for example, in AOV-graph of Fig. 1, the *constraint* attribute is created to affect the pointcut 15.1.

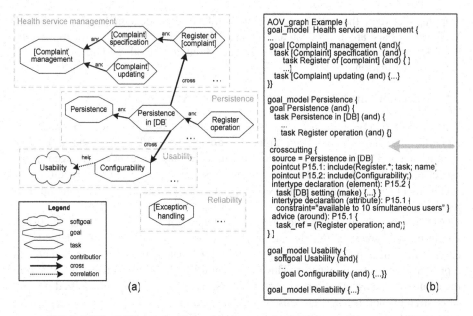

Fig. 1. HW in AOV-graph: (a) graphical representation (b) textual representation

To illustrate how a crosscutting relationship can be applied to requirements models, the AOV-graph language [23] was created as an instance of AORML. AOV-graph consists of *goals*, *softgoals* and *tasks*. Goals represent concrete objectives to be achieved for the system; Softgoals represent abstract objectives, frequently associated with non-functional requirements; and Tasks represent actions (or functional requirements) to be performed to achieve goals and softgoals. The AOV-graph model also contains the following relationships: contribution, correlation, and cross.

AOV-graphs are decomposition graphs or decomposition trees. Fig. 1 summarizes the Health Watcher AOV-graph: (a) illustrates the graphical representation, and (b) illustrates the textual representation. Although AOV-graph is essentially a graphical language, it was implemented in [23] as a textual language in order to facilitate its manipulation and verification (at the moment only textual representations are manipulated in this approach). In Fig. 1, there are four goal models: *Health service management*, *Persistence*, *Realiability* and *Usability*. These goal models represent different trees that can be connected by some relationship type. Each element of the tree (goal, softgoal or task) consists of a name and a contribution relationship: in the name, the words in brackets are *topics* and the others are *types*; the contribution relationship consists of the label attached to the relationship between that element and its parent, in brackets after the element name. In this same Figure, there is a crosscutting relationship whose source is the *Persistence_in_DB* task and two pointcuts are defined: the first one includes every task whose name begins with *Register* string, this pointcut is affected by the *Make register operation* task, defined in the advice. The second pointcut includes the *Configurability* goal that is affected by the *Set DB* task, defined in intertype declaration.

In AOV-graph, crosscutting relationships allow the grouping of tasks, goals and softgoals that, in a conventional requirements model, are spread and tangled over other elements. However, the option of defining a relationship instead of specifying a first order element for modularizing crosscutting concerns is justified for the following reasons: (i) the separation of "what" concerns are crosscutting, represented by the elements of the requirements model, from "how" these concerns are crosscutting, represented by the crosscutting relationship; and (ii) this AO extension is less intrusive to the requirements modeling language. As crosscutting and non-crosscutting concerns are represented through the same elements, the features of the modeling language remain valid to all system requirements, tangled or not; so (iii) it is possible to reuse these concerns in different projects.

2.3 Aspect-Oriented Software Architecture and AspectualACME

Architecture Description Languages (ADLs) provide elements to the architectural description of systems and promotes the separation of concerns (SoC) by separating elements that represent computation (components) and elements that represent the connection between components (connectors). *Components, connectors* and *configurations* are the basic elements that compose an architectural description [10]. Components and connectors have an *interface*. The component interface is a set of interaction points between the component and the external world. Such an interface specifies the services (messages, operations and variables) provided and required by a component. The services are also called *ports*. Connectors specify rules that govern the interaction between components. The connector interface specifies the interaction points between the connector and the components that they connect. Configurations define the architectural structure by specifying the connection of components and connectors.

In order to support the modularization of crosscutting concerns at the architectural level, several aspect-oriented description languages (AO ADLs) have been proposed [2][18][19]. Examples of architectural crosscutting concerns range from: (i) widely-scoped concerns initially handled in requirements specifications, such as persistence, usability, and reliability (Section 2.1), and/or (ii) different kinds of crosscutting concerns emerging due to certain design choices made at the architectural stage, such as event propagation [22], code mobility [9], transaction management [15], and exception handling policies [8][5].

In order to support modular representation of both types of architectural crosscutting concerns, the authors in [2] propose the concept of *Aspectual Connector* as the only abstraction needed to express crosscutting relationships at the architectural level. The aspectual connector is based on the traditional distinction existing in ADLs between *computation* and *interaction*. It follows the same idea to model interaction between components and crosscutting concerns. Computational elements, which implement crosscutting concerns or non-crosscutting concerns, are modeled as components. The distinction between aspectual components and traditional components is in the way that they compose with other elements.

The aspectual connector follows the connector philosophy and defines a new interface that distinguishes the roles of the internal elements of the connector in a crosscutting relationship. A role is to be bound to the component affected (base component) by other component (aspectual component). The interface of the aspectual connector defines: (i) a base role, (ii) a crosscutting role, and (iii) a glue clause. Fig. 2 contains a textual (a) and a graphical (b) specification of the aspectual connector. AspectualACME is essentially a textual language, but there is a graphical view in order to facilitate its visualization (in this work, only textual representations are specified by users).

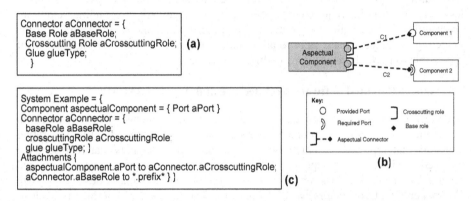

Fig. 2. AspectualACME aspectual connector: (a) textual notation (b) graphical notation (c) a description example

Fig. 2(b) illustrates an example of composition of an aspectual component and other components. C1 and C2 are examples of aspectual connectors. The aspectual component and the component are represented by the same abstraction. In the figure, the different color (white and gray) is just to differentiate them.

A base role is connected to a port of the component affected by the crosscutting concern – base component – and the crosscutting role is connected to the port of the aspectual component. The pair base-crosscutting roles do not impose the constraint, common of ADLs, of connecting input ports (provided ports) and output ports (required ports). A crosscutting role defines the place where the aspectual component connects to the connector. Fig. 2(b) illustrates an aspectual connector C1 that connects the provided port of the aspectual component with the provided port of the component 1. The glue clause specifies the details about the aspectual connection, such as, the moment of the aspectual interaction – after, before, around.

The aspectual connector idea is generic and can be instantiated by different ADLs. A broad discussion about this subject that comments why the notion of aspectual connector could be seen as a generalization of other existing AO extensions to ADLs can be found in [2]. In addition, [8] presents AspectualACME, an extension of the ACME ADL including the aspectual connector and a quantification mechanism that simplifies, syntactically, the reference of a set of join points in an architectural description. The basic elements of ACME are components, connectors and attachments. The attachments section (configuration) defines a set of port/role associations. Thus, it defines the place where the structural join points are identified in ACME. The quantification mechanism is used in the configuration through wildcards (*) that represent part of the component name or ports. Fig. 2(c) illustrates an example in AspectualACME where the *aspectualComponent* is connected, via the *aConnector*, to all components that contain a port with the name beginning with *prefix*.

Representations and *Properties* are other ACME elements. *Representations* are alternative decompositions of a given element (component, connector, port or role) to describe it in greater detail. Thus, the representation may be seen as a more refined depiction of an element. For instance, ports may have a representation to encapsulate a large set of API calls as a single port. Inside the representation, a set of ports is used to represent individual API calls. *Properties* of interest are *<name, type, value>* triples that can be attached to any ACME elements as annotations. Properties are a mechanism for annotating design elements with detailed, generally non-structural information.

3 Mapping Requirements to Architecture

The mapping from AOV-graph [23] to AspectualACME [2] exploits some similarities of the two modeling approaches. Both focus on the modeling of crosscutting concerns emerging in complementary development phase – requirements specification and architecture design. Both use general-purpose models and are based on some common symmetric aspect-oriented extensions, as we discussed in Section 1.

In both languages, the tangling and the scattering of crosscutting concerns are represented by the way that such concerns compose with other elements. The information about the composition is in the crosscutting relationship (in AOV-graph) and in the aspectual connector (in AspectualACME). Thus, crosscutting relationships of AOV-graph are mapped to aspectual connectors and attachments of AspectualACME. The concerns of the system are represented in AOV-Graph by *softgoals*, *goals* and *tasks* and in AspectualACME by *components* and *ports*. The mapping between these elements is possible because there is a semantic correspondence between *softgoals/goals/tasks* and *components/ports*; all of them can be seen as services that the system or its parts provide or require. Therefore, through softgoals, goals and tasks have different abstraction levels, they are mapped to services provided or required in the software architecture. On the other hand, components represent services provided by the system and ports represent services provided or required by the components in order to achieve their goals.

In this section, we present and explain the rules defined for the mapping from AOV-graph specifications to AspectualACME descriptions. In summary, the process to map AOV-graph into AspectualACME consists of: (i) mapping the hierarchy of goals, sofgoals and tasks into components, representations and ports; (ii) mapping goals, softgoals and tasks that are in pointcuts, advice and intertype declarations into ports and after that, generating *bindings* between these ports and ports of components that are in a higher level of the component hierarchy (bindings are links between external and internal interfaces); and (iii) mapping crosscutting relationships into aspectual connectors and attachments.

(i) Mapping the hierarchy of goals, softgoals and tasks into components, ports, properties and representations of AspectualACME – each element (goal/softgoal/task) of AOV-graph maps to a component or a port of

AspectualACME. This decision is based on the position that each goal/softgoal/task has in the hierarchy: root elements map to components, subelements that are not leaves (in the AOV-graph tree) map to components in representations, and subelements that are leaves map to ports. In addition, when a component and a port are generated, some properties are also inserted in order to register the source of each of them, see Fig. 3(b). These properties register some information about requirements in the architectural model and they will make the inverse mapping possible - from AspectualACME to AOV-graph.

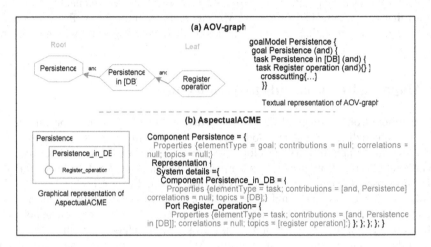

Fig. 3. Mapping goals, softgoals and tasks into components and ports of AspectualACME

For instance, Fig. 3(a) shows the *Persistence* goal model. In this model (i) the *Persistence* goal is the root of the tree, (ii) *Persistence in [DB]* is a subelement and (iii) *Register operation* is a subelement and a leaf of the tree. Fig. 3(b) illustrates the generated AspectualACME specification: (i) the *Persistence* goal generates the *Persistence* component, (ii) *Persistence in [DB]* generates a representation of the *Persistence* component, containing the component, *Persistence_in_DB*, and (iii) *Register operation* generates a port in *Persistence_in_DB*, called *Register_operation*. Each component and port has the following properties: *elementType* – describes the type of element that originated that component or port; *contributions* – describe the pairs [decomposition label, its parent element]; *correlations* – describe the pairs [correlation label, correlated element]; and *topics* – describe its topics, i.e., the strings in brackets, for example *[DB]* in *Persistence [DB]* task.

Following this process it would be possible to generate subcomponents or ports with similar names in different components because the same element (in AOV-graph) can contribute to more than one element in different trees. In these cases, these elements do not generate subcomponents, but components that are associated through common connectors.

(ii) Mapping pointcuts and intertype declarations of AOV-graph into ports and bindings of AspectualACME – some concepts in crosscutting relationships can also map to ports: (i) each element of an intertype declaration body, (ii) each element of an advice body; and (iii) each element of a pointcut. Semantically, crosscutting relationships group several relationships among goals, tasks and softgoals, i.e., they represent interactions that in architecture will be represented by connectors linking ports. For instance, in Fig. 4(a) the *[DB] setting* task of the first crosscutting relationship maps to the *DB_setting* port in the *Persistence_in_DB* component because this element is of an intertype declaration body in the crosscutting relationship whose source is *Persistence in [DB]*. Furthermore, each element of pointcuts (in each crosscutting relationhsip) maps to a port in components whose name is similar to the name of the parent element. For instance, in the second crosscutting relationship of Fig. 4(a), there is a pointcut with the element *Persistence in [DB]*, this element maps to the *Persistence_in_DB* port of the *Persistence* component (because *Persistence* is the parent of *Persistence_in_DB* in the goal tree). However, now there is a port and a subcomponent with similar names in the *Persistence* component, *Persistence_in_DB*. Both of them refer to the same service, and this is the reason to create a port *self* in the *Persistence_in_DB* component and a binding linking the *Persistence_in_DB* port with the *self* port.

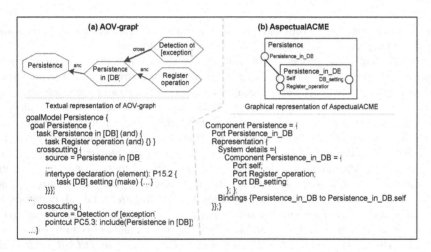

Fig. 4. Mapping pointcuts and intertype declarations to ports and bindings

(iii) Mapping crosscutting relationships into connectors and attachments – each advice and intertype declaration is associated to a set of pointcuts, for instance in Fig. 5(a) the intertype declaration is associated to the pointcut P15.2. This association means the *[DB] setting* task pertains to *Persistence_in_DB* and affects (or interacts with) the *Configurability* goal. Therefore, each advice and intertype declaration maps to an aspectual connector. In principle we named *sink* and *source* any *base role* and *crosscutting role* of aspectual connectors, respectively. The type of glue clause is determined by the advice type if the connector is generated from advice, it is *around* if it is generated from the intertype declarations with "element" type, and if it is generated from intertype declaration with "attribute" type then the glue has the value defined in the attribute of the intertype declaration. Therefore, from Fig. 5(a) we

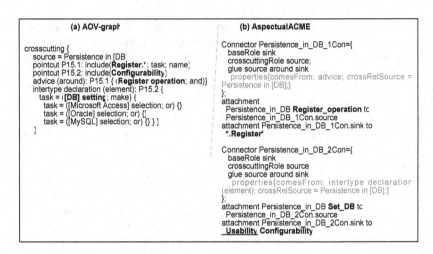

Fig. 5. Mapping crosscutting relationships to connectors and attachments

generate two connectors, illustrated in Fig. 5(b): the first connector comes from the advice and the second one comes from the intertype declaration.

We also add some properties in each connector in order to report their origin. Furthermore, for each relation between an element of the advice (or in the intertype) and an element of the pointcut, attachments are generated: (i) an attachment from the element of the advice (or of the intertype declaration) to the crosscutting role, and (ii) an attachment from the base role to the element of the pointcut. For instance, *Register operation* of the advice is associated to the pointcut 15.1 that refer to all elements with the string "Register". This relation *Register operation→Register.** maps to the two first attachments in Fig. 5(b): the first one is from *Persistence_in_DB.Register_operation* to *Persistence_in_DB_1Con.source*, and second one is from *Persistence_in_DB_1Con.sink* to **.Register**, i.e., all components that have ports beginning with the string *Register*. The second example is the *[DB] setting→Configurability* relation, and Configurability is a child of Usability (in AOV-graph). Thus, the mapping is: attachment *Persistence_in_DB.DB_setting* to *Persistence_in_DB_2Con.source* and attachment *Persistence_in_DB_2Con.sink* to *Usability.Configurability*.

Table 1 summarizes the mapping from AOV-graph to AspectualACME. These mapping rules make the generation of AspectualACME architectures from AOV-graph possible, and therefore, decrease the gap between the Requirements and Architecture activities. However, in AOV-graph, goals, softgoals and tasks can be written and organized by using different abstraction levels. Therefore, in order to guarantee the creation of a consistent and coherent architecture, human intervention is necessary in order to exclude, decompose or group components that are abstract or specialized too much.

Although these mapping rules have been created to specific models (AOV-graph and AspectualACME) they can be reused for the mapping of other languages based on or related to the elements in our base languages, V-graph and ACME. The rules 3

Table 1. Mapping AOV-graph to AspectualACME

Mapping		
	AOV-graph	**AspectualACME**

1	goals, softgoals and tasks that are not leaves and do not have grandchildren; as well as goals, softgoals and tasks that are source of crosscutting relationships; and parents of elements that are in pointcuts
	For each goal, softgoal and task that has grand children it is necessary generate a **representation** in order to organize their subcomponents.
		Component componentName {
		… // ports
		properties{
		elementType (can be goal, softgoal or task)
		contributions (list of [label, affected goal/softgoal/task]; label can be make, help, unknown, hurt, break, or, and)
		correlations (list of [label, affected goal/softgoal/task]; label can be make, help, unknown, hurt, break)
		topic (list of the words in brackets)}}

2	goals, softgoals and tasks that are leaves; as well as goals, softgoals and tasks that are in advice bodies, intertype declaration bodies and pointcuts	**Port portName** { **properties**{ (identical to component properties) **elementType, contributions, correlations, topic**}} For each port generated in a component that has a subcomponent with the same name it is necessary generate a **port self** in this subcomponent and generate a **binding** linking these two ports.

3	For each advice in the Crosscutting relationship	**Connector** connectorName {
		baseRole sink;
		crosscuttingRole source;
		glue source <advicetype in crosscutting relationship> sink
		properties {
		source <source in crosscutting relationship>;
		comesFrom advice}}

4	For each intertype declaration with "element" type in the Crosscutting relationship	**Connector** connectorName {
		baseRole sink;
		crosscuttingRole source;
		glue source around sink
		properties {
		source <source in crosscutting relationship>;
		comesFrom intertype_declaration_element}}

5	For each intertype declaration with "attribute" type in the Crosscutting relationship	**Connector** connectorName {
		baseRole sink;
		crosscuttingRole source;
		glue source <type and value in crosscutting relationship> sink
		properties {
		source <source in crosscutting relationship>;
		comesFrom intertype_declaration_attribute}}

6	For each relation advice → pointcut	**attachment** <port defined by elements into advice> **to** <connectorName.source>; **attachment** <connectorName.sink> **to** <port defined by operands into pointcut>;
7	For each relation intertype declaration (with "attribute" type) → pointcut	**attachment** <port defined by source of crosscutting relationship> **to** <connectorName.source>; **attachment** <connectorName. sink> **to** <port defined by operands into pointcut>;
8	For each relation intertype declaration (with "element" type) → pointcut	**attachment** <port defined by elements into intertype declaration> **to** <connectorName.source>; **attachment** <connectorName. sink> **to** <port defined by operands into pointcut>;

to 8 (in Table 1) are related to the mapping between crosscutting relationship and aspectual connector meta-models. While the rules 1 and 2 are related to the component model of the language. Therefore, the rules 1 and 2 have to be redefined if other models are used and the rules 3 to 8 can be reused with little change. Furthermore, as ACME is a general-purpose ADL, its elements are also present in other ADLs. AOV-graph meta-model also defines abstractions that can be found in other goal models.

4 Case Study

In this section, we discuss some details about the mapping from AOV-graph to AspectualACME in the context of the HealthWatcher system (HW). HW is a well-known example that has been used by different researchers in order to validate and demonstrate their aspect-oriented approaches. Health Watcher's goals are to collect and to control complaints and notifications, and to provide important information to the citizens about the Health System. In the event of a complaint, it will be registered on the system and addressed by a specific department which will be able to carry out the procedure and return an answer when the analysis is accomplished. This solution will be registered on the system, being available for queries.

```
Goal_model Manage [health service]{
 ..
 goal [Complaints] management (and) {
  task [Complaint] specification (and) {
    task [Kind of complaint] selection (and) {}
    task Register of complaint [kind], [date], [time] (and) {}
    task [Complaint information] request (and) {}
    task Register of [complaint information] (and) {}
    task Display of [complaint code] (and) {} }

  task [Complaint] updating (and) {
    task [Complaint code] request (and) {}
    task Display of [complaint information] (and) {}
    task [Conclusion] request (and) {}
    task Register of [conclusion] and [employee] (and) {}
 } }}
```

(a) AOV-graph

```
Component Complaints_management = {
 Representation {
  System details ={
    Component Complaint_specification = {
      Port Kind_of_complaint_selection;
      Port Register_of_complaint_kind_date_time
      Port Complaint_information_request
      Port Register_of_complaint_information;
      Port Display_of_complaint_code
      };

    Component Complaint_updating = {
      Port Complaint_code_request;
      Port Display_of_complaint_information;
      Port Conclusion_request
      Port Register_of_conclusion_and_employee;
 };  }; }; };
```

(b) AspectualACME

Fig. 6. Mapping of the Health service management

The modeling of HealthWatcher in AOV-graph consists of six goal models: Persistence, Realiability, Performance, Usability, Security and Health service management. Although these models had been specified in a simple way, it is easy to see the benefits of aspect-oriented approaches, such as: (i) early notion of which concerns are scattered and tangled, (ii) separation of these concerns in order to facilitate their analysis and change.

In Section 3, we presented the *Persistence* goal model and its mapping to AspectualACME. In the following, we present part of the *Health service management* and *Realiability* goal models and their mapping.

Fig. 6(a) depicts part of the *Health service management* goal model. This part is mapped to the AspectualACME specification in Fig. 6(b). In this case, we map the hierarchy of goal model to a hierarchy of components, following the mapping rules presented in Section 3. As shown in Section 3, the *Persistence_in_DB* component affects all ports whose name begins with the *Register* word, i.e., some ports in *Complaint_specification* and in *Complaint_updating* are affected by the *Persistence_in_DB* service. See the summarized *cross* relationships in Fig. 7 (bold relationships).

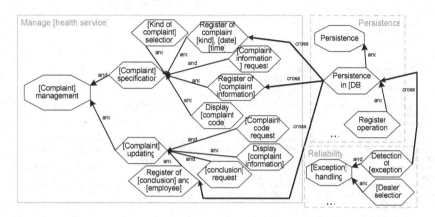

Fig. 7. Health Watcher AOV-graph

Fig. 8(a) depicts the *Realiability* goal model. In this case it only represents the Handling exception goal. This hierarchy is mapped to an *Exception_handling* component with the *Detection_of_exception* and *Dealer_selection* ports. In Fig. 8(b) this mapping follows the first activity in the process presented in Section 3. However, in Fig. 8(a) there is a crosscutting relationship whose source is *Detection of exception* and there are three intertype declarations. Therefore, applying the second step of the mapping process, *Detection of exception* is mapped to a subcomponent of *Exception_handling* and the elements of intertype declarations are mapped to ports of this subcomponent. Furthermore, a *self* port is created in this same subcomponent and a binding linking *Detection_of_exception* port to *Detection_of_exception.self*, see Fig. 8(b). In the same way, each element of pointcuts is mapped to a port in the components that are their parents, for example: *Persistence in [DB]* (in the first pointcut) is mapped to a port of *Persistence* component as we showed in Section 3.

After that, the connectors and attachments are generated from this same crosscutting relationship: (i) each intertype declaration is mapped to an aspectual connector with *around* gluetype (representing the composition moment), and the values intertype declaration (element) and *Detection of exception* to the properties *comesFrom* and *crossRelSource*, respectively; (ii) each relation intertype declaration → pointcut is mapped to an attachment associating the elements of intertype declaration to a crosscutting role and another one associating the base role to elements of pointcuts. For

```
goal_model Reliability {
goal Exception handling  (and) {                          (a) AOV-graph
   task Detection of [exception] (and) {}
   task Dealer selection (and) {} }
crosscutting {
   source = Detection of [exception]
   pointcut PC5.3: include(Persistence in [DB])
   pointcut PC5.4: include(Authentication by Login)
   pointcut PC5.5: include(Availability)
   intertype declaration (element): PC5.3 { task Detection of [persistence exception] (and) {} }
   intertype declaration (element): PC5.4 { task Detection of [authentication exception] (and) {} }
   intertype declaration (element): PC5.5 { task Detection of [availability exception] (and) {} } } } }
```
— —
```
Component Exception_handling={                         (b) AspectualACME
Port Detection_of_exception
Port Dealer_selection;
Representation{
   System details ={
      Component Detection_of_exception = {
         Port self
         Port Detection_of_persistence_exception;
         Port Detection_of_authentication_exception
         Port Detection_of_availability_exception;    };}
      Bindings {Detection_of_exception to Detection_of_exception.self};}
   Connector Detection_of_exceptionCon1, Detection_of_exceptionCon2, Detection_of_exceptionCon3 ={
      baseRole sink
      crosscuttingRole source
      glue source around sink
      properties{comesFrom: intertype declaration (element); crossRelSource = Detection_of_exception;};}
   attachment Detection_of_exception.Detection_of_persistence_exception to Detection_of_exceptionCon1.source;
   attachment Detection_of_exceptionCon1.sink to Persistence.Persistence_in_DB;
   attachment Detection_of_exception.Detection_of_authentication_exception to Detection_of_exceptionCon2.source
   attachment Detection_of_exceptionCon2.sink to Authentication.Authentication_by_login
   attachment Detection_of_exception.Detection_of_availability_exception to Detection_of_exceptionCon3.source
   attachment Detection_of_exceptionCon3.sink to Security.Availability
```

Fig. 8. Mapping the reliability requirement

example, the two first attachments associate *Detection_of_exception.- Detection_of_persistence_exception* to *Detection_of_exceptionCon1.source* and *Detection_of_exceptionCon1.sink* to *Persistence.Persistence_in_DB*. As we can observe, *Persistence_in_DB* affects some services and is affected by *Detection_of_exception*, i.e, any concern can cut across any other concern.

Fig. 9 depicts the graphic representation of the AspectualACME specification showed above. In this figure we can see how the components *Health service management*, *Persistence* and *Detection of exception* are related and how some services provided by *Persistence* and *Detection of exception* affect some services in an intrusive way. These connections could be seen like non-scalable (contrary to the quantification ideas), but new graphical views can be created to the architectural specification, such as those proposed in [23] to AOV-graph: a view showing the architecture before composition and other view of architecture after composition.

Fig. 9 was manually generated, but we are working in an extension of ACME Studio in order to make it support the aspectual connectors. ACME Studio contains a plug-in to Eclipse and it generates a graphical view from textual specifications in ACME. We are also working on architecturally-relevant quantification mechanisms for AspectualACME, essentially different from syntax-based mechanisms of AspectJ, but this is out of the scope of this work – a paper about such architecture-level quantification mechanisms have been submitted to FSE2007.

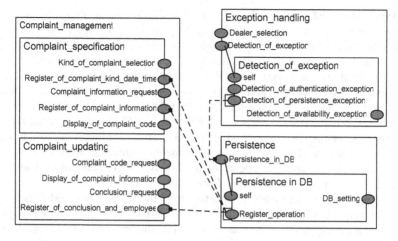

Fig. 9. Graphic representation of the Health Watcher architecture

By accomplishing the mapping between AOV-graph and AspectualACME, we provide an architecture that reflects the requirements of the system, representing an architecture baseline that can later be modified in order to accommodate architectural details.

5 Related Work

In order to bridging the gap between requirements and architecture several approaches define guidelines or mapping rules to produce the architecture design from requirements. However, there are three general problems with these approaches: (i) artifacts based on different meta-models and with different aims (requirements models portray the problem domain and architectural models portray the solution domain) are used, so all of these approaches only generate preliminary models; (ii) the proposed methods are to specific languages (meta-models). Therefore, it is difficult to extrapolate the guidelines or mapping rules to other languages; and (iii) the trace is defined only from requirements to architecture, but not vice-versa. Therefore, the architects can benefit from requirements models, but requirements engineers can not easily propagate architectural decisions or limitations to requirements specifications.

Our approach suffers from this first problem, because it also generates only a preliminary architectural description. Architectural issues have to be added after this mapping. However, our approach is also concerned with the generalizations of the mapping rules to other languages and tracing from architecture to requirements. As shown in Section 3, part of our mapping rules can be reused if input-languages use a symmetric approach to represent crosscutting concerns. If different abstractions are used to modularize crosscutting concerns, our mapping rules can even be used as a guide to map them.

Non-Aspect-oriented approaches: The CBSP (Component-Bus-System, and Properties) approach [4][11] helps the refinement of a set of given requirements into potential architectures by applying a taxonomy of six architectural dimensions. Input to this method can be a set of (incomplete) requirements captured in textual or formal descriptions that are categorized on 6 dimensions by the stakeholders. The result of CBSP is an intermediate and incomplete architecture model that captures "architectural decisions" of requirements. In [4], CBSP is applied in context of EasyWinWin, a requirements elicitation technique, and C2, an architectural language for distributed systems. In this method the categorization, conflict resolution is a skill-intensive manual task. This approach is fundamentally different from ours, because: (i) it is completely manual and depends on the experience of the architect; and (ii) it is not applied to change the requirements from architecture.

In [16], a method to derive the architecture from the KAOS goal models is defined. In this method: (i) software specifications are derived from requirements; (ii) an abstract architectural draft is then derived from functional specifications; (iii) this draft is refined to meet domain-specific architectural constraints; (iv) the resulting architecture is then recursively refined to meet the various non-functional goals modeled and analyzed during the requirements engineering process [13]. Contrasting this approach with our proposal, we have that: (i) the input of the mapping process of this approach is also a type of goal model. However, goal models in KAOS consist of a graphical tree and a formal language to define pre- and post-conditions for each goal while V-graph is only a well-structured model, but non-formal; (ii) this approach only defines the mapping from requirements to architecture, but not vice-versa; (iii) on the other hand, this approach provides guidelines to the refinement of the architecture by applying architectural styles and patterns, while we only provide the first draft of the architecture.

Aspect-oriented approaches: In [20] and [25] aspect candidates (represented in natural language and NFR graphs, respectively) are mapped to functions, architectural decisions or aspects in the architecture. This mapping is only based in the developer's experience and it does not provide guidelines to map non aspects candidates.

In [12] use cases are mapped to component diagrams (UML). Requirements are represented by use cases and crosscutting concerns are extensions to those use cases. Use case diagrams are refined in order to design the component diagrams. The use case diagram as well as the component diagram does not make explicit which concerns are crosscutting. On the other hand, the UML models are well-known and used, and there are also a lot of methods and tools to map one model into others.

In [21] an automated process that derives an AO architecture from an AO requirements specification is defined. This process is based on MDD (Model-Driven Development) and uses QVT (Query, View, Transformations) to define the transformation rules. The input is requirements models represented by a UML Profile and the output is an architectural description, represented in UML 2.0 Profile for CAM [19]. Although the authors mention that the process can be used with other source and target languages, the transformations rules are specific to UML diagrams and it provides transformation from requirements to architecture but non vice-versa.

In [14], it is defined an aspect-oriented generative approach and maps an extension of the features model to an extension of the UML component diagram. These extensions make the crosscutting concerns explicit. On the other hand, features models do not make explicit which concerns are functional or non-functional as the AOV-graph portrays. Furthermore, the component diagram of UML is only a graphical language.

As we previously described, most of these approaches map requirements to detailed project models such as UML class diagram and UML interaction diagram. The main drawback of these approaches is that the architect must to deal with some unnecessary details to the architectural analysis. The generative approach defined in [14] and the use case approach defined in [12] provide an alternative to this problem as they map requirements described in use case models and in features diagrams to component diagrams. The advantage of mapping a requirement model to an ADL, instead of mapping to a graphical language such as UML, is the possibility of using tools that include specification verification facilities. ACME, for instance, provides ACME Studio, a graphical development environment associated with a formal verification tool that verifies the constraints specified in the architectural description.

Our proposal of mapping is also different of those because we consider that both requirement engineering and architectural design can have benefits from this mapping. The symbiosis provides business strategies and stakeholders' requirements from requirements to architecture; and provides technology requirements and constraints from architecture to requirements.

6 Final Remarks

This paper presented a set of rules to map symmetric AO-requirements artifacts - defined as AOV-Graph models - to symmetric AO-ADL artifacts, structured as AspectualACME specifications. The mapping rules were defined to produce two symbiotically related models (requirement and architectural models) that guarantee the correspondence between the models and allow easy traceability and change propagation. We assessed the mapping rules using the HW system that can be used as a benchmark to the mapping rules as it is a real system that presents different types of crosscutting concerns. Also, as these two modeling languages offer abstractions that are supported by other symmetric AO requirements models and AO-ADLs, the mapping rules can be mirrored in other symmetric models and languages with minor adjustments. As previously discussed, the mappings from crosscutting relationships to aspectual connectors and attachments can also be reused in other similar contexts.

A number of advantages in defining the mapping from AO-requirements model to AO-architecture model: (i) it can be used by a tool to implement the automatic generation of the initial AO candidate architecture; (ii) it defines the correspondences between the information modeled in both models; (iii) it makes it possible the propagation of changes carried out in the requirements to the architecture; (iv) it makes it possible the syntactic verification of the specification by some existing tools; (v) it can be used to map and to trace crosscutting concerns from AOV-graph to AspectualACME.

Some problems can also arise due to the defined mappings such as: (i) semantic loss – some information represented in AOV-graph has no direct correspondence in AspectualACME and vice-versa. We deal with this problem by adding properties in the architectural description, so the architect can know if a component or port was derived from a goal, a softgoal or a task and he can decide if that component or port has to be directly represented in architecture. However, an automatic generation of the architecture from the requirements can result in an incomplete model because some architectural decisions are not represented in AOV-graph; (ii) limited creativity – the mapping rules are not so flexible and assume that the requirements were decomposed in the correct way. This does not make the architecture design process less creative because architectural information should be added. We have worked with the idea of that there is an information baseline, and it has to be repeated (and mapped to) in many of the models created during the software development process; therefore architects do not have to write this common information from scratch, he can add or change a pre-structure that was obtained from requirements.

The mapping presented in this paper is part of our effort in understanding how to represent crosscutting concerns in different software development phases and also in evaluating if there is a complete or a partial correspondence of the requirement and the architectural model. We conclude that the correspondence is very close when the models adopt similar concepts and an automatic tool can be used with a minimal human intervention. We are already developing a tool that implements the automatic mapping. Because of the limited space, the mapping from AspectualACME to AOV-graph will be addressed in another paper. As a future work we intend to evaluate the mapping rules with other case studies and to perform a deep evaluation of the traceability from the architecture to the requirements model.

References

1. Baniassad, E., Clarke, S.: Theme: An approach for aspect-oriented analysis and design. In: 7th International Conference on Software Engineering (ICSE 2004), pp. 158–167, Scotland (2004).
2. Batista, T., et al.: Reflections on Architectural Connection: Seven Issues on Aspects and ADLs. In: Workshop on Early Aspects, ICSE 2006, pp. 178–187, Shanghai (2006)
3. Chitchyan, R., et al.: Modelling and Traceability of Composition Semantics in Requirements. In: Workshop on Early Aspects, AOSD 2006, pp. 139–151, Born (2006)
4. Egyed, A., Grunbacher, P., Medvidovic, N.: Refinement and Evolution Issues in Bridging Requirements and Architecture - the CBSP Approach. In: From Requirements to Architecture Workshop (co-located with ICSE 2001), pp. 42–47, Toronto (2001)
5. Filho, F., et al.: Exceptions and Aspects: the Devil is in the Details. In: 14th International Conference on Foundations on Software Engineering (FSE-14), pp. 5–11, Portland (2006)
6. Filman, R., et al.: Aspect-Oriented Software Development. Addison-Wesley, San Francisco (2005)
7. Garcia, A., Chavez, C., Choren, R.: An Aspect-Oriented Modeling Framework for MAS Design. In: Padgham, L., Zambonelli, F. (eds.) AOSE 2006. LNCS, vol. 4405, Springer, Heidelberg (2007)
8. Garcia, A., et al.: On the Modular Representation of Architectural Aspects. In: The 3rd. European Workshop on Software Architecture, Nantes, pp. 82–97, Nantes (2006)
9. Garcia, A., Lucena, C.: Taming Heterogeneous Agent Architectures with Aspects. Communications of the ACM (accepted to appear)
10. Garlan, D., Monroe, R., Wile, D.: ACME: An Architecture Description Interchange Language. In: Conference of the Centre for Advanced Studies on Collaborative research (CASCON 1997), pp. 169–183, Toronto (1997)

11. Grunbacher, P., Egyed, A., Medvidovic, N.: Reconciling Software Requirements and Architectures: the CBSP Approach, Requirements Engineering, IEEE Computer Society, pp. 202–211, Springer Verlag, Heidelberg (2001)
12. Jacobson, I., Ng, P.: Aspect-Oriented Software Development with Use Cases. Addison-Wesley, San Francisco (2005)
13. SJani, D., et al.: Deriving Architecture Specifications from KAOS Specifications: A Research Case Study. In: Morrison, R., Oquendo, F. (eds.) EWSA 2005. LNCS, vol. 3527, pp. 185–202. Springer, Heidelberg (2005)
14. Kulesza, U., Garcia, A., Lucena, C.: Towards a method for the development of aspect-oriented generative approaches. In: Workshop on Early Aspects - Aspect-Oriented Requirements Engineering and Architecture Design (OOPSLA 2004), Vancouver (2004)
15. Kulesza, U., et al.: Quantifying the Effects of Aspect-Oriented Programming: A Maintenance Study. In: The 9th Int. Conf. on Soft. Maintenance (ICSM 2006), pp. 223–233, Philadelphia (2006)
16. Lamsweerde, A.v.: From System Goals to Software Architecture. In: Bernardo, M., Inverardi, P. (eds.) SFM 2003. LNCS, vol. 2804, Springer, Heidelberg (2003)
17. Moreira, A., et al.: Multi-Dimensional Separation of Concerns in Requirements Engineering. In: RE 2005. The 13th Int. Conf. on Requirements Eng, Paris, pp. 285–296. IEEE Computer Society, Los Alamitos (2005)
18. Pérez, J., et al.: PRISMA: Towards Quality, Aspect-Oriented and Dynamic Software Architectures. In: The 3rd IEEE Intl Conf. on Quality Software (QSIC 2003), pp. 59–66, Dallas (2003)
19. Pinto, M., Fuentes, L., Troya, J.: A Dynamic Component and Aspect Platform. The Computer Journal 48(4), 401–420 (2005)
20. Rashid, A., et al.: Modularization and composition of aspectual requirements. In: 2nd Int. Conf. on Aspect-Oriented Software Development, Boston, pp. 11–20. ACM (2003)
21. Sanchez, P., et al.: Towards MDD Transformations from AO Requirements into AO Architecture. In: Gruhn, V., Oquendo, F. (eds.) EWSA 2006. LNCS, vol. 4344, pp. 159–174. Springer, Heidelberg (2006)
22. Sant'Anna, C., et al.: On the Quantitative Assessment of Modular Multi-Agent Architectures. In: Multiagent Systems and Software Architecture (MASSA) - Special Track Net.Object Days, pp. 761–770, Erfut (2006)
23. Silva, L.: An Aspect-Oriented Approach to Model Requirements. In: The Doctoral Consortium on Requirements Engineering in conj. with Requirement Engineering Conference, Paris (2005)
24. Soares, S., et al.: Implementing Distribution and Persistence Aspects with AspectJ. In: 17th Annual ACM Conference on Object-Oriented Programming, Systems, Languages and applications (OOPSLA 2002), pp. 174–190, Seatle (2002)
25. Sousa, G., Silva, G., Castro, J.: Adapting the NFR framework to aspect-oriented requirements engineering. In: The 17th Brazilian Symposium on Software Engineering (SBES), Manaus (2003)
26. Sousa, G., et al.: Separation of crosscutting concerns from requirements to design: Adapting the use case driven approach. In: The Early Aspects Workshop at AOSD, Lancaster (2004)
27. Yu, Y., Leite, J., Mylopolous, J.: From goals to aspects: discovering aspects from requirements goal models. In: IEEE Int. Symp. on Requirements Engineering (RE 2004), pp. 38–47, Kyoto (2004)

AO-ADL: An ADL for Describing Aspect-Oriented Architectures

Mónica Pinto and Lidia Fuentes

Dpto. Lenguajes y Ciencias de la Computación, GISUM Research Group
University of Málaga, Málaga, Spain
{pinto,lff}@lcc.uma.es
http://caosd.lcc.uma.es/

Abstract. Architecture description languages are a sound and convenient approach to software architecture representation. The majority of well-known ADLs provide separation of computation and communication in components and connectors, respectively. However, computation and communication are not the only crosscutting concerns that may appear in a software architecture description. Traditional ADLs do not normally provide appropriate support to separate any kind of crosscutting concerns, which frequently result in poor architectures descriptions with highly coupled components. In this paper we present the AO-ADL language, based on a symmetric decomposition model that considers components and connectors as the basic structural elements (similar to traditional ADLs). We will show how aspects are treated as specific types of components that are composed by means of connectors. In order to cope with the separation of concerns we enrich the semantic and expressivity of traditional connectors to support either aspectual and non-aspectual component interactions.

Keywords: Aspect-oriented software architectures, ADLs, connectors, connector templates.

1 Introduction

Architecture Description Languages (ADLs) are a sound and convenient approach to software architecture representation. They have been recognized as an important tool for supporting the systematic reasoning about system components and their relationships early in the development process [1]. ADLs traditionally separate computation and communication into two different architectural elements, i.e. components to encapsulate computation, and connectors to encapsulate communication.

However, computation and communication are not the only crosscutting concerns that may arise during software architecture description. Other functional and extra-functional concerns, such as security, availability, etc., may also be tangled – i.e. several concerns are observed in the same component, or scattered – i.e. same concern is observed in more than one component. The lack of

A. Moreira and J. Grundy (Eds.): Early Aspects 2007 Workshop, LNCS 4765, pp. 94–114, 2007.

appropriate support to represent these crosscutting behaviors at the architectural level frequently result in poor descriptions of software architectures – with highly coupled components and loose of information about the interactions and dependencies among them.

On the other hand, the aim of Aspect-Oriented Software Development (AOSD) [2] is the identification and modeling of crosscutting concerns from requirements to implementation. Several approaches already exist for AO requirements, detailed design and implementation languages, but much more effort should be put in the specification of appropriate languages to describe AO architectures [3].

The answer to both challenges is the definition of ADLs able to support the separation and composition of any kind of crosscutting concerns by extending the expressivity of traditional ADLs. In this paper we present the AO-ADL (Aspect Oriented-Architecture Description Language) language [4]. Similar to traditional ADLs, AO-ADL considers components and connectors as the basic structural elements. Thus AO-ADL preserves the main architectural blocks of traditional ADLs that will be shown as enough to specify AO architectures. Notice that AO-ADL is not a completely new ADL. It is a generalization and evolution of our previous work named DAOP-ADL [5], which was specifically described for specifying component- and aspect-based software architectures running on top of the CAM/DAOP [6] platform. Other existing aspect-oriented ADLs are detailed in the related work section.

AO-ADL considers that components model either crosscutting (named *aspectual component*) or non-crosscutting behavior (named *base component*) exhibiting a symmetric decomposition model. Instead of defining a new entity to model aspects or extending the component with new kind of interfaces, as other aspect-oriented ADLs [5,7], a component is considered as an aspect when it participates in an aspectual interaction. This approach increases the reusability of components, which may play an aspectual or non-aspectual role depending on the particular interactions in which they participates. The symmetric nature of AO-ADL is one of the contributions of this language.

Following a symmetric approach, the crosscutting nature of a component only depends on the connections with other components, which in ADLs are specified in connectors. Thus, the second contribution of AO-ADL is the extension of the semantic of traditional connectors to represent the crosscutting effect of 'aspectual' components. This means that AO-ADL connectors provide support to describe different kinds of interactions among components – not only typical communication as in traditional ADLs, but also crosscutting influences among them. That is, AO-ADL connectors specify how 'aspectual' components are weaved with 'base' components during components' communication. In order to show the main characteristics of the AO-ADL language, we use the ATM model problem taken from the software architecture literature.

After this introduction, in section 2 we discuss the related work on aspect-oriented ADLs. In section 3 we describe the ATM case study that we will follow throughout the paper. Then, the AO-ADL language is presented in section 4. We briefly discuss components to then focus mainly on the definition of connectors.

We finish this section presenting the complete AO-ADL description of the ATM system. After the presentation of AO-ADL, in section 5 we discuss the main advantage of using our approach. The last section presents our conclusions and future directions.

2   Related Work

Non aspect-oriented ADLs have been extensively described and compared in the bibliography. Concretely, a comparison of some of the most relevant ones, like ACME [8], C2 [9] and Rapide [10], can be found in [1]. As stated in the introduction, these ADLs lack of support to specify crosscutting concerns and aspectual interactions. So, in this paper we focus on the related work about aspect-oriented ADLs.

Concretely, in order to define an aspect-oriented ADL, there are at least two questions that need to be answered: (1) which are the main architectural blocks of the language?, and (2) how composition between 'base' and 'aspectual' components is represented?

With respect to the first issue, there is not a consensus between existing AO architectural approaches [3,11]. While some of them add a new building block named aspect to model crosscutting concerns, others represent aspects as components with a different semantic, or as components that provide or require special 'crosscutting' interfaces.

In this sense, DAOP-ADL [5,6] (our previous work) and Fractal [7,12] extend traditional components with new kind of interfaces. In DAOP-ADL aspects are fist-order entities defining an *evaluated interface*. This interface specifies how aspects affect component's interfaces. Similarly, in Fractal a new kind of component named *Aspectual Component* is defined that contains a special *aspect component interface* that provides a set of methods to introspect a join point[1] Finally, in PRISMA [13] aspects are a new abstraction used to define the internal structure of both components and connectors. For a more extensive comparison of these proposals see [3,11].

Considering the lessons learned from our previous work DAOP-ADL (a asymmetric ADL), we concluded that the distinction between components and aspects at architectural level drastically decreases the possibilities for components reuse. Instead, the same building block (e.g. a component) can be used to represent either non-crosscutting and crosscutting concerns. Another proposal following this approach is AspectualACME [14], which is an aspect-oriented extension of ACME where aspects are modeled as ACME components. FuseJ [15] is also a symmetric approach that combines components and aspects and includes the concept of XML-based configurations to specify the weaving information. The main difference is that FuseJ is a Java based programming model and not an

---

[1] AO ADLs do not always share the same definition of symmetry. Notice that we consider that an aspect-oriented ADL is symmetric when the same building block (without new kind of interfaces or other structural elements) is used to model both base and aspectual behaviors. Otherwise, we consider that the ADL is asymmetric.

ADL. Finally, in [16] aspect-oriented software architectures are described in LEDA, where aspects are LEDA components; the support for aspect-orientation is provided by including special kind of components to the architecture.

With respect to the second issue, though there are differences on existing aspect-oriented ADLs, most of them agree on that the semantic of the compositions has to be somehow extended to incorporate aspects to an ADL. Once again, an interesting analysis and comparison of this issue has been performed in [3,11]. In [16] the semantic of connectors is not modified since in addition to the components modeling aspects, a new kind of component with the role of 'coordinators' have to be included in order to describe an aspect-oriented software architecture. These components behave as an aspect manager modeling the interception of join points and the invocation of aspects. In PRISMA [13], since aspects are part of either the components and connectors specification, also the composition specification follows a different approach, being specified inside both components and connectors.

In DAOP-ADL [5], the antecedent of AO-ADL, connections are defined outside either components and connectors, in a specific composition section. They are defined in terms of a set of composition rules, which specify component communication, and a set of aspect evaluation rules, which specify component and aspect weaving. This is basically the same information that AO-ADL encapsulates as part of the specification of connectors. A similar approach is followed by Fractal and FuseJ that define an XML-based aspect binding section and linklets specification, respectively, in order to describe components and aspects compositions. These specifications are equivalent to those in DAOP-ADL. Thus, the main difference between AO-ADL and DAOP-ADL, Fractal and FuseJ is that in the later the concept of connector is not explicit and the component and aspect bindings play the role of both connections and configurations. Beside that, the composition information in AO-ADL is not completely new, since it is an evolution of the information described in the DAOP-ADL composition rules.

In AspectualACME [14], the specification of connectors model composition by defining base and crosscutting roles and configurations, being very similar to AO-ADL connectors. This proposal extends ACME connectors to support crosscutting roles. The main difference with respect to our approach is on the definition of pointcuts. While in AspectualACME pointcuts are defined as part of ACME's attachments, in AO-ADL pointcuts are defined inside connectors. Other difference is that, though both languages allow the use of quantifications[2] in the specification of pointcuts, in AO-ADL the roles of connectors can also be specified using quantifications. As shown along the paper, this feature of AO-ADL improves the adaptability and reusability of connectors.

Finally, also the ConcernBASE proposal [17] is similar to ours in that it extends the semantic of connectors to capture new kind of interactions among components, though they follow a different approach. Concretely, ConcernBASE connectors defines a context to represent various kinds of interactions simultaneously. It defines a set of crosscutting interaction categories that can be specified

---

[2] We understand quantifications as the use of wildcard and binary operators.

inside connectors, such as data access, arbitrator, linkage, distributor and adaptor. The main contribution of this work is that it extends the taxonomy of software connectors proposed by Medvidovic in [18], though the main shortcoming is that the list of crosscutting categories is limited and therefore it does not provide support to separate any kind of crosscutting concern.

3   A Case Study: The Automated Teller Machine System

As mentioned in the introduction, in order to show the contributions of our approach we will use the automated teller machine model problem, taken from the software architecture literature. In order to illustrate the separation of concerns in software architectures, additionally to the ATM system, we have also experience using the AO-ADL language for describing the software architecture of the Health Watcher [19] and the Auction system [20] case studies.

A simplified description of the system[3] is the following: *"In the automated teller machines (ATMs) system each bank in a consortium provides its own computer to maintain its own accounts and process transactions against them. Human cashiers enter account and transaction data. Automated teller machines communicate with a central computer which clears transactions with the appropriate banks. An automated teller machine accepts a cash card, interacts with the user, communicates with the central system to carry out the transaction, dispenses cash, and prints receipts. The system requires appropriate security provisions. The system must handle concurrent accesses to the same account correctly. The banks will provide their own software for their own computers.".*

A partial description of the software architecture of the ATM system, where mainly the core functionality is represented, is shown in Fig. 1. According to Fig. 1, the ATM-GUI component represents the user graphical interface and interacts with the ATM component, which encapsulates the main behavior of an ATM. The bank (Bank component) is always an intermediary of the interactions between the ATM (ATM component) and the customers' accounts (Account). Finally, in order to maintain a backup copy of the accounts, the Account component is responsible for updating the BAccount component. This description has been partially extracted from [21], where a non-aspect oriented description of the ATM model problem is described[4],[5]

This description needs to be completed with the representation of extra-functional or non-functional requirements, which are of our interest to show the main contributions of our approach. Concretely, throughout the paper we focus on four of the non-functional requirements specified in [21] for the ATM system:

---

[3] As it appears in http://www.cs.cmu.edu/~ModProb/

[4] We have not used the solution in [21] since it was not described with an ADL.

[5] To the best of our knowledge, a complete specification of the ATM system using an ADL is not available; and normally these descriptions do not address extra-functional concerns, the most important ones to illustrate the benefits of our AO approach.

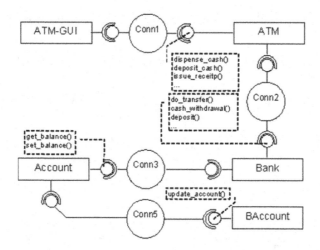

Fig. 1. Partial software architecture of the core functionality of the ATM System

- NFR1. *Heterogeneity.* In [21] this is interpreted as providing inter-communication mechanisms between two heterogeneous banking system.
- NFR2. *Concurrency.* The system must handle concurrent accesses to the same account preserving the integrity of the data account.
- NFR3. *Security.* In [21] security implies the *authentication* of customers that interact with the ATM, the *authorization* in the access to the bank's accounts and the *confidentiality* in the interactions between the ATM and the bank accounts. We extend *confidentiality* as a requirement to be satisfied by all the interactions between components in the ATM system.
- NFR4. *Availability.* Customer services should be available 999/1000 requests. In [21] availability is achieved by maintaining a replica of the accounts.

In the following sections we first describe the AO-ADL language and how to represent crosscutting concerns in the Component and Connector architectural view. Then, we show the completed aspect-oriented solution for the ATM system specified in AO-ADL. We will make special emphasis on the advantages introduced by the enriched semantic of AO-ADL connectors.

4   The AO-ADL Language

AO-ADL is a new XML-based architecture description language specifically well-suited for describing aspect-oriented architectures. Likewise traditional ADLs [1] the main architectural elements of AO-ADL are components and connectors. Instead of extending ADLs with concepts introduced by aspect-oriented programming (AOP) languages, we integrate all these concepts (e.g. join points, pointcuts, etc.) under the definition of components and connectors. We do not consider those concepts specific of AOP languages and close to implementation

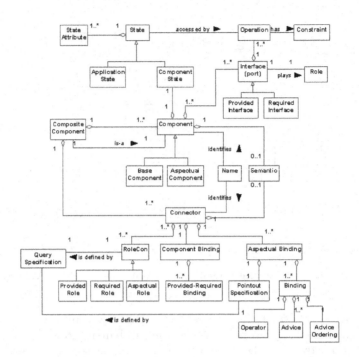

Fig. 2. AO-ADL Metamodel

such as introductions, since they not always help to capture the fundamental nature of software architecture descriptions.

As we already stated above, the main difference between crosscutting and non-crosscutting concerns is merely in the role they play in a particular composition binding and not in the internal behavior itself. Therefore, instead of inventing a new structural element, we redefine the connector and extend its semantics with aspectual bindings. Notice that a software architect has also the possibility of specifying a traditional connector without including the specification of neither aspectual roles nor aspectual bindings. This means that when there is not crosscutting behavior to be specified, the software architect can use connectors as in traditional ADLs. Moreover, software architects non-experts in aspect-orientation would not need to learn AO concepts. Instead, connectors can be specified in two iterations. First, provided and required roles and component bindings are specified. Then, this connector is extended to incorporate aspectual roles and aspectual bindings.

Notice that we have opted for defining a new language, even when many ADLs already exist that could have been extended with AO characteristics [1]. Even when the extension of an existing language would require less effort than the definition of a new one from scratch, the prior approach has also significant drawbacks. Concretely, the main problem of extending a language is obscuring the semantics of the elements of the new language. For instance, ACME [22] defines the *property* concept to extend a component or connector with new characteristics. If we want to extend ACME for AO-ADL, all AO-ADL distinctive features would be ACME properties. This means that the semantics of all AO-ADL new elements would be hidden under a unique concept, the property. A similar reasoning can be done for xADL [23], a highly-extensible XML-based ADL that provides a set of extensible schemas[6]. From our experience it was not worth extending an existing ADL, since AO-ADL required a number of innovative characteristics the semantics of which we wanted to keep clear.

Figure 2 shows the meta-model of our language. The different parts of the meta-model are explained in next subsections using the ATM system case study.

4.1   AO-ADL Components

As discussed above, the first contribution of AO-ADL is the representation of both components and aspects, without distinction, with a single architectural element, the component (Component in Fig. 2). In AO-ADL the specification of components is the same than in other ADLs [1]. From the case study described before, the Account component is represented in AO-ADL as specified in Fig. 3.

As shown in Fig. 3, components are identified by a required unique name inside a particular architectural design (Name in Fig. 2). They are described by means of their provided (ProvidedInterface in Fig. 2) and required (RequiredInterface in Fig. 2) interfaces (the *ports* of the components). The interfaces are defined by the <interface> tag (see Fig. 3). When reusing an interface definition as part of a component the software architect assigns a unique identifier to each interface, the role name (Role in Fig. 2), that refers to the role the component can play or require in a particular architectural design. For example, the Account component in Fig. 3 plays the role of managing the balance of the account (BalanceMgm) and requires the role of managing backup copies (BackupMgm).

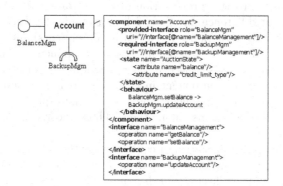

Fig. 3. AO-ADL description of the Account 'base' component

Components can also expose their public state (State in Fig. 2). For the Account component, the balance and credit_limit_type state attributes have been defined.

---

[6] We extended this language for our previous work DAOP-ADL (DAOPxADL [24]) but the resulting architectural specifications are more complex and awkward.

Finally, components can optionally expose their semantics (Semantic in Fig. 2), which is a high-level model of a component's behavior. This behavior is expressed in terms of the interaction protocol between components. The interaction protocol specifies the ordering of the occurrence between the reception of operations in provided interfaces and the sending of operations through required interfaces. In the Account component the behavior section specifies that once the setBalance operation is received in the provided interface with role name BalanceMgm, the updateAccount operation of the required interface with role name BackupMgm is sent. Note that AO-ADL allows embedding of domain-specific languages for specifying components semantics. This feature is used by other ADLs as well (e.g. ACME). Its main benefit is the possibility of reusing existing standard or well-adopted (formal) notations. Other concepts of AO-ADL, which are out of the scope of this paper, are composite components and application state.

Following the symmetric approach, the decision about if a component specification defines a crosscutting or non-crosscutting behavior will be taken during the architecture configuration definition. This means that the connector of a given components interaction will specify if a component is 'base' or 'aspectual'. Note that in the latter case, any operation defined as part of a provided interface of the component can be considered an *advice*.

4.2   AO-ADL Connectors

In traditional ADLs connectors are the building block used to model interactions among components and rules that govern those interactions [1]. Similarly, the connector is the architectural element for composition in AO-ADL, but extended with additional features to support interactions with 'aspectual' components.

There are two main differences between the representation of connectors in traditional ADLs, and the representation of connectors in AO-ADL (Connector in Fig. 2). The first difference and most relevant one is the distinction between *component bindings* (interactions among 'base' components) and *aspectual bindings* (interactions between 'aspectual' and 'base' components). This means that components referenced in the aspectual binding section of a connector are playing the role of an 'aspectual' component in the specified interaction. Later in this section we show how the component bindings and the aspectual bindings differ due to the different interactions among them. Thus, Second difference is the use of quantifications to specify the connector roles.

Fig. 4 shows the BalanceManagement connector for the ATM system. The ATM requirements state that the Bank component (which required interface's role is specified in the provided-role clause of the connector in lines 2 to 6) is the responsible for setting the balance of the Account component (which provided interface's role is specified in the required-role clause of the connector in lines 7 to 11). The composition binding between these components is specified in the component-Binding clause of the connector in lines 17 to 22. Furthermore, the 'availability' requirement previously described in section 3 (NFR4) is a crosscutting requirement that affect the interaction between the Bank and the Account components. Basically, this requirement states that a backup account, represented by the component BAccount, needs to be updated when a new balance is set in the Account component. Applying the AOSD principles, we consider Replication as an 'aspectual' component (which provided interface's role is specified in the

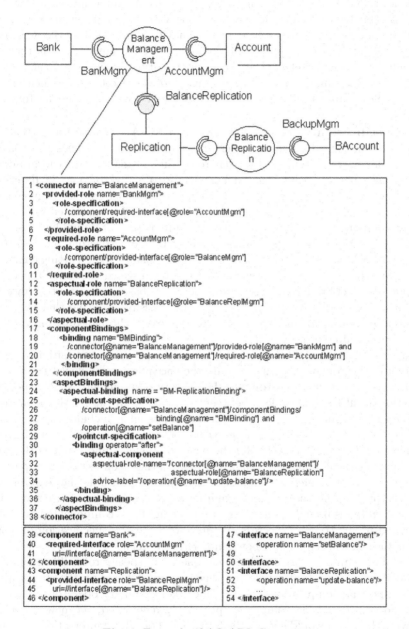

```
1  <connector name="BalanceManagement">
2    <provided-role name="BankMgm">
3      <role-specification>
4        /component/required-interface[@role="AccountMgm"]
5      </role-specification>
6    </provided-role>
7    <required-role name="AccountMgm">
8      <role-specification>
9        /component/provided-interface[@role="BalanceMgm"]
10     </role-specification>
11   </required-role>
12   <aspectual-role name="BalanceReplication">
13     <role-specification>
14       /component/provided-interface[@role="BalanceReplMgm"]
15     </role-specification>
16   </aspectual-role>
17   <componentBindings>
18     <binding name="BMBinding">
19       /connector[@name="BalanceManagement"]/provided-role[@name="BankMgm"] and
20       /connector[@name="BalanceManagement"]/required-role[@name="AccountMgm"]
21     </binding>
22   </componentBindings>
23   <aspectBindings>
24     <aspectual-binding name = "BM-ReplicationBinding">
25       <pointcut-specification>
26         /connector[@name="BalanceManagement"]/componentBindings/
27                              binding[@name= "BMBinding"] and
28         /operation[@name="setBalance"]
29       </pointcut-specification>
30       <binding operator="after">
31         <aspectual-component
32           aspectual-role-name="/connector[@name="BalanceManagement"]/
33                              aspectual-role[@name="BalanceReplication"]
34           advice-label="/operation[@name="update-balance"]/>
35         </binding>
36     </aspectual-binding>
37   </aspectBindings>
38 </connector>
```

```
39 <component name="Bank">                        47 <interface name="BalanceManagement">
40   <required-interface role="AccountMgm"         48   <operation name="setBalance"/>
41     uri=//interface[@name="BalanceManagement"]/>  49      ...
42 </component>                                    50 </interface>
43 <component name="Replication">                  51 <interface name="BalanceReplication">
44   <provided-interface role="BalanceReplMgm"     52   <operation name="update-balance"/>
45     uri=//interface[@name="BalanceReplication"]/>  53      ...
46 </component>                                    54 </interface>
```

Fig. 4. Example of AO-ADL Connector

aspectual-role clause of the connector in lines 12 to 16) that affects the interaction between the Bank and the Account components (specified in the pointcut-specification of the connector in lines 25 to 29).

Notice that the above implies the removal of the required interface with role name BackupMgm from the Account component that was shown in Fig. 3. Instead, in an aspect-oriented solution this behavior is provided by the Replication component, acting as an 'aspectual' component. The main benefit is that the Account component is released of the responsibility of maintaining the backup copy, which was tangled with the core concern of the Account component.

In the next subsections we describe the different parts of the connectors[7].

Role Specification. An important novelty of AO-ADL connectors is that the connector roles can be defined specifying a query that identifies the component(s) that may be connected to that role. This means that instead of always associating a particular interface to a connector role, this role may be described by a query matching 'any component playing a particular role', or 'any component containing a set of particular operations in one of its provided interfaces', or 'any component having a particular attribute as part of its public state'.

This is particularly useful for the specification of aspectual bindings (described below). Since 'aspectual' components encapsulate crosscutting concerns, this means that the usual situation would be one in which the same 'aspectual' component affects different connections between 'base' components. However, without using queries to specify roles, it is not possible to avoid that the same aspectual composition rules would appear replicated through different connectors of the architecture.

An example of the replication of the same aspectual composition rules in different connectors occurs when we add the Encryption component to our architecture. Assuming that, according to the security requirement (NFR3) specified in section 3, all the interactions between components in the ATM system need to be encrypted, in Fig. 5.a the Encryption component is included as an 'aspectual' component that affects the interactions between the ATM-GUI and the ATM components, between the ATM and the Bank components and between the Bank and the Account component. As shown in Fig. 5.a these connections are specified by three different connectors. Consequently, an aspectual-role clause specifying the encryption 'aspectual' behavior and an aspectual-binding clause specifying how encryption is bound to the interaction among 'base' components have to be replicated in the three connectors. We have omitted the specification of Conn2 that is the same specification shown in Conn1 and Conn3[8].

The above can be easily avoided using queries to specify roles. The main idea is to define an 'aspectual' connector which mainly focuses on the specification of the aspectual compositions, using wildcards and binary operators to specify roles. For the Encryption component previously mentioned, the new connector (shown in Fig. 5.b) would specify the following: 'For all the interactions between

---

[7] A more formal statement of the connector semantics is part of our future work.

[8] Only the part of the connector that would be replicated is shown.

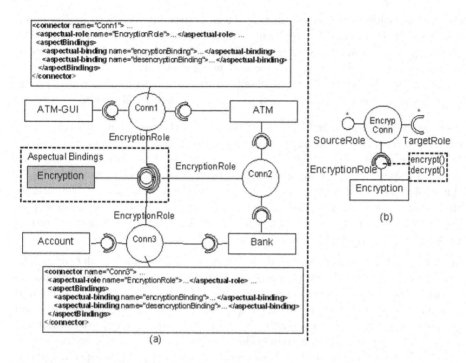

Fig. 5. Examples of (a)Scattered aspectual composition; (b)Use of quantified ports

any source and target component in the ATM system, a component playing the role EncryptionRole in one of its provided interfaces is attached'. In our case study that component is the Encryption component.

Furthermore, the connectors' roles establish the scope of the join points that can be referenced by the connector's pointcuts (described below). The idea is that we can easily represent different weaving scenarios with connectors by using queries on the definition of the connectors' roles.

For instance, at the architectural level typical join points would be: the 'reception of an operation defined in the provided interface of the component', where the source component is omitted from the pointcut specification; the 'sending of an operation defined in the required interface of a component', where the target component is omitted from the pointcut specification; the 'interaction among two components', where both the source and the target component are identified; the 'occurrence of a particular component's state or application's state', what is called a state-based join point, etc. The only requirement is that we need to expose, in the specification of the connector roles, all the information that we will then refer during the specification of the pointcuts.

Base Component Composition. The specification of the 'base' component bindings (ComponentBinding in Fig. 2) inside the connector describes the connections among 'base' components. For instance, the componentBindings clause in the connector shown in Fig. 4 describes the interaction between the Bank and the Account components by connecting the corresponding provided and required roles previously described in the connector (component binding with name 'BM-Binding' in lines 17 to 23). Note that we do not discuss the kind of interactions or communication mechanisms among components that may be considered in AO-ADL, i.e. the type of connector (message-oriented infrastructures, pipes, filters, etc.). Interested readers are referred to [18,25] for such a discussion.

Aspectual Component Composition. This is the main novelty of AO-ADL connectors with respect to traditional connectors. The specification of the aspect bindings (AspectBinding in Fig. 2) inside the connector describes the connections between 'aspectual' components and 'base' components. For instance, in Fig. 4 the Replication component is an 'aspectual' component that affects the interaction between the Bank and the Account components. Concretely, in an aspectual binding (e.g. the aspectual binding with name 'BM-ReplicationBinding' in lines 23 to 36) the following information is provided:

1. **Pointcut Specification.** The description of the pointcuts identifying the join points that will be intercepted. As mentioned before these join points are defined in terms of: (1) a provided role of the connector; (2) a required role of the connector, or (3) a composition binding previously described in the same connector. In the first two cases the pointcut is expressed omitting the other party in the communication. The example of Fig. 4 is an instance of the third case, where the join point captured by the pointcut specification is the interaction between the components connected to the provided-role and required-role of the connector (which in our example would be the Bank and the Account components respectively) by means of the setBalance() operation (specified in the pointcut specification in lines 25 to 28 in Fig. 4). Pointcuts can be specified using wildcards and binary operators. The only requirement is that the pointcut specification will only refer to join points previously exposed in the roles of the connector.

2. **Binding.** A different binding section is defined for each kind of advice (before, after, around) to be included in the definition of the aspect bindings. For instance, the set of 'aspectual' components being composed 'before' a join point may be different from the set of 'aspectual' components composed 'after' a join point.

   (a) **Operator.** The kind of advice is specified in the operator. Basic AO-ADL operators are before, after, around and concurrent-with. Operators take the form 'X before Y', where X is an advice and Y is a join point. A detailed description of all the possible AO-ADL operators as well as the semantic of each operator is out of the scope of this paper, but it is similar to other approaches. Thus, we will explain those that are used in the examples as they appear. For instance, in Fig. 4, the operator is after, indicating that the Replication component is injected always after the interaction among the Bank and the Account component.

   (b) **Constraint.** A constraint restricting the injection of aspects under certain circumstances. Constraints can be expressed as pre-conditions, post-conditions or invariants.

(c) **Advice.** For each kind of advice, the list of 'aspectual' components to be composed is specified. This makes reference to the aspectual-role clause previously defined in the connector (lines 12 to 16 in Fig. 4) and to the name of one of the operations in the referenced interface. The behavior specified by this operation is the behavior to be composed at the matched join points. In Fig. 4, the update-balance operation (line 34) of a component with a provided interface with role name BalanceReplMgm (line 14) is specified as the advice to be executed (line 32-34).

(d) **Advice Ordering.** Several aspects being composed at the same join point need to be appropriately ordered. This information is provided for each aspect binding, since the ordering among a set of aspects may be different depending on the context in which they are composed. The operators before, after, around and concurrent-with previously described are also used to indicate the order of execution of advice. Once again the complete list of ordering operators is out of the scope of this paper.

Notice that this composition information is defined in an aspect-oriented fashion, including common terms of aspect-orientation such as *pointcut specification*, *advice* and *advice ordering/sequencing*. Consequently, it is possible the specification of new relationships (aspect-oriented relationships) between components,

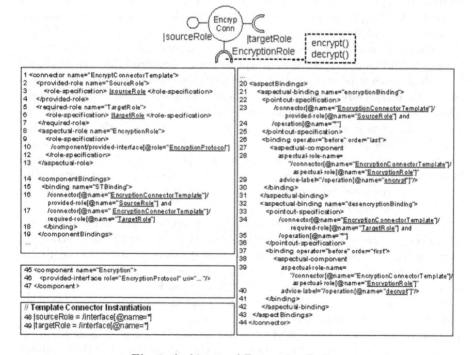

Fig. 6. Architectural Encryption Pattern

which are not supported by the component bindings usually specified inside connectors by non-aspect-oriented ADLs.

4.3   Connector Templates

Another interesting feature of AO-ADL is the definition of connector templates. The idea behind connector templates is that the definition of the connections between 'aspectual' and 'base' components from scratch is not a very practical solution since it requires a lot of effort and, potentially, it is an important locus of errors. Also, it would be very useful to have a mechanism to reuse some recurrent aspect-oriented architectural solutions. An alternative option would be that the software architect has available a set of aspect-oriented architectural patterns or templates for well-known crosscutting concerns. Then, these templates would have to be instantiated in particular software architectures.

For instance, in Fig. 5.b we have shown how to satisfy the confidentiality part of NFR3 in AO-ADL by adding the Encryption 'aspectual' component. However, since encryption is a well-known recurrent crosscutting concern, an alternative to the inclusion of this component from scratch would be the use of an AO-ADL template that indicates us how to compose this component with the rest of components in our software architecture. Concretely, we may have reused the connector template shown in Fig. 6.

The template is interpreted as follows: The behavior of the Encryption 'aspectual' component is the same independently of the particular components connected to the provided and required role of this connector (notice the use of |sourceRole and |targetRole formal parameters in lines 3 and 6 respectively). The template states that, always before sending a message the encrypt advice of the component connected to the encryption port is executed (lines 26 to 30). In case where other aspects have to be injected simultaneously to the encryption aspect, the encrypt advice will be the last one in being evaluated (see the ordering information in line 26). This makes sense since the content of the message should not be encrypted if other aspects need to access to it. Similarly, always before receiving a message, the decrypt advice is executed (lines 37 to 41). When other aspects also need to be injected in the same join point, the ordering information in line 37 indicates that the decrypt advice is the first one to be evaluated. This makes sense since the content of the message should be decrypted before any other aspect access to it.

Then, the |sourceRole and |targetRole formal parameters need to be substituted by particular interface names or queries in order to instantiate the pattern, as shown in the lower part of Fig. 6 (lines 48 and 49). Notice that the shown instantiation, using wildcards to specify both the source and the target components, corresponds to the connector previously described in Fig. 5.b.

In this example, we are assuming that all the interactions among the components need to be encrypted (notice the use of the * wildcard to specify the intercepted messages). However, this is not always the case. In general, in order to define more complex interactions, and still be able to reuse the pointcuts specification, we need to also parameterize those operations of the provided and required roles of the connector that are going to be intercepted by the aspectual components. This is possible in AO-ADL using queries to specify the connector's roles (section 4.2).

For instance, analyzing NFR2, the Account component is a critical resource that can be simultaneously accessed by several instances of the Bank component in order to read (the Bank as a consumer) and write (the Bank as a producer) the balance of the account. This can be identified by the software architect as a typical producer/consumer synchronization problem, for which AO-ADL will provide a connector template. In this case the connector template would define: (1) a required role |reader with at least a |...read() operation; (2) a required role |writer with at least a |...write() operation; (3) a provided role |criticalResource with at least the |...read() and |...write() operations, and (4) an aspectual role |RWsynchronization with the |...beforeRead(...), |...afterRead(...), |...beforeWrite(...) and |...afterWrite(...) operations[9].

Then, in order to instantiate the template: (1) the |reader and the |writer parameters would be instantiated with a required interface of the Bank component containing the get_balance() and set_balance() operations respectively; (2) the |criticalResource parameter would be instantiated with a provided interface of the Auction component also containing the get_balance() and set_balance() operations; (3) the |RWsynchronization with a provided interface of the Concurrency component; (4) the |...read() parameter with the get_balance() operation; (5) the |write(...) parameter with the set_balance() operation, and so on. Since the specification of the pointcuts inside the connector is defined in terms of these parameters, it can be reused for different instantiations of the connector template.

Finally, notice that the use of the notation |param to identify the template's parameters is only a syntactic sugar used to simplify the description of the templates. We are now implementing an Eclipse plug-in that uses the Java Emitter Templates (JET)[10] technology for defining and instantiating the AO-ADL connector templates. JET is part of the Eclipse Modeling Framework Technologies (EMFT) and uses a JSP-like syntax to write templates, as well as the instantiation parameters[11].

4.4   The Complete Architecture of the ATM System in AO-ADL

To finish with our example we will show the complete software architecture of the ATM system presented in section 3.

Fig. 7 shows the aspect-oriented software architecture of the ATM system, which includes the components of Fig. 1 plus the components representing crosscutting concerns[12]. The 'aspectual' components are shown in grey color and

---

[9] The ... in |...m(...) means any parameters of any type.

[10] Web Site: www.eclipse.org/emft/projects/jet/

[11] More information about this can be found in http://caosd.lcc.uma.es/AO-ADL

[12] In this particular example the 'aspectual' components model the non-functional requirements described in section 2. In other scenarios, functional requirements may also be modeled as 'aspectual' components.

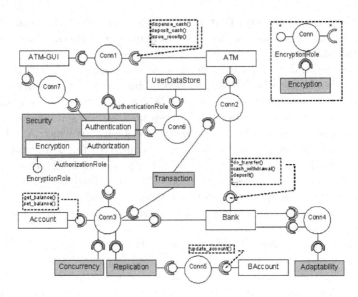

Fig. 7. AO version of the architecture of the ATM System

are the Security, the Transaction, the Concurrency, the Replication and the Adaptability components. We have omitted the XML descriptions for simplicity.

Notice that this is a high-level abstraction of the software architecture. More refined versions of these components may be also specified in AO-ADL, by decomposing each component in a set of components and interconnections among them (though it is out of the scope of this paper).

5   Main Features of AO-ADL

In this section we will outline the main contributions of the AO-ADL language and assess the advantages of these characteristics in the specification of AO architectures.

The modularity of components is improved, for either 'base' and 'aspectual' components. This is achieved by modeling crosscutting concerns as separated components (i.e. 'aspectual' components). In this sense it is possible to specify aspect-oriented architectures, solving the tangled and the scattered behavior problem earlier, at the architectural level.

The pointcut specification is not part of the 'aspectual' component definition. This is shared with most AO ADLs nowadays, including our previous work DAOP-ADL. Thus, the main contribution is that in AO-ADL the pointcut definition is part of the connector aspectual binding specification. Also, when a component plays the role of an 'aspectual' component the advice can be any operation defined as part of its provided interface. All this improves the reusability and evolution of 'aspectual' components.

AO-ADL defines a symmetric decomposition model. As previously mentioned, this feature of our language increases the possibilities of reusing a component, which may play an aspectual or non-aspectual role depending on the particular interactions in which that component participates. That means that the same component can be (re)used either as a 'base' component or as an 'aspectual' component in different software architecture specifications.

Explicit representation of all the dependencies of each aspect. Likewise components in traditional ADLs and IDLs, the 'aspectual' component specification explicitly shows all the dependencies that the 'aspectual' component has with other components by means of its provided and required interfaces. Moreover, AO-ADL provides an homogeneous way of representing such dependencies, without making distinction between 'base' and ' aspectual' components. This information is very useful for the study of the interactions among aspects [26].

Single architectural view to represent crosscutting and non-crosscutting concerns and its interactions. It is possible to clearly identify which are the concerns modeled in a particular software architecture just by looking at the component and connector view (see Fig. 7). This will improve the communication with stakeholders, as well as the evolution and maintainability of both functional and non-functional concerns. Notice that other solutions, such as the one presented in [21], use different levels of abstraction to represent different kinds of concerns. For instance, while *security* is represented as UML constraints in a class diagram, *availability* is represented by adding a new component and required interface into the system and *heterogeneity* is modeled by the use of a design pattern. Consequently, there is not a single architectural view in which all the functional and non-functional concerns of the system can be clearly identified. Notice that it is not our intention to say that other architectural views are not necessary to complete the specification of the software architecture, but that the homogeneous representation of all the concerns in the component and connector view helps to improve the understanding of software architectures and the traceability of concerns among views.

AO-ADL connector specification promotes the refinement of components interactions. Core functionality can be specified first or independently of crosscutting and non-functional concerns. Then, 'aspectual' components can be added or removed from a software architecture without affecting the connections among 'base' components. Since the binding information for 'base' and 'aspectual' component is organized in different sections of the connector, only the 'aspectBindings' section needs to be modified to add/remove 'aspectual' components. An example of this are Fig. 1 and Fig. 7, being the later one an extension of the prior, in which 'aspectual' components were added. The interconnections among components in Fig. 1 remains the same in Fig. 7.

Connector templates. Existing catalogues of crosscutting concerns define nonfunctional or extra-functional concerns that are typical of an application domain. Based on these catalogues, the software architect can identify aspect-oriented architectural solutions for certain recurrent crosscutting concerns. In AO-ADL these aspect-oriented architectural solutions for recurrent crosscutting concerns can be captured by the specification of connector templates. These templates can then be reused in different architectural configurations as shown in Fig. 6.

6 Conclusions and Future Work

In this paper we have presented AO-ADL, an XML-based aspect-oriented architecture description language. The main contributions of AO-ADL are: (1) The symmetric decomposition model, which defines the component as the architectural block to model both functionality and aspectual behavior, and (2) The extended semantic of connectors to specify aspectual composition information.

Another interesting feature of AO-ADL, which improves the definition and evolution of aspect-oriented software architectures, is the definition of connector templates. Currently, we are working on the definition of a library of aspect-oriented architectural patterns. We are mainly focusing on the definition of connector templates for modeling well-known crosscutting concerns. This will allow reusing these concerns in different software architectures.

The use of XML has important advantages, such as using the built-in XML tool support to define and manipulate architectural descriptions, or the possibility for a runtime execution environment of using this information during the application execution [6]. However, it also has an important drawback regarding the readability of the software architecture in the communication with stakeholders. In order to cope with this shortcoming we are now defining a tool suite that will provide support to define, manipulate and reuse AO-ADL specifications. This tool makes use of the XML-to-Ecore mapping technology provided by the Eclipse Modeling Framework (EMF)[13] in order to provide an ECore model of AO-ADL. An additional goal is the definition of a mapping process, in the MDD (Model-Driven Development) sense, to define a correspondence between the AO-ADL ECore model and the UML 2.0 Ecore model. This correspondence bases on the mapping process from architecture to design defined in [27] and will provide a UML 2.0 standard representation of AO-ADL software architectures.

Finally, we would like to remark that AO-ADL is the aspect-oriented integrated ADL of AOSD-Europe[14]. Concretely, in this project we are now collaborating on the definition of COMPASS [20,28], an approach that offers a systematic means to derive an aspect-oriented architecture, described in AO-ADL, from a given aspect-oriented requirements specification, described in RDL (Requirements Description Language) [29]. This approach is a constituent part of the aspect-oriented mapping process that is being defined in this project from requirements to architecture and from there to design and implementation [27]. Concretely, the AO-ADL tool support discussed in the previous paragraph is being defined as part of this project.

---

[13] Web Site: www.eclipse.org/emft/projects/
[14] European Network of Excellence on AOSD.

Acknowledgment

We are very grateful to the anonymous referees for their insightful suggestions, that greatly helped improving the contents of the paper. This work is supported by European Commission FP6 Grant AOSD-Europe (IST-2-004349), European Commission STREP Project AMPLE (IST-033710), and Spanish Commission of Science and Technology (TIN2005-09405-C02-01).

References

1. Medvidovic, N., Taylor, R.: A Classification and Comparison Framework for Software Architecture Description Languages. IEEE Transaction on Software Engineering 26(1), 70–93 (2000)
2. Aspect-Oriented Software Development Web Site, http://www.aosd.net
3. Chitchyan, R., Rashid, A., Sawyer, P., Garcia, A., Pinto, M., Bakker, J., Tekinerdogan, B., Clarke, S., Jackson, A.: Survey of (Aspect-Oriented) Analysis and Design Approaches. AOSD-Europe project Report AOSD-Europe-ULANC-9 (2005)
4. Krechetov, I., Tekinerdogan, B., Pinto, M., Fuentes, L.: Initial Version of Aspect-Oriented Architecture Design Approach. AOSD-Europe project report AOSD-Europe-UT-D37 (February 2006)
5. Pinto, M., Fuentes, L., Troya, J.M.: DAOP-ADL: An Architecture Description Language for Dynamic Component and Aspect-Based Development. In: Pfenning, F., Smaragdakis, Y. (eds.) GPCE 2003. LNCS, vol. 2830, pp. 118–137. Springer, Heidelberg (2003)
6. Fuentes, L., Pinto, M., Troya, J.M.: Supporting the Development of CAM/DAOP Applications: an Integrated Development Process. Software Practice and Experience 37(1), 21–64 (2007)
7. Pessemier, N., Seinturier, L., Coupaye, T., Duchien, L.: A Model for Developing Component-Based and Aspect-Oriented Systems. In: Löwe, W., Südholt, M. (eds.) SC 2006. LNCS, vol. 4089, Springer, Heidelberg (2006)
8. Garlan, D., Monroe, R., Wile, D.: ACME: An Architecture Description Interchange Language. In: Proc. of CASCON 1997 (November 1997)
9. Medvidovic, N., Oreizy, P., Robbins J.E., Taylor, R.N.: Using Object-Oriented Typing to Support Architectural Design in the C2 Style. In: Proc. of ACM SIGSOFT 1996, USA, pp. 24–32 (October 1996)
10. Luckham, D., et al.: Specification and Analysis of System Architecture Using Rapide. IEEE Trans. Soft. Eng. 21(4), 336–355 (1995)
11. Batista, T., Chavez, C., Garcia, A., SantAnna, C., Kulesza, U., Rashid, A., Filho, F.C.: Reflections on Architectural Connection: Seven Issues on Aspects and ADLs. In: Proc. of EA 2006, China (May 2006)
12. Pessemier, N., Seinturier, L., Duchien, L.: Components, ADL and AOP: Towards a Common Approach. In: Proc. of the Workshop ECOOP RAMSE 2004 (June 2004)
13. Pérez, J., Ramos, I., Jaén, J., Letelier, P., Navarro, E.: PRISMA: Towards Quality, Aspect-Oriented and Dynamic Software Architectures. In: Proc. of 3rd IEEE Intl Conf. on Quality Software, USA (November 2003)
14. Garcia, A., Chavez, C., Batista, T., SantAnna, C., Kulesza, U., Rashid, A., Lucena, C.: On the Modular Representation of Architectural Aspects. In: Gruhn, V., Oquendo, F. (eds.) EWSA 2006. LNCS, vol. 4344, pp. 82–97. Springer, Heidelberg (2006)

15. Suvée, D., De Fraine, B., Vanderperren, W.: A Symmetric and Unified Approach Towards Combining Aspect-Oriented and Component-Based Software Development. In: Gorton, I., Heineman, G.T., Crnkovic, I., Schmidt, H.W., Stafford, J.A., Szyperski, C.A., Wallnau, K. (eds.) CBSE 2006. LNCS, vol. 4063, pp. 114–122. Springer, Heidelberg (2006)
16. Navasa, A., Pérez, M.A., Murillo, J.M.: Aspect Modelling at Architecture Design. In: Morrison, R., Oquendo, F. (eds.) EWSA 2005. LNCS, vol. 3527, pp. 41–58. Springer, Heidelberg (2005)
17. Kandé, M.M., Strohmeier, A.: On The Role of Multi-Dimensional Separation of Concerns in Software Architecture. In: Proc. of OOPSLA 2000 Workshop on Advanced SoC in Object-Oriented Systems, USA (October 2000)
18. Mehta, N.R., Medvidovic, N., Phadke, S.: Towards a taxonomy of software connectors. In: Proc. of the 22nd ICSE 2000, Ireland, pp. 178–187. ACM Press, New York (2000)
19. Pinto, M., Gámez, N., Fuentes, L.: Towards the architectural definition of the Health Watcher system with AO-ADL. In: Proc. of the Early Aspects Workshop at ICSE 2007, May, Minnesota, USA (2007)
20. Chitchyan, R., Pinto, M., Rashid, A., Fuentes, L: COMPASS: Composition-Centric Mapping of Aspectual Requirements to Architecture. Accepted for publication in TAOSD: Special Issue on Early Aspects
21. Choi, H., Yeom, K.: An Approach to Software Architecture Evaluation with the 4+1 View Model of Architecture. In: Proc. of the Ninth APSEC 2002 (2002)
22. Allen, R., Dounce, R., Garlan, D.: Specifying and Analyzing Dynamic Software Architectures. In: Astesiano, E. (ed.) ETAPS 1998 and FASE 1998. LNCS, vol. 1382, Springer, Heidelberg (1998)
23. Dashofy, E.M., Hoek, A., Taylor, R.N.: An Infrastructure for the Rapid Development of XML-based Architecture Description Languages. In: Proc. of the 24th International Conference on Software Engineering (ICSE'02), Orlando, Florida
24. Fuentes, L., Gámez, N., Pinto, M.: DAOPxADL: An extension of the xADL Architecture Description Language with Aspects. In: Proc. of the DSOA 2006 workshop collocated with JISBD 2006, Spain (2006)
25. Shaw, M., DeLine, R., Zelesnik, G.: Abstractions and Implementations for Architectural Connections. In: Proc. of (ICCDS 1996) (1996)
26. Sanen, F., et al.: Study on interaction issues AOSD-Europe Project Report, AOSD-Europe-KUL-7 (February 2006)
27. Chitchyan R., et al.: Mapping and Refinement of Requirements Level Aspects. AOSD-Europe project report No: AOSD-Europe-ULANC-24 (November 2006)
28. Chitchyan, R., Pinto, M., Fuentes, L., Rashid, A.: Relating AO Requirements to AO Architecture. In: Proc. of the Early Aspects Workshop(OOPSLA'05), USA (2005)
29. Chitchyan, R., Sampaio, A., Rashid, A., Sawyer, P., Khan, S.: Initial Version of Aspect-Oriented Requirements Engineering Model. AOSD-Europe project report No: AOSD-Europe-ULANC-17 (February 2006)

Composing Structural Views in xADL

Nelis Boucké[1], Alessandro Garcia[2], and Tom Holvoet[1]

[1] Distrinet, KULeuven
{nelis.boucke,tom.holvoet}@cs.kuleuven.be
[2] Computing Department, Lancaster University
garciaa@comp.lancs.ac.uk

Abstract. Experience with building an architecture for an industrial Automatic Guided Vehicle Transportation System (AGVTS) shows that several essential concerns crosscut the architectural views. To cope with this, a stronger separation proved to be necessary, i.e. using different views for different concerns. In practice this was difficult, since the support for relations between views is very limited. This makes separation of concerns in views hard, thereby increasing maintenance overhead and reducing reuse capabilities. Our claim is that specifying compositions of views is as important as specifying the views itself. This paper extends a representative architectural description language (xADL) which support for composing structural views, by introducing three relations, namely *refinement*, *mapping*, and *unification*. Improving separation of concerns in views and their explicit composition enhances architecture understandability and changeability. The feasibility of the relations is assessed by redesigning the AGVTS architecture. Based on a real maintenance scenario, we investigate to what extent these explicit compositions lead (or not) to enhanced architectural changeability for evolving the distribution strategy in the AGVTS system.

1 Introduction

The architecture of a software system defines the design structure or structures, which comprise software elements, the externally visible properties of those elements, and the relationships among them [3]. This implies that the core issue in architectural design is to define and compose the high-level design structures that are relevant to key stakeholders' concerns. Over the last decades several Architectural Description Languages (ADLs) have been proposed to describe architectures.

Experience with building a multiagent architecture (MAA) for an industrial Automatic Guided Vehicle Transportation System (AGVTS) shows that several concerns typically crosscut the architectural views. A crosscutting concern in an ADL description is a concern that is not effectively modularized using the abstractions of that ADL, in this case the modularization at the level of architectural views. Using MAA means structuring the system in several autonomous entities (agent components), connected to an environment component, working together (coordinating) to achieve the goals of the system [46]. We have observed that some architecturally-relevant concerns, such as control, coordination, and distribution, crosscut the decomposition in architectural views of the AGVTS system. The architects judged that a stronger separation was necessary to allow evolving individual concerns more easily and targeted a clean separation of the description of different concerns in different views.

A. Moreira and J. Grundy (Eds.): Early Aspects 2007 Workshop, LNCS 4765, pp. 115–138, 2007.
© Springer-Verlag Berlin Heidelberg 2007

In order to achieve the separation of such crosscutting architectural concerns, we encountered a fundamental problem that is the subject of this paper. Having divided to conquer, we must reunite to rule [29]. Once the concerns are separated using the views, there is a need to integrate the views to obtain the final system, and this is where the current architectural practice falls short. For integration, we need to define *relations* between views. In this context, we use the term *composition* for an aggregation of several views and relations. As a consequence, the *system* is a composition of all views and associated relations between the views.

Looking to architectural practice, there is good support to describe several views, but the support for describing relations between views is limited. For example, Clements and colleagues [12] use tables to define a mapping between elements in different views. Yet, the relation remains informal (relying on a textual explanation) and the support for different types of relations is too limited. The IEEE-1471 standard[27] requires that any inconsistencies between views are documented, but leaves completely open how this should happen. In other approaches the relations between views remain implicit or informal. Without proper support for relations, the architect has no choice but to leave the concerns mingled with each other in the views. Not separating important concerns makes it harder to comprehend the architecture and leads to increased maintenance and change overhead, reduced reuse capabilities, and generally results in architectural erosion over the system lifetime [4].

Our claim is that integrating the views is as important as specifying the views itself. Relations and compositions must become first class, and become an explicit and integral part of an ADL. Based on these observations, we extend a representative ADL with explicit support for composing structural views. In this first extension we limit ourselves to add relations between one type of view only, namely the structural view of xADL [14]. xADL is a general-purpose, extensible ADL to model architecturally-relevant structures. xADL supports the specification of structural views, but there is little to no support for the relations between views. Concretely, we introduce three types of relations, *refinement*, *mapping*, and *unification*, and use these relations to compose several structural views. The xADL language is used as an example, but similar composition rules could be of use to other ADLs as well. To assess the feasibility of the operators, we use them to refactor and evolve the AGVTS architecture in order to make the key concerns of the architect explicit, together with the associated structural views and relations between the views.

The proposed approach differs from existing aspect-oriented ADLs by focussing on composition of structural views. The current state of art in aspect-oriented ADLs concentrates on defining aspectual components and aspectual relations to add or change *behavior* on component interfaces, starting from the decomposition into components and connectors [4,37,39]. In another words, they tend to mimic AO composition mechanisms supported by the family of AspectJ [16]-like programming languages [32]. This paper focuses on the structural impact of a concern, starting from a decomposition into structural views and trying to compose these views together.

Overview: The remainder of this paper is structured as follows. Section 2 introduces ADLs. Section 3 introduces our case study and illustrates the lack of relations in a more concrete context. In section 4 we introduce compositions and relations in xADL and review an excerpt of the AGVTS in the context of these relations. Section 5 describes related work. Finally, we conclude in section 6.

2 Architectural Description Languages

In the last decades, several ADLs have been proposed to model architectures. ADLs exists in all kinds of shapes and forms. Several ADLs have a formal foundation (like ACME [24], xADL [15] and AADL [42]), but we also consider less formal approaches to define an ADL, like [12] or [40]. Some ADLs are meant to model a particular application domain, others are more general-purpose. We will use the xADL language in our illustrations. The motivation to use the xADL language is that it provides a core language with a simple set of general-purpose constructs to model an architecture. Additionally, it provides an easy way to extend the language definition and the associated tool support for new concepts, allowing fast prototyping of new ADL constructs.

xADL supports three types of views: (1) a view defining component types, called types or archType in xADL; (2) structural views describing component and connector types and how they are linked to each other, called architectural structure or archStructure in xADL; (3) instance views describing component and connector instances and how they are linked to each other, called architectural instances or archInstance in xADL. Both second and third are a kind of component and connector viewtype in the sense of [12]. The second one shows configuration types of components and connectors emphasizing on how they should be linked together (called structure by the xADL authors), while the third one shows component and connector instances to document the dynamics of the system. In this paper, we focus on the second type of view of xADL and call this a structural view on the system, inline with the terminology suggested by the xADL authors.

2.1 Basic Elements in xADL

An structural view in xADL is built around the following basic elements[1].

- **Components:** Components are the loci of computation in the architecture. Components have a unique identifier and a textual description, along with a set of interfaces.
- **Connectors:** Connectors are the loci of communication in the architecture design. Similar to components, connectors also have a unique identifier, a textual description, and a set of interfaces.
- **Interfaces:** Interfaces are components' and connectors' portals to the outside world. A "interface" in xADL is called "port" for components and "roles" for connectors in other languages like ACME ADL. Interfaces have a unique identifier, a textual description, and a direction. The direction indicates whether the interface is provided, required, or both.
- **Links:** Links are connections between interfaces, defining the topology of the architecture.

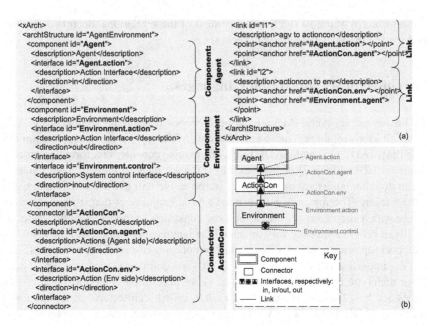

Fig. 1. Example xADL specification, showing the `Agent` and `Environment` component, connected with the `ActionCon` connector. We used the same abbreviated notation as the xADL authors used in [15] to improve readability of the specification. We will only once include a key, the other figures use the same graphical notation.

Figure 1a shows an example architectural description containing two components (`Agent` and `Environment`), one connector `ActionCon`, and links to attach the connector to the components. The environment in this picture is a software component providing operations to the agents to view and manipulate the world. In principle, the identifier of an interface can be any unique string. We follow the convention that the identifier is built following the pattern 'element-name-dot-interface-name', like `Agent.action`. References are represented by the href property, containing a unique identifier or an element after the sharp symbol.

xADL is supported by a tool set integrated in the Eclipse platform, called ArchStudio. We used ArchStudio 4.0, available since November 2006 [28]. ArchStudio contains both a visual editor, that allows to graphically manipulate the architecture (notation similar to fig. 1b) and a special-purpose specification editor, representing the architecture in the form of a tree.

Special Construct: Subarchitecture. xADL has an additional construct called *subarchitecture*, which we would like to explain here since one of our relations is inspired by it. Subarchitecture is a relation between a component or connector *type* and an architectural structure, defining that the architectural structure forms a subarchitecture of the component or connector type. We briefly describe types in xADL because they are used

---

[1] Based on [15]. The group element is left out because it is not used in this paper.

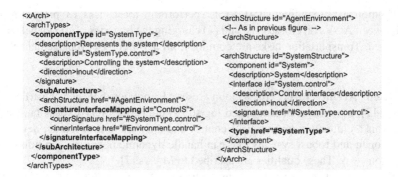

```
<xArch>                                              <archStructure id="AgentEnvironment">
  <archTypes>                                          <!-- As in previous figure -->
    <componentType id="SystemType">                  </archStructure>
      <description>Represents the system</description>
      <signature id="SystemType.control">            <archStructure id="SystemStructure">
        <description>Controlling the system</description>  <component id="System">
        <direction>inout</direction>                     <description>System</description>
      </signature>                                        <interface id="System.control">
      <subArchitecture>                                    <description>Control interface</description>
        <archStructure href="#AgentEnvironment">           <direction>inout</direction>
        <SignatureInterfaceMapping id="ControlS">          <signature href="#SystemType.control">
          <outerSignature href="#SystemType.control">    </interface>
          <innerInterface href="#Environment.control">   <type href="#SystemType">
        </signatureInterfaceMapping>                     </component>
      </subArchitecture>                                </archStructure>
    </componentType>                                  </xArch>
  </archTypes>
```

Fig. 2. Example with subarchitecture construct

the subarchitecture construct, but we will not come back to types in the remainder of this paper. Types are grouped in the archTypes section of an xADL document, specifying types for components, connectors and interfaces. Component and connector types are defined as a set of signatures. A signature prescribes what interface a component must offer to be of the type. Types are typically used if exactly the same component or connector type is needed in several structural views.

Figure 2 contains an example component type SystemType, having one signature called SystemType.control. The SystemStructure architectural structure uses the SystemType to construct the System component, and provides a href to show that the System.control interface covers the SystemType.control signature. The subarchitecture construct is contained within the type, e.g. in the SystemType component in fig. 2. Note that there appears an (indirect) relation between two architectural structures: SystemStructure is related with AgentEnvironment through its System component of type SystemType.

3   Case Study: Automatic Guided Vehicle Transportation System

This section introduces the industrial case study, an Automatic Guided Vehicle Transportation System (AGVTS). First, the application is briefly introduced in section 3.1. Next, we exploit an excerpt from an existing architectural description [5] to illustrate the problem of concerns that crosscut the structural views in section 3.2.

3.1   Automatic Guided Vehicle Transport System

An Automatic Guided Vehicle Transport System (AGVTS) is a fully automated industrial system that uses multiple AGVs to transport loads in a warehouse or production plant. An AGV is an unmanned, battery powered transportation vehicle. The AGVTS uses an external software system – called Ensor – running on the computer of each AGV vehicle that steers the vehicle based on high-level commands given by the AGVTS (like move, turn). The main functional requirements for the AGVTS are: (1) allocating transportation tasks to individual AGVs; (2) performing those tasks; (3) preventing conflicts between AGVs on crossroads; and (4) charging the batteries of AGVs before they are drained. Transportation tasks are coming from a Warehouse Management System (WMS).

Multiagent Architecture. In a joint research project between DistriNet and Egemin [17], a producer of automated logistic systems, the AGVTS was built with a MAA. This architecture decentralizes control and answers to new market demand for flexible, open and robust systems that can handle dynamic operating conditions in an autonomous way. These qualities are ascribed to MAAs [7].

Using a MAA means structuring the system in several autonomous entities (agent components) connected to an environment component. The agents and environment are built according to a reference architecture for multi-agent systems [44]. An agent component operates autonomously, but coordinates with other agent components to achieve the system goals. Each agent has three interfaces: (1) perception: to observe the environment; (2) action: to influence the environment; (3) communication: to communicate with other agents by sending messages through the environment. The environment is a software component, shielding the agents from technical details and providing abstractions to view and manipulate the real world [45]. The environment provides interfaces for perception, action and communication to the agents.

Concerns. In this paper, we will focus on three essential concerns for the software architect building an MAA for an AGVTS, namely control, coordination and distribution. The concerns are identified based on the experience of the architects building an AGVTS and each of them has a significant impact on the structural view of the system. We briefly discuss each of the concerns and describe the architectural implications of the respective concerns before going into details on crosscutting concerns in the next section.

The control concern covers the decomposition into agents and an environment (to realize decentralized control in the AGVTS). We consider this decomposition as the dominant decomposition in an MAA. In the architectural description we will mainly focus on the interaction between the agents and the environment and less on the internals of the respective components. In the AGVTS we identified three types of agents. There is an AGVAgent for each AGV vehicle, responsible for managing the tasks of an AGV. There is a Transport-Agent for each transportation task in the system, responsible for searching an appropriate AGV to perform a new transport and to follow up the dispatching of the tasks. Finally, there are one or more TransportManagerAgents, in charge of communicating with a WMS and managing (create, remove, etc.) the TransportAgents. For an AGVTS, the tasks of the Environment include providing the interfaces for perception, action and communication to the agents and the translation of high-level commands from the AGVAgent to Ensor, the software package for low-level control of the AGV vehicle.

Because agents operate autonomously, coordinating their behavior is essential to let the multiagent system operate as a whole. Because coordination is so important in the AGVTS, the architects decided to separate this concerns. The coordination concern

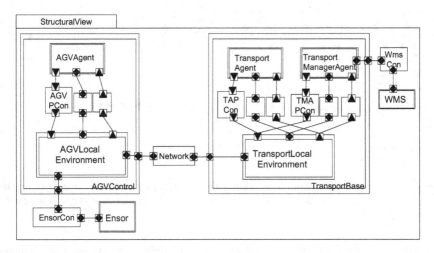

Fig. 3. First decomposition view of an existing architectural description of the AGVTS, to illustrate crosscutting of the control and distribution concern. Same graphical notation as fig. 1.

covers all types of coordination between different agents in the system, e.g. assigning transport or avoiding collisions on crossroads.

The third concern, distribution, covers the implications of building a software system on a physically distributed infrastructure. We focus on the decomposition into subsystems to allow easy deployment on a physical infrastructure and any additional support needed for this, like remoting or synchronization support. Note that we specifically look for the impact of distribution on the *structure* of the software (thus in structural views), independent of the deployment view. Distribution is specifically important for an AGVTS, since the physical infrastructure exists of an industrial computer on each AGV vehicle and one or several server systems, connected through a wireless network.

3.2   Concerns Crosscutting Structural Views

As defined in the introduction, a crosscutting concern in an ADL description is a concern that is not effectively modularized using the abstractions of that ADL [4]. Any type of decomposition implies that there are concerns that crosscut with that decomposition. If an architect decides to decompose the system in several structural views, there will be concerns that crosscut these structural views.

To illustrate crosscutting and the need for a stronger separation we start from the original architectural documentation and show how the concerns control, distribution and coordination crosscut in the architectural views of the AGVTS.

Control and Distribution. Figure 3 shows the first decomposition view of the architectural description of the AGVTS. Careful analysis reveals that this decomposition mixes up at least two of the concerns: control and distribution.

To understand better which part of the decomposition is done for which concerns, fig. 4 shows separate structural views per concerns. The left part shows the Control view, outlining a decentralized control architecture defining

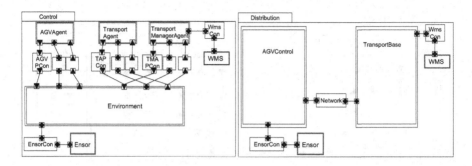

Fig. 4. Left: Control view, showing the decomposition into agents and environment. Right: Distribution view, showing the decomposition into subsystems for deployment. Same graphical notation as fig. 1.

the types of agents and an environment. The right part shows the Distribution view, defining two subsystems (AGVControl and TransportBase), to be deployed on an AGV vehicle and a server respectively. Note that the Environment component in the Control view corresponds to the AGVLocalEnvironment and TransportLocalEnvironment components in the StructuralView. But in the StructuralView it is implicit which part belongs to which concern and what the relations between different concerns are, mingling up the two concerns. Additionally, there are several other views mingling up the same concerns, leading to crosscutting.

In the introduction some well-known drawbacks of crosscutting concerns are mentioned. Here we illustrate one specific consequence, namely that it is harder to change the architecture with respect to one of the concerns. The architects encountered this problem during a revision the AGVTS architecture. The original architecture located an agent on each AGV vehicle. During the project Egemin realized that switching to a distributed MAA is a big step with far-reaching effects for the company, not only for the software but for the whole organization[2]. Therefore, Egemin proposed a stepwise integration starting with an architecture having all agents located on a single computer system with remote access to the AGV vehicles. In principle, the impact of such a revision would be limited since only the distribution concern is changed. Unfortunately, due to the concerns crosscutting the views, they had to adapt most of software architecture and change nearly every individual view.

Control and Coordination. To illustrate that crosscutting concerns have a even more broadly scoped impact on the views, we annotated the table of content of the existing architectural description of the AGVTS with two concerns: control and coordination. Figure 5 shows the annotated table of content, showing both static and runtime views. View names marked in bold include fragments of the control concern, underlined names include fragments of the coordination concern. Views that are both bold and underlined intermingle the definition of coordination with agents, illustrating that the two

---

[2] This is inline with the observations of Bass et al. [3] that an architecture affects the developing organization.

– Static views
 1. Layered: The ATS (AGVs transportation system)
 2. Decomposition: **The ATS, Transport base, AGVControl, Local environment**, Transport agent, AGV agent, <u>Decisions</u>
 3. Uses: **Transport Base, AGV Control system**
 4. Generalization: **Agents**
– Runtime views (instances)
 1. Shared date: **Agent, <u>Local virtual environment</u>, Protocol description**
 2. Process views: **Move action, Sending-Receive action, Background processes**
– Mixed views: <u>ObjectPlaces middleware</u>, <u>collision avoidance</u>

Fig. 5. List of design models made for the AGV transportation system. Model names in bold include the control concern, underlined model names include the coordination concern.

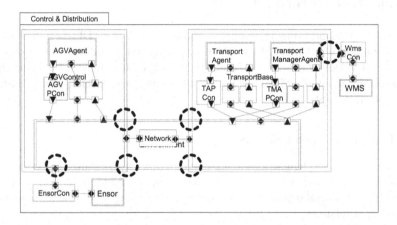

Fig. 6. Illustration of overlap between both views. The dashed circles point to strange overlap between the elements, for the remainder we use the same graphical notation as fig. 1.

concerns crosscut each other in the views. Notice that this illustration involves several types of view, including static, run-time and deployment types of views. This illustrates the broadly scoped influence of coordination and control on the architectural views.

Relations. Why do the concerns crosscut each other? In the first version of the architecture, the architects did not explicitly consider a set of essential concerns to separate, obviously leading to crosscutting concerns as just illustrated.

Based on the changes to the distribution concerns and the analysis revealing crosscutting concerns, the architects judged that a stronger separation was necessary. During a revision of the architecture, they wanted to separate the description of different concerns in different views. The two views in fig. 4 could be an example of this. That is when the architects encountered the lack of appropriate relations, preventing them from using such strong separation between concerns in views.

The challenges to relate the Control view and Distribution view are:

1. The same element appear in different structural views, e.g. Ensor, WMS and the respective connectors.
2. Some components must become subcomponents of other components, e.g. AGVAgent must become subcomponent of AGVControl.
3. If the components would be drawn in the same view, one component would crosscut the border of other components. To illustrate this, we constructed a view mixing the elements of the Control and Distribution view (called Control&Distribution view) in fig. 6. One can see that the Environment component cuts across the border of the AGVControl and TransportBase components.

4   Composing Structural Views

This section illustrates how to compose structural views in xADL. Section 4.1 introduces the necessary changes to the xADL language, adding the concepts of composition and introducing three types of relations. Section 4.2 uses the extended language to refactor an excerpt of the AGVTS architecture covering two concerns introduced earlier in this paper: control and distribution.

4.1   Compositions and Relations

Firstly, we add a new element to the xADL description called architectural composition (denoted <archComposition> in the XML specification), describing a concrete composition of several structural views and the associated relations. Next, we introduce three types of relations.

- **unification:** Unifies elements (components or connectors) from different structural views with each other, i.e. declares that the elements are exactly the same element. The unified elements must either have exactly the same interfaces, or the architect must define the corresponding interfaces.
- **mapping:** Maps individual or groups of elements (called subjects) from one structural view on a single element of another structural view (called target). The subjects then become subelements of the target element. The join points used in the mapping rule are the interfaces, the architect must define corresponding interfaces between the target and the subject.
- **refinement:** Defines that a specific structural view (referred to as inner structure) describes a substructure for an architectural component (referred to as outer component) of another structural view. The join points used in the mapping rule are again the interfaces, the architect must define corresponding interfaces between the outer component and interfaces in the inner structure.

Figure 7 shows an example architectural composition using the refinement relation. The figure shows three structural views (represented by a UML package symbol: Struct1, Struct2 and Struct3) and a composition specification. A composition specification always consists of a unique identifier, a description and a set of relations between the views.

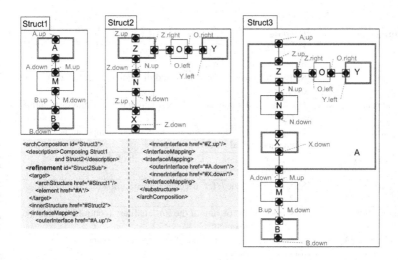

Fig. 7. Example composition using the refinement relation. Struct2 refines component A of Struct1, resulting in Struct3. Same graphical notation as fig. 1.

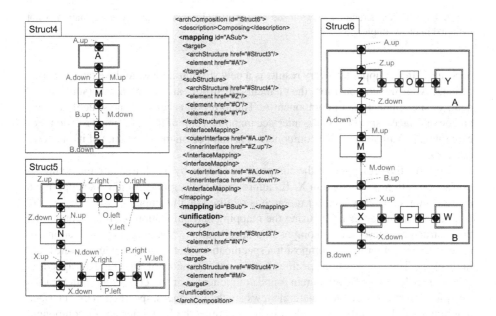

Fig. 8. Example composition using the mapping and unification relations. Parts of Struct2 are mapped on component A and B of Struct1, resulting in Struct3. Same graphical notation as fig. 1.

In our specific solution, a composition results in a new view that is a reification of the relations and can be used in further compositions (the view has the name of the identifier of the composition). The composition specifies that Struct2 refines component A

Structural view	Purpose	Concern	Step
Control	Describes the agent types, environment and associated relations.	control	1
Centralized	Subsystems needed for centralized deployment.	distribution (centralized)	2C
EnsorConnectorInternal	Describes a refinement of the EnsorConnector.	auxiliary (control&distribution)	3C
ControlExtendedAlt1	Composition of Control and EnsorConnectorInternal	result of composition	3C
CentralizedAGVSystem	Composition of ControlExtendedAlt1 and Centralized	result of composition	4C
Decentralized	Subsystems needed for decentralized deployment.	distribution (decentralized)	2D
EnvironmentInternal	Describes a substructure of the Environment component.	auxiliary (control&distribution)	3D
ControlExtendedAlt2	Composition of Control and EnvironmentInternal	result of composition	3D
DecentralizedAGVSystem	Composition of ControlExtendedAlt2 and Decentralized	result of composition	4D

Fig. 9. The different structural views made for the AGVTS. For simplicity, coordination is not included in the example.

of Struct1. In our approach every results is a new structural view, in the example called Struct3. After the composition, the elements of Struct2 are sub elements (sub components or sub connectors) of component A. The join-points between the structural views are the interfaces, specified in the interface mappings part of the refinement relation. For example, the A.up interface of component A is mapped on interface Z.up of its subcomponent Z.

Currently, the reification of the composition is done by hand. Because the composition specification is specified in XML, appropriate tool support could make applying a composition really easy. Further research is required on this point.

Figure 8 shows an example using the mapping and unification relations, containing three structural views and a composition specification. Mapping and unification are mostly used together in one composition specification, that is why we demonstrate them in this way. The composition specifies that several elements of Struct2 are mapped on (i.e. are subelements of) component A and component B of Struct1, resulting in Struct3. The join-points between the structural views are the interfaces, specified in the interface mapping part of the refinement relation. For example, the B.up interface of component B is mapped on interface X.up of its subcomponent X.

We introduce specifically these three relations to cope with the challenges identified in section 3.2. We briefly recall the challenges and mention the relation coping with the particular challenge.

1. The same element appears in different structural views, e.g. Ensor, WMS and the respective connectors. This is where *unification* can be used.

2. Some components must become subcomponents of other components, e.g. AGVAgent must become subcomponent of AGVControl. In that case, *refinement* can be used to refine one of the components to prevent this crosscutting.
3. If the components would be drawn in the same view, one component would crosscut the border of other components. This is the type of crosscutting where the relations can cope with. This is where *mapping* can be used.

Notice that there are several important differences between the existing subarchitecture construct (described in section 2.1) and the refinement composition operator. Firstly, subarchitecture defines a relation between a *type* and a structural view. Refinement is a relation between two structural views, resulting in a more direct relation between structural views. Secondly, refinement is not described in the component type, as for subarchitecture, but in a separate composition specification section. This has the advantage that refinement can be varied depending on the context of the target composition.

4.2 Example of Composing Structural Views in the AGVTS

Figure 9 provides an overview of the structural views we have described for the AGVTS, with a short description of the purpose, the associated concern and the step in which the structural view is used. In the concern column we either provide the associated concerns, or mentioned where the view originates from.

The scenario in the AGVTS application is built up as follows. First we define the control concern, by decomposing the system in agents and an environment in step 1. In the next step, distribution is added to the picture, considering two alternative distribution schemas leading to two different systems. Steps 2C to 4C describe a centralized distribution schema, with associated relations to the control concerns. Steps 2D to 4D describe a decentralized distribution schema.

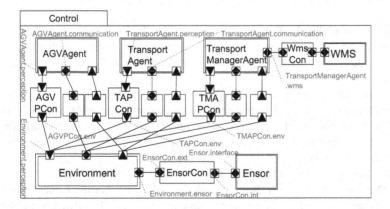

Fig. 10. The Control view showing the agent types, the Environment component and the relations with external components (WMS and Ensor). To simplify the figure, we only showed the names of connectors and interfaces used in the composition specifications. Same graphical notation as fig. 1.

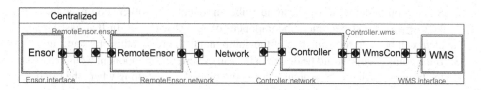

Fig. 11. Centralized view. Same graphical notation as fig. 1.

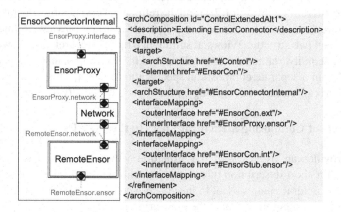

Fig. 12. Left: EnsorConnectorInternal view. Right: Composition specification to compose the EnsorConnectorInternal (at the left) and the Control view (fig. 10), using the same graphical notation as fig. 1.

Step 1 - Control Concern. The Control view shown in fig. 10 has already been described in detail in section 3.2 and is the same as the left part of fig. 4. The view shows a decomposition in agents and an environment.

Step 2C - Centralized. The goal of the first distribution schema (centralized) is to allocate all agents and the environment to a single server. To allow such allocation, we must provide remote access to the `Ensor` component which is situated on the AGV vehicle.

We start with defining two subsystems, shown in fig. 11, `Controller` and `RemoteEnsor`. They will be deployed on a single server and an AGV vehicle, respectively. Both have an interface for remote communication (connected to each other via `Network`). Furthermore, the `Controller` is connected to the WMS, `RemoteEnsor` to the `Ensor` system.

Next, we want to define the relation between the Centralized view and the Control view. The connector between `Environment` and `Ensor` in the Control view does not have appropriate support for remote communication yet. To solve this problem, we refine the `EnsorCon` in the next step.

Step 3C - EnsorConnectorInternal. To refine the EnsorConnector, we first define an auxiliary view and then compose this auxiliary view with the Control view.

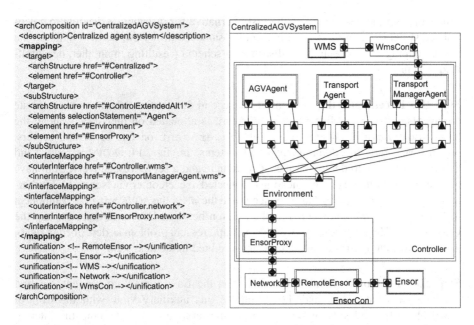

```
<archComposition id="CentralizedAGVSystem">
  <description>Centralized agent system</description>
  <mapping>
    <target>
      <archStructure href="#Centralized">
      <element href="#Controller">
    </target>
    <subStructure>
      <archStructure href="#ControlExtendedAlt1">
      <elements selectionStatement="*Agent">
      <element href="#Environment">
      <element href="#EnsorProxy">
    </subStructure>
    <interfaceMapping>
      <outerInterface href="#Controller.wms">
      <innerInterface href="#TransportManagerAgent.wms">
    </interfaceMapping>
    <interfaceMapping>
      <outerInterface href="#Controller.network">
      <innerInterface href="#EnsorProxy.network">
    </interfaceMapping>
  </mapping>
  <unification> <!-- RemoteEnsor --></unification>
  <unification><!-- Ensor --></unification>
  <unification><!-- WMS --></unification>
  <unification><!-- Network --></unification>
  <unification><!-- WmsCon --></unification>
</archComposition>
```

Fig. 13. Final composition in centralized agent system for AGVTS. Left: composition specification composing the Centralized view (fig. 11) and the ControlExtendedAlt1 view (fig. 12). Right: the resulting view after this composition, called CentralizedAGVSystem, using the same graphical notation as fig. 1.

Figure 12 shows an auxiliary view called EnsorConnectorInternal defining the internal structure of the EnsorCon. This structural view contains two subcomponents connected to each other by a connector: EnsorProxy and RemoteEnsor. EnsorProxy will act as a proxy for Ensor from the perspective of the Environment component.

Next, we compose this auxiliary view (EnsorConnectorInternal) with the Control view using the *refinement* relation. The composition specification is shown at the right hand side of fig. 12. The composition results in the ControlExtendedAlt1 view that is used in the next step to be composed with the Centralized view.

Step 4C - CentralizedAGVSystem. Finally, the Centralized view is composed with the ControlExtendedAlt1 view in fig. 13. We use both *mapping* and *unification* for this. The EnsorProxy component and all agents and the Environment component are mapped on the Controller. We unify the pairs of RemoteEnsor, Ensor and WMS components with each other. This results in the CentralizedAGVSystem view (shown at the right hand side of fig. 13). Notice that there is no explicit connector between Environment and EnsorProxy, or between RemoteEnsor and Ensor. At first glance this might seem strange, but the links between the respective components pass the border of EnsorCon. This is a result of describing a refinement of EnsorCon, meaning that the interfaces of the EnsorCon are delegated to internal components.

This wraps up the description of the first alternative for distribution, leading to a centralized system. The next step starts from the same Control view, but will build up the system aiming at a decentralized distribution schema (resulting in another, decentralized system).

Step 2D - Decentralized. The goal of the second distribution schema is to distribute the agents. In such a schema, the `AGVAgent` is allocated on the AGV vehicle, the `TransportAgent` and `TransportManagerAgent` on one or several servers. Again, we start by defining two subsystems in fig. 14, `AGVControl` and `TranportBase`, to deploy on the AGV vehicle and a server respectively. Both have an interface for remote communication (connected to each other via Network). Furthermore the `TranportBase` has a connection to the `WMS`, the `AGVControl` component to `Ensor`. Next, we want to define the relation between Decentralized view and the Control view. Here we have to solve the overlap/crosscut problem as described in fig. 6. To solve this, the Environment component is refined in the next step.

Step 3D - EnvironmentInternal. To refine the Environment component, we first define an auxiliary view and then compose this auxiliary view with the Control view. The left hand side of fig. 15 shows the auxiliary view defining the internal structure of the environment. The environment is split up in two local environment, `AGVLocalEnvironment` and `TransportLocalEnvironment`. These two local environments synchronize state take care of communication, and together they form a virtual representation of a single Environment component.

Defining the composition with this auxiliary view using the *refinement* relation is less trivial than the previous example. The `Environment` is split in two components, but three interfaces (perception, communication, action) are offered by both the `AGVLocalEnvironment` and the `TransportLocalEnvironment`, asking for a more complex interface mapping. In the composition specification we provide several alternative mappings and specify which connector uses which alternative. The right hand side of fig. 15 shows the composition specification. The composition results in the ControlExtendedAlt2 view that is used in the next step to compose with the Decentralized view.

Step 4D - DecentralizedAGVSystem. Finally, we can compose the system together to form a decentralized version of the AGVTS. Figure 16 contains the composition

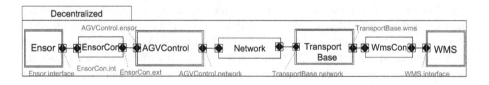

Fig. 14. Decentralized view. This is the same view as the right hand side of fig.4, with resized elements to allow compacter presentation. Same graphical notation as fig. 1.

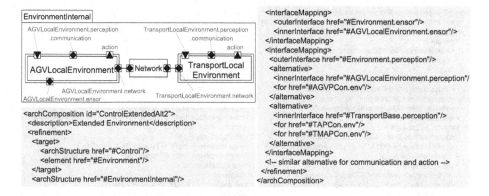

Fig. 15. (a) EnvironmentInternal structural view. Same graphical notation as fig. 1. (b) Specification to compose EnvironmentInternal with Control.

specification using the mapping and unification relations. This results in the Decentral-izedAGVSystem view, looking exactly like fig. 3. This wraps up the description of the second alternative for distribution, leading to a decentralized system.

4.3 Discussion

Relations Between Structural Views Made Explicit. Using structural views to separate concerns and adding explicit compositions between structural views proves to be valuable from different perspectives. By using separate structural views, an architect can effectively separate several important concerns. With the extension to the xADL language, an architect can explicitly define the relations between different structural views. As discussed in the first section, this helps to improve the understandability and changeability of individual architectural concerns, such as in the distribution-specific scenario in the AGVTS architecture. It also becomes easier to compare two different distribution schemas for the same control view.

Notice that the resulting decentralized architecture looks the same as the original crosscutting design. The main difference is the process followed by the architect to design this structural view. The new decomposition has clearly separated the concerns and provided explicit composition specifications between the structural views.

Lessons learned. First, it became clear that using relations and compositions does not necessarily simplify the architectural description. There is a tradeoff between extensive&explicit specification and simplicity. Leaving assumptions and relations implicit is without doubt much simpler, requires less effort, and it may be easier to have an overall view of the system. But explicit specification does make the assumptions associated with individual concerns explicit, together with the relations between the structures. This makes it easier to manage and change the architectural description, clear advantages of the proposed solution that are essential for some architectures. One suggestion to improve the understanding of the overall view of the system is to include some re-

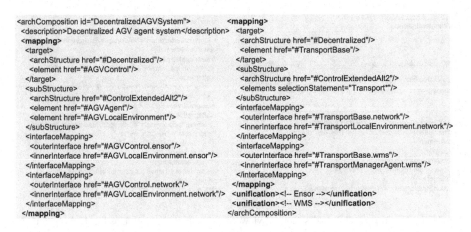

```
<archComposition id="DecentralizedAGVSystem">          <mapping>
  <description>Decentralized AGV agent system</description>    <target>
  <mapping>                                                   <archStructure href="#Decentralized"/>
    <target>                                                  <element href="#TransportBase"/>
      <archStructure href="#Decentralized"/>              </target>
      <element href="#AGVControl"/>                       <subStructure>
    </target>                                               <archStructure href="#ControlExtendedAlt2"/>
    <subStructure>                                          <elements selectionStatement="Transport*"/>
      <archStructure href="#ControlExtendedAlt2"/>       </subStructure>
      <element href="#AGVAgent"/>                        <interfaceMapping>
      <element href="#AGVLocalEnvironment"/>               <outerInterface href="#TransportBase.network"/>
    </subStructure>                                         <innerInterface href="#TransportLocalEnvironment.network"/>
    <interfaceMapping>                                   </interfaceMapping>
      <outerInterface href="#AGVControl.ensor"/>        <interfaceMapping>
      <innerInterface href="#AGVLocalEnvironment.ensor"/>  <outerInterface href="#TransportBase.wms"/>
    </interfaceMapping>                                     <innerInterface href="#TransportManagerAgent.wms"/>
    <interfaceMapping>                                   </interfaceMapping>
      <outerInterface href="#AGVControl.network"/>    </mapping>
      <innerInterface href="#AGVLocalEnvironment.network"/>  <unification><!-- Ensor --></unification>
    </interfaceMapping>                                <unification><!-- WMS --></unification>
  </mapping>                                           </archComposition>
```

Fig. 16. Final composition in decentralized agent system for AGVTS. The refication of this composition is the same as fig. 3 and is repeated in fig. 14.

sults of the composition in the architectural documentation. Tool support is essential to make this feasible.

The second lesson we learned is that compositions are a natural extension to architectural description. Adding compositions to the xADL language was possible without touching the existing architectural concepts in the language. Additionally, there are already first hints in important architectural works that relations are important, as illustrated in the introduction. Yet, these relations receive only limited attention and are not explicitly embedded in the ADL. In this paper we go one step further by explicitly grouping the views and associated relations in compositions.

The idea behind the relations only relies on basic ADL elements, such as components, interfaces and connectors. As consequence, integration with for example the ACME ADL should be straightforward. Of course, the syntax needs to be adapted. Integration with ACME ADL is a matter of future work.

Limitations. The relations rely on specifying correspondence between interfaces (interface mapping). This restriction to one-to-one mapping might not work well in some cases. For example, one structural view could contain two interfaces which map on one interface in another structural view. Another example is the problem with the refinement in step 4D, in which an interface occurs on two subcomponents. The latter problem is solved by adding an alternative specification to refinement, but this might not always be possible. In some situations there will be no other choice but to refactor the interfaces of one of the structural view.

This paper focuses on structural views and composition of structural views. Other types of views are also possible and relations between these views need further investigation. We briefly discuss first insights into the matter, distinguishing between relations between the same type of views and relations between different types of views.

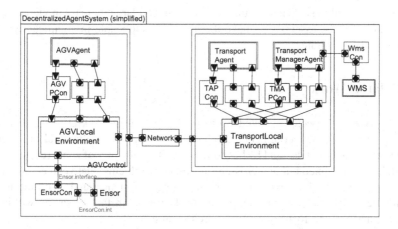

Fig. 17. Decentralized agent system for AGVTS, result after composition in fig. 16. We left out the `Environment` component (containing the `AGVLocalEnvironment` and the `TransportLocalEnvironment`) to make the figure more readable.

Firstly, we discuss relations between the same type of view. We expect that each type of view may need its own set of relations. That is because each type of view has its own set of basic elements and different semantics, like component and connector types as building blocks of a structural view or processes and communication channels as building blocks for a process view. Relations are described in terms of the basic building blocks and are only meaningful within the specific semantics of that particular view. This seems to confirm our expectations.

Secondly, we discuss relations between different types of views. We suspect that each pair of types of views may need its own set of relations, for the same reason as explained above. Several relations between different types of views are already supported in ADLs. For example, in an xADL instance view an architect can describe that this component is of a particular type described in a structural view.

Notice that for an architectural description, not every type of view needs direct relations with all other types of views. Some relations between views can be indirect, i.e. through another type of view. Describing meaningful relations in general in the context of heterogeneous representations is a challenging problem [36], because there exist a large quantity of types of views each with its own notation and semantics.

We proposed three relations. Each of the relations serves a specific purpose as outlined at the end of section 4.1. However, in other situations other relations might be needed. Other possible relations include relations to solve interferences between identifiers of software elements, relations to solve non-corresponding interfaces, etc. An important remark is that the total set of relations should stay rather small so that it remains easily comprehensible and usable for a software architect.

Further exploratory studies are required to assess the scalability of the approach. Currently, we only considered an excerpt from the architecture of the AGVTS. Further studies are needed to see what the impact is in case of a large increase in views. Again, tool support will be essential to make the approach applicable in significantly larger architectural case studies.

5 Related Work

With the rise of Aspect-Orientated Software Development (AOSD [20]), there is a growing awareness that certain concerns have a structural and behavioral crosscutting impact on architectural design [1,2]. Additionally, the outcomes of some recent empirical studies have pointed out that crosscutting-related problems relative to certain architectural concerns, such as exception handling [18], persistence, and distribution [33], can manifest early in design decompositions. The work in this paper fits within this trend, but has a strong focus on software architecture.

Some aspect oriented techniques for programming (e.g. HyperJ [43]) and requirements engineering (e.g. [11,34,41]) provide structural relations for enabling the separation of certain recurring crosscutting concerns. Surprisingly, composition mechanisms for modularizing architectural crosscutting structural views have been neglected in most of the available literature [4,13] focusing on discussing the interplay of aspects and ADLs. Batista and colleagues [4] have identified seven issues related to the appropriateness of abstractions in conventional and AO ADLs for representing crosscutting concerns. However, the analyzed composition-related issues mostly focus on connectors and attachments can be extended to allow behavior-dependent aspect composition. In addition, existing AO ADLs [21,26,35,39,37,38] expose join points as nodes in a dynamic component or object call graph. Modularizing crosscutting concerns in structural views is not supported by this behavioral compositions mechanisms for software architectures, leading to another approach as advocated by this paper.

The presented approach is closely related to multi-dimentional separation of concerns (MDSOC) as introduced by Tarr et al. [43]. Each of the views corresponds to a hyperslice. The architectural composition we propose corresponds to a hypermodule. A hypermodule is a set of hyperslices, together with a composition rule that specifies how the hyperslices must be composed to form a single, new hyperslice that synthesizes and integrates their units. We defined a composition specification as an aggregation of several views and relations. Just as a hypermodule defines a new hyperslice, a composition specification defines a new view. The implication of such choice in our specific solution need further research, but at first sight such hierarchical composition can be beneficial for the scalability of the approach. Our relations correspond to the composition rules of MDSOC.

Quantification [19] over architectural elements is found in the selection statement for the elements specification. In the example, the expressions are rather limited (text and wildcards), but they can easily be extended.

In the field of software architecture, there is little support for relations between views. Rozanski and Woods [40] identify that quality concerns crosscut several views. The authors introduce architectural perspectives as complementary to views in the sense that they define a set of activities, tactics and guidelines to ensure that the view fulfils a quality. IEEE-Std-1471 [27] provides a strong conceptual model relating stakeholders, concerns and views, but lacks a way to describe relations between different views. Clements et al. [12] provides some support for relations between views by integrating information beyond views in the form tables and an associated informal description.

Several approaches combine aspect orientation with multi-agent systems. Kendall et al. [30,31] describe the use of aspect orientation while designing and implementing role models for multi-agent systems (more recently continued in [8]). Contrary to this paper, the authors focus on implementation. In [23], Garcia et al. observe that several agent concerns such as autonomy, learning, and mobility crosscut each other and the basic functionality of an agent. The authors propose an aspect-oriented approach extrapolating implementation mechanisms to the architecture. More recently, Garcia et al. [22] identified crosscutting concerns for agent systems described in the ANote modeling language. Our work differs in its focus on relating architectural views. Boucké et al. [6] did some experiments to extrapolate the approach to the architectural level. The main conclusion was that the basic idea behind Theme/UML proved very interesting, but the language itself is less suited for architectural design. We introduce a language that is based on the same foundation (MDSOC, discussed before) but is embedded in an architectural description language.

6 Conclusion

The lack of explicit relations between structural views in an architectural description is a severe problem, leading to improper documentation of concerns that affect multiple structural views. Based on a concrete set of non-trivial examples, this paper illustrated that several relevant concerns crosscut the architecture structural views of an industrial automatic transportation system. Our systematic analysis of the architecture decompositions identified several challenges to relate structural views and we proposed an initial set of relations in xADL to cope with these challenges.

Through a first case study, this paper has illustrated the feasibility of composition and the concrete relations, namely refinement, mapping and unification. We have used these relations to refactor the architecture of a transportation system. One of the advantages is that distribution is clearly separated from control, making it easier to compare alternative distribution schemas. Within the limited setting of this paper, the results look promising. In future work, we plan to formally extend xADL by integrating the relations in the language definition and to investigate tool support to apply the compositions.

We should highlight that from our experience in previous case studies [18,25,33,10] the three relations and the composition seem to be recurrently demanding in architecture design processes. For instance, concerns such as error handling, distribution, and persistence, have been identified as crosscutting in the architecture of a Web-based information system [33,18], Eclipse CVS plugin [18,25], a reflective middleware system [10,9], and a traveller information system [18,25]. We have observed that in all these cases, advice-pointcut mechanisms, as supported by most AO ADLs, are not sufficient to cope with the separation and composition of such concerns. The reason is that issues like error detection, timeout control, and data synchronization [25] demand structural composition, and advice-pointcut is an inherently dynamic mechanism. Thus, we believe that the relations proposed in this paper are promising general-purpose

ADL additions to improve the stability of an architectural specification in the presence of change. We intend to perform further studies in order to confirm or refute our expectations.

Acknowledgments. Nelis is supported by the Institute for the Promotion of Innovation through Science and Technology in Flanders (IWT-Vlaanderen). Nelis and Alessandro are also partially supported by European Commission as part of the grant IST-2-004349: European Network of Excellence on Aspect- Oriented Software Development (AOSD-Europe), 2004-2008. Thanks to Danny Weyns, Dimitri Van Landuyt, the reviewers and the attendants of the Early Aspect workshop at AOSD 2007 for the discussions about the paper.

References

1. Araujo, J., Baniassad, E., Clements, P., Moreira, A., Rashid, A., Tekinerdogan, B.: Version 1 of the early aspects landscape report. Published on (2005),
   http://www.early-aspects.net
2. Baniassad, E., Clements, P.C., Araujo, J., Moreira, A., Rashid, A., Tekinerdogan, B.: Discovering early aspects. IEEE Softw. 23(1), 61–70 (2006)
3. Bass, L., Clements, P., Kazman, R.: Software Architectures in Practice, 2nd edn. Addison-Wesley, Reading (2003)
4. Batista, T., Chavez, C., Garcia, A., SantAnna, C., Kulesza, U., Rashid, A., Filho, F.: Reflections on architectural connection: Seven issues on aspects and ADLs. In: Workshop on Early Aspects held at ICSE 2006 (2006)
5. Boucké, N., Holvoet, T., Lefever, T., Sempels, R., Schelfthout, K., Weyns, D., Wielemans, J.: Applying the Architecture Tradeoff Analysis Method (ATAM) to an industrial multi-agent system application. Technical Report CW431, Dept. of Computer Sience, KULeuven (2005)
6. Boucké, N., Weyns, D., Holvoet, T.: Experiences with Theme/UML for architectural design of a multiagent system. In: Multiagent Systems and Software Architecture, Proceedings of the Special Track at Net.ObjectDays 2006, pp. 87–110. Net.ObjectDays, K.U.Leuven (2006)
7. Boucké, N., Weyns, D., Schelfthout, K., Holvoet, T.: Applying the ATAM to an architecture for decentralized control of a transportation system. In: Hofmeister, C., Crnkovic, I., Reussner, R. (eds.) QoSA 2006. LNCS, vol. 4214, Springer, Heidelberg (2006)
8. Cabri, G., Leonardi, L., Zambonelli, F.: Modeling role-based interactions for agents. In: The Workshop on Agent-oriented methodologies at OOPSLA (2002)
9. Cacho, N., Batista, T., Garcia, A., Sant'Anna, C., Blair, G.: Improving modularity of reflective middleware with aspect-oriented programming. In: International Workshop on Software Engineering for Middleware (SEM 2006) (2006)
10. Cacho, N., SantAnna, C., Figueiredo, E., Garcia, A., Batista, T., Lucena, C.: Composing design patterns: A scalability study of aspect-oriented programming. In: 5th International Conference on Aspect-Oriented Software Development (AOSD 2006) (2006)
11. Chitchyan, R., Rashid, A., Rayson, P., Waters, R.: Semantics-based composition for aspect-oriented requirements engineering. In: Aspect Oriented Software Development conf (2007)
12. Clements, P., Bachman, F., Bass, L., Garlan, D., Ivers, J., Little, R., Nord, R., Stafford, J.: Documenting Software Architectures, Views and Beyond. Addison Wesley, Reading (2003)
13. Cuesta, C., Romay, M., Fuente, P., Barrio-Solorzano, M.: Architectural aspects of architectural aspects. In: Morrison, R., Oquendo, F. (eds.) EWSA 2005. LNCS, vol. 3527, pp. 247–262. Springer, Heidelberg (2005)

14. Dashofy, E.M., van der Hoek, A., Taylor, R.N.: An infrastructure for the rapid development of xml-based architecture description languages. In: Proceedings of the 24th International Conference on Software Engineering (ICSE2002) (2002)

15. Dashofy, E.M., van der Hoek, A., Taylor, R.N.: A comprehensive approach for the development of modular software architecture description languages. ACM Transactions on Software Engineering and Methodology (TOSEM) 14(2), 199–245 (2005)

16. Eclipse. Aspectj project, www.eclipse.org/aspectj/

17. Egemin. Egemin website, www.egemin.com

18. Filho, F., Cacho, N., Ferreira, R., Figueiredo, E., Garcia, A., Rubira, C.: Exceptions and Aspects: The Devil is in the Details. In: Proc. Int. Conf. on Foundations on Software Engineering (2006)

19. Filman, R., Friedman, D.: Aspect-oriented programming is quantification and obliviousness. In: Proceedings of the workshop on Advanced Separation of Concerns, OOPSLA (2000)

20. Filman, R.E., Elrad, T., Clarke, S., Akşit, M. (eds.): Aspect-Oriented Software Development. Addison-Wesley, Reading (2005)

21. Garcia, A., Chavez, C., Batista, T., Sant'anna, C., Kulesza, U., Rashid, A., Lucena, C.: On the modular representation of architectural aspects. In: Proc. of the European Workshop on Software Architecture (2006)

22. Garcia, A., Chavez, C., Choren, R.: Enhancing agent-oriented models with aspects. In: Proceedings of the ACM Fifth International Joint Conference on Autonomous Agents & Multi Agent Systems (2006)

23. Garcia, A., Kulesza, U., Lucena, C.: Aspectizing multi-agent systems: From architecture to implementation. In: Choren, R., Garcia, A., Lucena, C., Romanovsky, A. (eds.) SELMAS 2004. LNCS, vol. 3390, pp. 121–143. Springer, Heidelberg (2005)

24. Garlan, D., Monroe, R.T., Wile, D.: ACME: Architectural description of component-based systems. In: Foundations of Component-Based Systems, Cambridge University Press, Cambridge (2000)

25. Greenwood, P., Bartolomei, T., Figueiredo, E., Dosea, M., Garcia, A., Cacho, N., Sant'Anna, C., Soares, S., Borba, P., Kulesza, U., Rashid, A.: On the impact of aspectual decompositions on design stability: An empirical study. In: Ernst, E. (ed.) ECOOP 2007. LNCS, vol. 4609, pp. 176–200. Springer, Heidelberg (2007)

26. Grundy, J.: Multi-perspective specification, design and implementation of components using aspects. International Journal of Software Engineering and Knowledge Engineering 10(6) (December 2000)

27. IEEE. Recommended practice for architectural description of software-intensive systems (ansi/ieee-std-1471) (September 2000)

28. ISR, Institute for Software Reseach. Archstudio 4.0 tool set for the xadl language, http://www.isr.uci.edu/projects/archstudio/

29. Jackson, M.A.: Some complexities in computer-based systems and their implications for system development. In: Proceedings of CompEuro 1990, IEEE Computer Society Press, Los Alamitos (1990)

30. Kendall, E.A.: Role model designs and implementations with aspect-oriented programming. In: OOPSLA 1999. Proceedings of the 14th ACM SIGPLAN conference on Object-oriented programming, systems, languages, and applications, pp. 353–369. ACM Press, New York (1999)

31. Kendall, E.A.: Role modelling for agent systems analysis, design and implementation. IEEE Concurrency 8, 34–41 (2000)

32. Kojarski, S., Lorenz, D.H.: Modeling aspect mechanisms: A top-down approach. In: In Proc. Int. Conf. on Software Engineering, pp. 212–221 (2006)

33. Kulesza, U., SantAnna, C., Garcia, A., Coelho, R., von Staa, A., Lucena, C.: Quantifying the Effects of Aspect-Oriented Programming: A Maintenance Study. In: Proceedings of 9th International Conference on Software Maintenance - ICSM 2006 (2006)
34. Moreira, A., Rashid, A., Araujo, J.: Multi-dimensional separation of concerns in requirements engineering. In: The 13th International Conference on Requirements Engineering (RE 2005), pp. 285–296 (2005)
35. Navasa, A., Pérez, M., Murillo, J., Hernández, J.: Aspect oriented software architecture: a structural perspective. In: Workshop on Early Aspects, AOSD 2002 (2002)
36. Nuseibeh, B., Kramer, J., Finkelstein, A.: Viewpoints: meaningful relationships are difficult! In: ICSE 2003. Proceedings of the 25th International Conference on Software Engineering, Washington, DC, USA, pp. 676–681. IEEE Computer Society, Los Alamitos (2003)
37. Perez, J., Ramos, I., Jaen, J., Letelier, P., Navarro, E.: Prisma: Towards quality, aspect oriented and dynamic software architectures. In: Int. Conf. On Quality Software (2003)
38. Pessemier, N., Seinturier, L., Duchien, L.: Components, adl and aop: Towards a common approach. In: Workshop ECOOP Reflection, AOP and Meta-Data for Software Evolution (RAM-SE04) (2004)
39. Pinto, M., Fuentes, L., Troya, J.M.: A dynamic component and aspect-oriented platform. Computing Journal 48(4), 401–420 (2005)
40. Rozanski, N., Woods, E.: Software Systems Architecture. Addison-Wesley, Reading (2005)
41. Silva, L.: An aspect-oriented approach to model requirements. In: Proc. of the Doctoral Consortium on Requirements Engineering (with RE conference) (2005)
42. Software Engineering Institute.The sae aadl standard info site,
    http://www.aadl.info/
43. Tarr, P., Ossher, H., Harrison, W., Sutton, S.: N degrees of separation: Multi-dimensional separation of concerns. In: Int. Conf. on Software Engineering, pp. 107–119 (1999)
44. Weyns, D., Holvoet, T.: A reference architecture for situated multiagent systems. In: Weyns, D., Van Dyke Paruak, H., Michel, F. (eds.) E4MAS 2006. LNCS, vol. 4389, Springer, Heidelberg (2006)
45. Weyns, D., Parunak, H.V.D., Michel, F., Holvoet, T., Ferber, J.: Environments for multiagent systems: State-of-the-art and research challenges. In: Weyns, D., Parunak, H.V.D., Michel, F. (eds.) E4MAS 2004. LNCS (LNAI), vol. 3374, Springer, Heidelberg (2005)
46. Wooldridge, M.: An introduction to Multiagent Systems. John Wiley & Sons, Chichester (2002)

Using Aspects in Architectural Description

Rich Hilliard

r.hilliard@computer.org

Dedicated to the memory of Douglas T. Ross (21 December 1929 – 31 January 2007), creator of plex and Structured Analysis.

Abstract. This paper sketches an approach to using aspects for architectural description within the conceptual framework of IEEE 1471. I propose a definition of *architectural aspect* within that framework and examine its consequences and motivations. I show that architectural aspects can be accommodated within the current conceptual framework of IEEE 1471 without modification; and outline extensions to the framework which could be candidates for further standardization work, or incorporated into aspect-oriented architectural methods.

Keywords: software systems architecture, architectural description, architectural aspects, architectural viewpoints and views, architectural models.

1 Introduction

1.1 Aspect-Oriented Software Development

Work in Aspect-Oriented Programming (AOP) has led to insights in how crosscutting concerns can be captured and implemented – leading to new approaches to modularization of programs which improve program clarity, understandability, modifiability and maintainability. The theme of work in Aspect-Oriented Software Development (AOSD) and the Early Aspects community is to extend these insights throughout all phases of software development to develop "techniques [which] provide systematic means for the identification, modularisation, representation and composition of crosscutting concerns such as security, mobility and real-time constraints" [http://www.early-aspects.net/]. It is hoped that the insights of AOP can provide similar benefits by providing means for managing crosscutting concerns both throughout the software life cycle, and between life cycle phases – if there are uniform concepts of aspects available.

1.2 Aspects in Architecture

Architecting is an important activity of system construction; the term denotes both a specific phase in the life cycle, and a continuing focus on managing certain essential concerns over the life time of a system:

A. Moreira and J. Grundy (Eds.): Early Aspects 2007 Workshop, LNCS 4765, pp. 139–154, 2007.
© Springer-Verlag Berlin Heidelberg 2007

IEEE 1471 defines *architecture* as "the fundamental organization of a system embodied in its components, their relationships to each other, and to the environment, and the principles guiding its design and evolution" [1].

Software systems architects routinely practice separation of concerns and must deal with crosscutting concerns because a primary job of the architect is to insure the quality of a system. While functionality is relatively easy to identify, specify and localize, other qualities (frequently lumped together as simply "non-functional concerns") are pervasive, prevailing architectural concerns. The essence of the architect's job is to negotiate and balance these conflicting concerns of many diverse stakeholders to construct a feasible, functioning system.

The characterization in the previous paragraph is analogous to the situation in programming which motivated the invention of aspects. Perhaps the force of crosscutting concerns is even stronger at the architectural level than in implementation – at least if we take "Boehm's Law" seriously. Qualities dominate the architect's job, whereas functionality is often a consideration which can be deferred to subsequent design and implementation.

Further, this is equally true in systems architecture as in software architecture; so it would be useful to have solutions which are applicable in either domain, since both are frequently parts of major system developments [2].

Therefore, it is worth asking whether there is a role for aspects, or aspect-like constructs, within Architecting. This is a big question and not a new question; it has been raised already in the Early Aspects community. This paper will focus on one topic within the larger question:

How can aspects be used within Architectural Description?

This focus is justified by observing that aspects are largely an approach to modularization, and therefore a syntactic notion. So answers to this question should be offered within the context of existing representational resources. Note that the representational resources for architectural description are quite different from those used in design and implementation. In AOP, aspects crosscut program texts, whereas in modern architectural practices, architectural descriptions are organized using multiple views – can we make sense of aspects crosscutting architectural views? What problems and opportunities does this present?

1.3   Outline for the Remainder of Paper

In the next section, I outline the conceptual framework for architectural description which forms the basis for IEEE 1471. I go into some detail, because its details make possible the introduction of aspects without modification to the framework. In section 3, I apply the conceptual framework to derive a working definition of architectural aspect and then suggest extensions to the framework which clarify some matters and may be useful for developing aspect-oriented architectural methods. In section 4, I survey related work: the question of the role of aspects in Architecting has been raised by others. I contrast the current approach with other work. The final section contains some conclusions.

2   A Conceptual Framework for Architectural Description

2.1   IEEE 1471

IEEE Std 1471, *Recommended Practice for Architectural Description of Software-Intensive Systems* [1] was the first formal standard to address what is an architectural description (AD). It was developed by the IEEE Architecture Working Group between 1995 and 2000 with representation from industry, other standards bodies and academia, and was subject to intensive reviews by over 150 international reviewers, prior to its publication in 2000.

In 2006, IEEE 1471 became an draft international standard (ISO/IEC DIS 42010) and is now undergoing joint revision by IEEE and ISO (http://www.iso-architecture.org/ieee-1471/). One of the motivations for this paper is to examine what changes are needed in IEEE 1471 to support aspect-oriented architecting.

IEEE 1471 establishes a set of content requirements on an architectural description (any collection of products used to document an architecture) on how ADs should be organized and their information content, while: (*i*) abstracting away from specific media (e.g., text, HTML, XML); (*ii*) being method-neutral (it is being used with a variety of existing and new architectural methods and techniques); and (*iii*) being notation-independent (recognizing that diverse notations are needed for recording various facets of architectures).

IEEE 1471 is built upon a conceptual framework for architectural description (see Figure 1).

The content requirements of an AD per IEEE 1471 are stated using the terms and concepts of the conceptual framework. These rules define what it means for an architectural description (AD) to conform to the Standard. The key concepts needed for discussing architectural aspects are summarized in the remainder of this section.

2.2   Architectures and Architectural Descriptions

I have cited IEEE 1471's definition of "architecture" in the Introduction, and its focus on *architectural descriptions* (ADs): work products used to document the architecture of a software-intensive system.

Although perhaps obvious to some, the conceptual framework distinguishes architectures from architectural descriptions. Architectures are conceptual entities. Architectural descriptions are concrete artifacts.

Architects do their best to express their concepts in a concrete representation which can be captured, managed, reasoned about and shared with others. The force of the standard is on ADs – that which can be concretely captured. Being clear about conceptual entities (architectures) versus artifacts (ADs) will be useful when concerns and aspects are discussed below.

2.3   Stakeholders and Concerns

The audiences for an AD are the various stakeholders of the system.

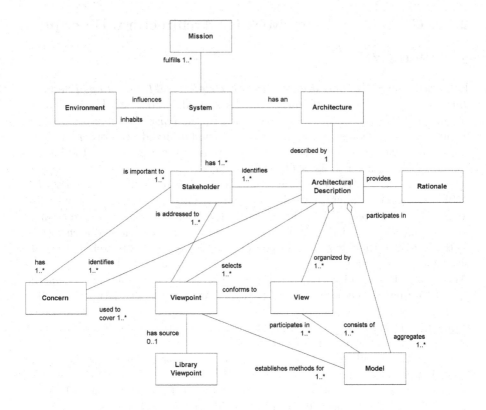

Fig. 1. IEEE 1471 Conceptual Framework

A *stakeholder* is any person, organization or other entity with an interest in the architecture of the system.

The recognition of the role of stakeholders in the AD reflects the multi-dimensional, multi-disciplinary nature of Architecting [4] and facilitates the architectural understanding of their interests with respect to the system.

Within IEEE 1471, those interests are called *architectural concerns* (or *concerns* for short).

Concerns are those stakeholder interests pertaining to the system's development, design, operation, or any other area, which are critical to its architecture. Each concern is an issue which the architecture, and therefore the architectural description, must address. Familiar concerns include: functionality, security, performance, constructibility, reliability – all of which are often considered to be associated with early aspects.

Concerns arise at all stages of a system's construction and operation – it often takes an Architect to recognize which concerns are architecturally significant and cannot be deferred. IEEE 1471 says nothing about the granularity of a concern: it may be as broad as data distribution or as specific as operator security policy.

The sum total of these concerns presents the Architect with a set of problems to solve; the Architect's job is to describe a system manifesting properties that will allow the needs and concerns of the stakeholders for the system to be met.

Therefore, an AD should be explicit in addressing these stakeholders. Under the rules of IEEE 1471, an architectural description must explicitly identify the stakeholders of the system's architecture and enumerate each architectural concern. If an AD does not address all identified stakeholders' concerns it is, by definition, incomplete.

2.4   Architectural Viewpoints and Views

What the Viewer brings to the Viewed in the Viewing, yields the View.
– Douglas T. Ross

It is routine among architectural methods and frameworks to use multiple *architectural views* as a fundamental organizing principle of architectural descriptions to capture information about an architecture (e.g., [5,6,7,8,9,10,11]).

In IEEE 1471, an AD is organized into one or more architectural views. An *architectural view* is defined to be "a representation of a whole system from the perspective of a related set of concerns".

There are many reasons for introducing views, pertaining to separation of concerns and management of complexity (for discussion see [12]). However, early work on architectural views was relatively informal with respect to what constituted a view and how its contents were to be created and analyzed.

Although the use of multiple views was hardly new in IEEE 1471, its contribution is three-fold:

(*i*) to provide conventions for rigorously defining, and therefore using, the contents of a view;

(*ii*) to motivate the selection of views for use through their ability to address specific concerns of specific stakeholders; and

(*iii*) to articulate a "wholeness condition" on views that contributes to the relevance, well-formedness, consistency and completeness of ADs.

In IEEE 1471, the permissible contents of an architectural view is governed by specifying an *architectural viewpoint*.

The idea of a viewpoint first appeared in Ross' Structured Analysis (SADT) [13]. Nuseibeh, Kramer and Finkelstein, working in requirements engineering, treat viewpoints as first-class entities, with associated attributes and operations [14]. The ISO/IEC *Reference Model for Open Distributed Processing* (RM-ODP) defines "*viewpoint* (on a system): a form of abstraction achieved using a selected set of architectural concepts and structuring rules, in order to focus on particular concerns within a system" [15].

All of these precedents contributed to the IEEE 1471 notion:

an *architectural viewpoint* is "a specification of the conventions for constructing and using a view. A pattern or template from which to develop individual views by establishing the purposes and audience for a view and the techniques for its creation and analysis".

Each architectural viewpoint used in an AD must be "declared" before use (either "in line" in the AD or by reference to its source). Table 1 is a template for specifying a viewpoint in accordance with IEEE 1471.

Table 1. Ingredients of a Viewpoint (*based on IEEE 1471*)

A viewpoint is defined by:

- the viewpoint name;
- a set of architectural concerns to be framed by the viewpoint. Views conforming to that viewpoint must address each of those concerns;
- a set of representational resources to be used in constructing conforming views, such as viewpoint languages, modeling techniques and analytical methods; and,
- the source, if any, of the viewpoint (e.g., author, literature citation) if it is defined by reference.

A viewpoint definition may additionally include:

- any formal or informal consistency or completeness checks associated with the underlying method to be applied to models within the view;
- any evaluation or analysis techniques to be applied to models within the view; and
- any heuristics, patterns, or other guidelines which aid in the synthesis of an associated view or its models.

Each architectural view has a governing architectural viewpoint. The viewpoint provides the set of conventions for constructing, interpreting and analyzing a view, including the rules for determining whether it is well-formed.

Each identified stakeholder concern must be framed by at least one of the architectural viewpoints selected for use in an AD; if not, the AD is incomplete.

Making viewpoints first-class provides a means by which the variety of architectural techniques in use today can be uniformly described and therefore compared and perhaps made interoperable.

2.5   Architectural Models

In IEEE 1471, "a view may consist of one or more architectural models". Very little else is said about the use of such models in the 2000 edition of the standard, which has led to some confusion.

There were two motivations for introducing models into architectural views.

First, in order to address a related set of concerns, some views might need to employ more than one type of notation. Per the rules on viewpoint specifications (Figure 1), when a view requires more than one notation, this is captured within the viewpoint definition, specifying the multiple models to be used and the notations for each.

For example, Kruchten's 4+1 Logical viewpoint uses both UML class diagrams and UML component diagrams. These would each be determined in the associated viewpoint definition. Another example could be a Project Management viewpoint specifying that project management views include three types of model: GANTT charts, budgets and org charts to fully address project management concerns.

A second use of architectural models is to capture in one place some architectural detail that contributes to addressing distinct concerns in more than one view – without requiring explicit repetition of that detail in each view.

IEEE 1471 does not provide any further rules or guidance on the use of architectural models within views; this was left open to users of the Standard.

Clearly this latter usage of architectural models is close to the intended purpose of aspects. Architectural models are the essential element of the framework for supporting architectural aspects, as discussed in the next section.

3 Architectural Aspects

The previous section presented a somewhat detailed description of the IEEE 1471 conceptual framework. In this section, I propose a definition of architectural aspect and examine its implications within the IEEE 1471 conceptual framework, demonstrating that aspects can be directly accommodated therein. I then suggest some extensions to the conceptual framework which make its support for architectural aspects clearer, and which are independently motivated for improving that framework. I refer to existing concepts of AOP (including join points, point cuts, advice, base and aspect languages, symmetric and asymmetric paradigms) to motivate the presentation.

Let's begin with a definition. In the remainder of this section, I will examine its consequences and motivations, using the "AOP metaphor" to explore the applicability of aspects to Architectural Description.

DEFINITION. An *architectural aspect* is a shared architectural model addressing exactly one architectural concern.

Model sharing is the architectural analog of the primary motivation for aspects in AOP: to modularize a representation addressing concerns that would otherwise be scattered, and repeated, across multiple views. Sharing is thus crucial in the definition to capturing the crosscutting nature of aspects.[1] If an architec-

---

[1] At least within "asymmetric" approaches to aspects, which I will tentatively assume here, although it remains an open question. Under the asymmetric approach, aspects are added to the base – the set of views of the system. For practical reasons, I think Architectural Description will remain view-based because views are frequently organized for an architecture's diverse stakeholders. Adopting the symmetric paradigm would be a radical change for Architectural Description, and would blur the organization of information for stakeholders. This is different from the situation in AOP where, in a sense, there is a single stakeholder: the programmer.

tural model is not shared, then by the definition here, it is not an architectural aspect – it is merely a constituent of a view.

One immediate consequence of this definition is that it explains what entities architectural aspects crosscut: they crosscut views and the models which comprise those views.

A second consequence, following from the definitions and rules described in section 2, is that it classifies architectural aspects into:

1. *intra-view* aspects (aspects which apply within a single view); and
2. *cross-view* aspects (aspects which apply across two or more views).

More about these two classes below.

Finally, defining architectural aspects to be essentially a specialization of the existing construct of architectural model is consistent with other practices in AOSD (such as aspect-oriented design) and requires nothing new be added to the IEEE 1471 conceptual framework to support architectural aspects.

Architectural Concerns. Architectural concerns in IEEE 1471 appear to match the idea of concern in AOSD, although not necessarily used in a rigorous manner within that community. (There has been some recent work on concern-based modeling, see 4.)

A concern is a statement of an area of interest on the part of a stakeholder in the architecture of the system. A concern frames a problem to be solved by the architecture. A concern may be large or small, wide or narrow, requirements-, design- or constraint-oriented ... the essence is that it reflects a statement. The rigor arises as follows. Architectural concerns must be recorded and accounted for in the AD. Each identified architectural concern must be recorded such that an AD is *incomplete* if there are any concerns which have not been framed by at least one viewpoint.

There are concerns of varying granularities: a major concern may warrant a viewpoint of its own (e.g., Functionality, or Distribution). A minor concern might not require its own viewpoint, but could be grouped with others within a viewpoint (e.g., Extensibility of system functionality might be grouped with Functionality).

By limiting an aspect to a single concern in the definition, an aspect becomes the most fine-grained solution element expressible within the framework – without referring to elements of a particular viewpoint language.

It is worth noting that architectural aspects as defined above are quite distinct from aspects that might arise within aspectual (aspect-oriented) viewpoint languages. These are two distinct levels of description. There is no simple relationship between architectural aspects and aspectual languages used as viewpoint languages. Architectural aspects crosscut models and views; whereas aspectual languages within viewpoints would not introduce any crosscutting at an architectural level.

Insights from AOP. Key notions of AOP are join points, point cuts and advice; defined in relation to base and aspect languages. In this section, I briefly discuss the relevance of these notions within Architectural Description, leading up to a proposal at the end of this section.

Unlike the situation in AOP, in Architectural Description there is no single base language; since architectural aspects crosscut views, each viewpoint language is a potential *base language*.[2] Similarly, an architectural aspect could be written in any other viewpoint language chosen to address the identified concern. All languages used in an AD are, by definition, viewpoint languages and must be defined by some viewpoint. Given this, what can we say about base and aspect languages in an architectural setting?

Consider Figure 2, which depicts examples of the two kinds of architectural aspects: intra-view and cross-view aspects. For intra-view aspects, the viewpoint establishes the language to be used for each model. Typically, an intra-view aspect will use the same viewpoint language as the rest of the viewpoint because the concern addressed by the aspect may be subsumed by the concerns framed by the viewpoint – but not necessarily. The aspect may be encapsulating everything there is to say about its identified concern utilizing a language not used elsewhere, but it is still part of a single viewpoint.

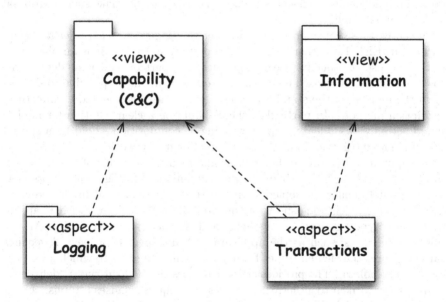

Fig. 2. Examples of intra-view and cross-view architectural aspects

For cross-view aspects, the issue of where the aspect language should be defined is not currently addressed by the Standard. There was a notion in IEEE 1471 that each model was: (*i*) defined by exactly one viewpoint: *Viewpoint establishes methods for one or more Models*) and (*ii*) possibly used in other

---

[2] We could say aspect-oriented architectural description does not enjoy the *Luxury of the Monolinguistic Base* – the flip side of the *Tyranny of Dominant Decomposition*.

views: *Model participates in one or more Views*); but this was reflected only in the diagram (Figure 1) – there were no rules based on this notion nor any further elaboration. This is an area for improvement in the on-going IEEE 1471 revision.

A *join point* is a location expressed in a base language at which an aspect is to be applied. These will be elements of viewpoint languages.

A *point cut* is an expression which picks out a set of join points based on some criteria. Such expressions will be part of the specification of an architectural aspect, and will determine where it applies. This may involve quantification of some kind [16]. *Advice* refers to the rules for combining aspects with base elements to yield the final result.

An architectural aspect can be similarly characterized by its interface (point cut expression) and its body (advice), as proposed below.

Improving Architectural Models. Addressing the considerations of the previous section (analogues of join points, point cuts, advice) for architectural aspects necessarily involves architectural models, since by definition, aspects are a specialization of models. In fact, it can be argued that mechanisms for these are useful independent of aspects. This section will briefly make such a proposal and offer an example.

Currently, these considerations fall under the slogan of *view (or model) integration*. In IEEE 1471, there are no rules pertaining to this; it is an obligation on the end user to specify integration rules as a part of viewpoint definitions. However, with an increased emphasis of models, it might be possible to do better in the revision of the standard, or as a part of aspect-oriented architectural description methods. In particular, there should be a clear solution for models shared across views. Ideally, aspect weaving or composition would be a special case of model integration, but this is an area for future work.

One approach is to revive the **provides** and **requires** language of module interconnection to state relations between views and models. In Figure 3, a cross-view aspect, **Fault Handling**, is depicted. In the UML cartoon, (and in the previous figure), views, models and aspects are denoted by UML packages, with an appropriate stereotype (≪view≫, ≪model≫ and ≪aspect≫, respectively). Arrows show dependencies; such as the application of an aspect to a view. A **requires** clause captures the element types from a viewpoint language to which an aspect applies (join points). The **provides** clause captures the element types "delivered" by the aspect. Taken together, the **provides** and **requires** clauses establish a contract between models. This is generally useful; not just for specifying aspects for any architectural models and views [17].

Another approach could be to introduce a generalized notion of architectural element, as a entity within a view associated with a sort or type defined by its viewpoint, over which to allow quantification.

Under either approach, I suspect universal quantification over types is sufficient for most architectural applications.

View integration in general, the nature of quantification needed, and the investigation of these alternatives, are topics for future work.

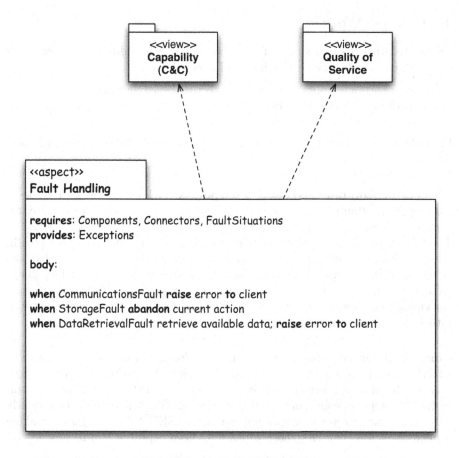

Fig. 3. Example: Fault Handling

Consider[3]:

model : ___ :: *view* : *viewpoint*

A viewpoint defines the rules on a view; where are model rules defined? In IEEE 1471 currently, model rules are part of the viewpoint definition (as per Figure 2), but, as noted above, that does not really address the case where a model (whether or not it is an aspect) is shared by two or more views (such as the cross-view aspects introduced above).

Mark Gerhardt has suggested that for the IEEE 1471 revision ___ should be filled by an architectural *model type* (or *metamodel*). A model type would identify the concerns addressed by its model (instances), the model language to be used, and any additional conventions. Viewpoint definitions could then reference these model types. The provides/requires contracts would contribute to defining model types.

---

[3] This notation is useful for expressing analogies: $a : b :: c : d$ which is to be read "a is to b as c is to d".

4   Related Work

There are three major themes of "related" work – in addition to a few other approaches – which may be classified as follows:

- aspects within a components and connectors-based viewpoint;
- concern-oriented approaches; and
- crosscutting architectural constructs.

Each elucidates some of the issues raised in this paper. I discuss each of these themes in turn.

Aspects in Component-Based Viewpoints. A body of work presumes a base representation of components and their connectors, as found in many architecture description languages (ADLs). These include AspectualACME [18], TranSAT [19], Fractal Aspect Component, CAM/DAOP [20], and FuseJ [21]. In these languages, aspects crosscut components and connectors which are elements of the viewpoint language, and the aspects themselves are viewpoint language (ADL) elements. This is in contrast to the present work in which aspects crosscut views. These might better be referred to as component or connector aspects, rather than architectural aspects.

Concern-Oriented Approaches. The introduction of architectural concerns into IEEE 1471 arose from attention to *separation of concerns* in software engineering. Recently, concerns have become of increasing interest in their own right within the Aspects community and elsewhere [22,23]. Sutton and Tarr rightly note that concerns are concepts not artifacts; IEEE 1471 focuses on making explicit *identified concerns*; those which have been captured and recorded:

> "If we consider a concern to be any matter of interest in a software system, then concerns subsume aspects as they are usually defined. The commonly accepted definition of aspect (in this context) is a program property that forces crosscutting in the implementation []. This definition recognizes the distinction between concerns (specifically properties) and artifacts (specifically implementations), and it calls attention to an important implementation issue. However, it is relatively narrow (focusing on properties and implementations), it categorizes concerns by their effects (rather than by more intrinsic characteristics), and it links the identification of those concerns to artifacts. In our view, a general notion of concern is needed for AOD (and AOSD in general), one that is not dependent on or linked to notions of artifact." [23]

Approaches to concern modeling could be used within the IEEE 1471 framework, and could lead to additional future requirements in this area for the revision.

Although starting from a different foundation than this paper, Katara and Katz develop several mechanisms which could be of use in the present context [24]. Their work could be used to extend the suggestions here for interpreting join points using the language of **provides** and **requires** for view integration.

Other Crosscutting Architectural Constructs. There are other crosscutting constructs proposed for architectural description that have uses similar to aspects. Two such constructs are architectural perspectives and textures.

Rozanski and Woods (R&W) define perspectives this way [8]: "An *architectural perspective* is a collection of activities, tactics, and guidelines that are used to ensure that a system exhibits a particular set of related quality properties that require consideration across a number of the system's architectural views."

Typically, R&W note, "Applying a perspective almost always leads to the creation of something – usually some sort of model – that provides an insight into the system's ability to meet a required quality property."

A perspective is so close to a viewpoint, which R&W are already using, it is not clear why they needed to introduce it. Like a viewpoint, a perspective defines a set of resources to be used to address a particular set of quality properties (i.e., concerns). Many of their perspectives (Security, Performance and Scalability, Evolution) would just as easily be defined as viewpoints, and R&W's template for perspectives is equivalent to the IEEE 1471 template for viewpoints (although more refined).

Alexander Ran and colleagues have described *architectural textures* as follows:

> "Texture is the recurring microstructure of the system. Crosscutting concerns (Kiczales et al., 1997; Ossher and Tarr, 1999) that cannot be localized in a single component must be addressed across multiple components repeatedly. In a well-designed system this must be done in a uniform fashion, which creates recurring microstructure–a definite texture of the system. Examples of crosscutting concerns include exception handling, execution tracing, overload control, flow control, resource reservation policies to mention a few."

That these two constructs have been proposed seems to align with the two types of aspects identified above, as follows: a perspective that crosscuts a defined set of viewpoints could be realized as a cross-view architectural aspect, as defined above. A texture could be captured as an intra-view aspect – the aspect would refer to multiple components at the same time, within a single viewpoint of concern. Treating a texture as an aspect allows the regularity of the "recurring microstructure" to be stated in one place.

Other Approaches. Several papers treat aspects as lightweight views, or do not regard views as essential to architectural description. Bass, Klein and Northrop suggest architectural analogues of join points and point cuts, but equate architectural aspects to architectural views, lacking a rigorous formulation of view [25].

Kim Mens' "Architectural Aspects" [26] is a good antidote to the tyranny of the single-view approach to architecture embodied in early academic work in software architecture, which focused on the components and connectors viewpoint to the exclusion of other viewpoints. However, Mens adopts the symmetric paradigm – equating all architectural elements to aspects. While the choice of paradigm for architectural description is an open question (see footnote 1), it would be a major change to the currently widespread practices of view-based architectural description.

Boucké and Holvoet (B&H) propose extending architectural descriptions with *architectural slices*: "since the architectural elements in a slice are meant to cover a specific driver, there is a direct traceability between drivers and the views describing them (and thus no tangling)" [27]. However, part of the problem B&H set out to solve is self-inflicted – they do not adopt a rigorous notion of view (cf. sections 2, 3 above) and do not use viewpoints to link architectural concerns with the resources used to create views as in IEEE 1471.

Firstly, B&H rightly note the need for stronger connections/relations between elements in distinct views and the relation of decisions and intent, as noted above, need to be better handled in architecture. "Secondly, the standard notion of views does not allow explicit definitions of 'open spots' (like abstract classes or parameters) that should be filled in later." Both of these issues are independent of the use of aspects, and need to be addressed anyway. (See my [28] for an early treatment of these issues.)

All of this could be accomplished within the framework outlined above, making B&H's *slice composition diagram* essentially an architectural viewpoint with matching and other operators to be operations of the associated viewpoint language. Alternatively, these could be defined with reference to an architectural elements metalanguage as suggested above.

5   Conclusions

I have shown how architectural aspects can be accommodated within the current conceptual framework of IEEE 1471 without modification. I have also outlined extensions to that framework which could be candidates for further standardization work, or incorporated into aspect-oriented architectural methods. Some of these are useful refinements of the conceptual framework independent of their relevance to aspect-oriented architectural methods, such as making the handling of architectural models more rigorous and providing an approach to view/model integration. Some of these ideas I hope to explore in the future.

But it is reasonable to ask (as one anonymous reviewer did): *Are aspects needed for architectural description?*

The situation in AD is different from that in programming. The dominant decomposition is multiple viewpoint language-based, and already concern-oriented. Views and models are the modules of an AD, determined by viewpoints, and organized by concerns.

The definition of architectural aspect I've proposed establishes a methodological constraint on when aspects are architecturally relevant within the current conceptual framework of IEEE 1471: when exactly one concern is being addressed; and when that aspect is shared: i.e., when it crosscuts views (or their models). This yields two kinds of aspects which seems to align with existing proposals about textures and perspectives. It also preserves the asymmetric paradigm which seems to inherent to current architectural practice.

Acknowledgments. I would like to thank: Mark Maier (Aerospace) for reading an earlier draft of this paper; the participants in the *First Workshop on Aspects in Architectural Description* (http://aosd.net/workshops/aarch/2007/) for their feedback on some of the ideas here; and the anonymous reviewers of this submission. Their comments made it possible to substantially improve this version.

References

1. IEEE: ANSI/IEEE Std 1471–2000 Recommended Practice for Architectural Description of Software-Intensive Systems (2000)
2. Maier, M.W., Emery, D., Hilliard, R.: ANSI/IEEE 1471 and systems engineering. Systems Engineering 7(3), 257–270 (2004)
3. IEEE 1471 – ISO/IEC 42010, Web site: http://www.iso-architecture.org/ieee-1471/
4. Maier, M.W., Rechtin, E.: The art of systems architecting, 2nd edn. CRC Press (2000)
5. Kruchten, P.B.: The 4+1 view model of architecture. IEEE Software 28(11), 42–50 (1995)
6. Emery, D.E., Hilliard, R., Rice, T.B.: Experiences applying a practical architectural method. In: Strohmeier, A. (ed.) Reliable Software Technologies - Ada Europe 96. LNCS, vol. 1088, Springer, Heidelberg (1996)
7. Hofmeister, C., Nord, R.L., Soni, D.: Applied Software Architecture. Addison-Wesley, Reading (2000)
8. Rozanski, N., Woods, E.: Software Systems Architecture: Viewpoint Oriented System Development. Addison-Wesley, Reading (2005)
9. Garland, J., Anthony, R.: Large Scale Software Architecture: A Practical Guide Using UML. Wiley, Chichester (2002)
10. Clements, P.C., Bachmann, F., Bass, L., Garlan, D., Ivers, J., Little, R., Nord, R., Stafford, J.: Documenting Software Architectures: views and beyond. Addison-Wesley, Reading (2003)
11. ISO: ISO/IEC 10746-1 Information Technology – Open Distributed Processing – Reference Model: Overview (1998)
12. Hilliard, R.: Views and viewpoints in software systems architecture. In: First Working IFIP Conference on Software Architecture, San Antonio, Position paper (1999)
13. Ross, D.T.: Structured Analysis (SA): a language for communicating ideas. IEEE Transactions on Software Engineering SE-3(1) (1977) 16-34 Also appears in Programming methodology : a collection of articles by members of IFIP WG2.3 edited by David Gries, Springer-Verlag, New York (1978)
14. Nuseibeh, B., Kramer, J., Finkelstein, A.: A framework for expressing the relationships between multiple views in requirements specification. IEEE Transactions on Software Engineering 20(10), 760–773 (1994)
15. ISO: ISO/IEC 10746-2 Information Technology – Open Distributed Processing – Reference Model: Foundations (1996)

16. Filman, R.E., Friedman, D.P.: Aspect-oriented programming is quantification and obliviousness. In: Filman, R.E., Elrad, T., Clarke, S., Akşit, M. (eds.) Aspect-Oriented Software Development, pp. 21–35. Addison-Wesley, Boston (2005)
17. Hilliard, R.: Views as modules. In: Balzer, B., Obbink, H. (eds.) Proceedings Fourth International Software Architecture Workshop (ISAW-4), 4 and 5 June, Limerick, Ireland, pp. 7–10 (2000)
18. Garcia, A., Chavez, C., Batista, T., Sant'anna, C., Kulesza, U., Rashid, A., Lucena, C.: On the modular representation of architectural aspects. In: Proceedings of the 3rd European Workshop on Software Architecture, Nantes, France (2006)
19. Barais, O., Cariou, E., Duchien, L., Pessemier, N., Seinturier, L.: TranSAT: A framework for the specification of software architecture evolution. In: ECOOP First International Workshop on Coordination and Adaptation Techniques for Software Entities (WCAT04), Oslo (2004)
20. Pinto, M., Fuentes, L., Troya, J.: A component and aspect dynamic platform. The Computer Journal 48(4), 401–420 (2005)
21. Suvée, D., Fraine, B.D., Vanderperren, W.: A symmetric and unified approach towards combining aspect-oriented and component-based software development. In: Gorton, I., Heineman, G.T., Crnkovic, I., Schmidt, H.W., Stafford, J.A., Szyperski, C.A., Wallnau, K. (eds.) CBSE 2006. LNCS, vol. 4063, Springer, Heidelberg (2006)
22. Kandé, M.M.: A Concern-oriented Approach to Software Architecture. PhD thesis, École Polytechnique Fédéral de Lausanne, These n. 2796 (2003)
23. Sutton Jr., S.M., Tarr, P.: Aspect-oriented design needs concern modeling. In: Proceedings of AOSD 2002 Workshop on Aspect-Oriented Design (2002)
24. Katara, M., Katz, S.: A concern architecture view for aspect-oriented software design. Software and Systems Modeling 5 (2006)
25. Bass, L., Klein, M., Northrop, L.: Identifying aspects using architectural reasoning. In: Proceedings Early Aspects Workshop (2004)
26. Mens, K.: Architectural aspects. In: Proceedings of AOSD 2002 Workshop on Early Aspects: Aspect-Oriented Requirements Engineering and Architecture Design (2002)
27. Boucké, N., Holvoet, T.: Relating architectural views with architectural concerns. In: EA 2006. Proceedings of the 2006 international workshop on Early aspects at ICSE, pp. 11–18. ACM Press, New York (2006)
28. Hilliard, R., Rice, T.B.: Expressiveness in architecture description languages. In: Magee, J.N., Perry, D.E. (eds.) Proceedings of the 3rd International Software Architecture Workshop, Orlando FL, November 1 and 2 1998, pp. 65–68. ACM Press, New York (1998)

Mapping Features to Aspects:
A Model-Based Generative Approach

Uirá Kulesza[1,2], Vander Alves[3,4], Alessandro Garcia[3],
Alberto Costa Neto[2], Elder Cirilo[1], Carlos J. P. de Lucena[1], and Paulo Borba[2]

[1] PUC-Rio, Computer Science Department, Rio de Janeiro - Brazil
{uira, lucena, ecirilo}@inf.puc-rio.br
[2] New University of Lisboa, FCT, Computer Science Department, Lisboa - Portugal
[3] Informatics Center, Federal University of Pernambuco, Recife - Brazil
{vra, acn, phmb}@cin.ufpe.br
[4] Lancaster University, Computing Department, Lancaster - United Kingdom
garciaa@comp.lancs.ac.uk

Abstract. Handling the various derivations of an aspect-oriented software family architecture can be a daunting and costly task if explicit support is not systematically provided throughout early and late development stages. Aspect-oriented software development (AOSD) has been recently explored as a technique that enables software product line customization. However, the application of AOSD has been limited to modularize specific crosscutting features encountered in the implementation of software product-line architectures or frameworks. Only a few works have investigated the development of product derivation approaches for AOSD. This paper presents a model-based generative approach to mapping features to aspects across different artifacts of a product line. Our main aim is to enable the smooth and systematic derivation of aspect-oriented software family architecture. Our approach is complementary to a set of previously-proposed modularization guidelines to implement aspect-oriented frameworks. We present details about the suite of mappings supported by our generative model, illustrate them in heterogeneous case studies, and discuss several implementation issues for its accomplishment.

1 Introduction

Aspect-Oriented Software Development (AOSD) [13, 19] is a software engineering approach to modularize crosscutting concerns that existing paradigms are not able to capture explicitly. Crosscutting concerns are broadly-scoped features or properties that often crosscut several modules in a software system. AOSD encourages modular descriptions of crosscutting concerns typically through a new modular unit, called *aspect*. Early aspects [5, 30] refer to the aspect-oriented (AO) approaches which address the explicit handling of crosscutting concerns at the requirements and architecture level. The majority of the existing development techniques, including the early aspects approaches, have explored the use of AO techniques to modularize traditional (such as logging and security) and domain-specific crosscutting concerns (e.g., [22]).

A. Moreira and J. Grundy (Eds.): Early Aspects 2007 Workshop, LNCS 4765, pp. 155 – 174, 2007.

The use of AOSD techniques in the development of frameworks and product lines have been only recently exploited [1, 2, 4, 14, 22-28, 33]. However, aspects have been notouriously used to modularize crosscutting features encountered in the implementation of aspect-oriented software family architectures. We have identified from our experience [22-24] the following benefits on the application of AO techniques in product line development: (i) clear separation and variation of crosscutting features starting at early phases; (ii) direct mapping of crosscutting features in aspects; (iii) simplified implementation of code generator, because the composition of crosscutting features is accomplished by aspect weavers; and (iv) improved reuse of artifacts associated with crosscutting features. However, the achievement of such benefits is fundamentally dependent on the provision of a set of guidelines to model, implement and compose non-crosscutting and crosscutting features. Also, it requires the definition of mapping rules between the different abstractions (such as, features, aspects, use cases) used in both the product line development and the product derivation stages.

This paper presents a model-based generative approach to mapping features from the problem space to aspects from the solution space. It is centered on the development of a generative model [7] composed of three elements: (i) an architecture model; (ii) a feature model; and (iii) a configuration model. Our main aim is to support automatic product derivation of family architectures which are implemented using aspect-oriented programming. Our approach is complementary to a set of previously proposed modularization guidelines [23, 24] to implement framework and product lines using aspect-oriented programming. We also present mapping rules between the kinds of features and implementation elements which guide the specification of our configuration model, and illustrate our approach with case studies.

This paper is organized as follows. Section 2 gives an overview of our AO approach for framework development. Section 3 presents our model-based generative approach by detailing the different models used in the product derivation stage. Section 4 illustrates the approach with a case study in the mobile games domain. Section 5 discusses a set of lessons learned from the use of the proposed guidelines and mapping rules. Related work is discussed in Section 6. Concluding remarks are offered in Section 7.

2   An Aspect-Oriented Framework Development Approach

Our previous work [23] has proposed an approach for developing application frameworks using aspect-oriented programming. This section briefly shows an overview of our framework development approach (Section 2.1) and the use of the approach in the JUnit framework (Section 2.2).

2.1   Approach Overview

In our approach, an OO framework specifies and implements not only its common and variable behavior using OO classes, but it also exposes a set of extension join points (EJPs) [23, 24] which can be used to also extend its functionality. EJPs establish a contract between the framework classes and a set of aspects extending the framework functionality. They aim at increasing the framework variability and integrability with other implementation artifacts (such as components, frameworks or APIs) by serving two purposes: (i) to offer a set of join points spread and tangled in the framework classes into which the implementation of crosscutting optional and alternative features can be included; and (ii) to expose a set of framework events that can be used to notify or to facilitate a crosscutting integration with other software elements (such as, frameworks or components).

In this context, EJPs document crosscutting extension points for software developers who need to instantiate and evolve the framework. They can also be viewed as a set of constraints imposed on the whole space of available join points in the framework design, thereby promoting safe extension and reuse. EJPs are a specialization of the Crosscutting Interface (XPI) concept [15, 31] applied in the context of framework/product line development. Similar to XPIs [16, 30], EJPs establish a contractual interface between the framework classes and a set of aspects extending the framework functionality. However, EJPs focus specifically on the definition of candidate join points to be extended by aspects to introduce implementations of additional framework variabilities or crosscutting compositions with other artifacts (components, frameworks) [23, 24]. One of the main aims of EJPs and XPIs is to decrease the coupling between the base code and its aspects. A key characteristic of EJPs is that framework developers and users do not need to learn totally new abstractions to use them, as they can mostly be implemented using the mechanisms of AOP languages. We have presented guidelines to implement EJPs using AspectJ [24]. Following these guidelines, each EJP is implemented as: (i) an aspect that exposes relevant framework join points through a set of public pointcuts; and (ii) an aspect that codifies runtime and compile-time contracts to address the specification of constraints between the framework and its respective extension aspects.

Our approach promotes framework development as a composition of a core structure and a set of extensions. A framework extension can define one of the following: (i) the implementation of optional or alternative framework features; or (ii) the integration with an additional component or framework. The composition between the framework core and the framework extensions is accomplished by different types of extension aspects, each one defining a crosscutting composition with the framework by means of its exposed EJPs. We next describe the main concepts of our approach:

(i) *framework core* – implements the mandatory functionality of a software family. Similar to a traditional OO framework, this core structure contains the frozen-spots that represent the common features of the software family and hot-spot classes that represent non-crosscutting variabilities from the domain addressed;

(ii) *aspects in the core* – implement and modularize existing crosscutting concerns or roles in the framework core. They represent the traditional use of AOP to simplify the understanding and evolution of the framework core;

(iii) *variability aspects* – implement optional or alternative features existing in the framework core. These elements extend the framework EJPs with any additional crosscutting behavior;

(iv) *integration aspects* – define crosscutting compositions between the framework core and other existing extensions, such as an API or an OO framework. These elements also rely on the EJPs specification to define their implementation.

Figure 1 shows the design of an OO framework with aspects following our approach. Both variability and integration aspects intercept only join points matched by pointcuts in the EJPs provided by the framework; further, such aspects must comply with all the constraints defined by the EJPs. This brings systematization to the framework extension and composition with other artifacts, providing a number of benefits [23], such as enhanced understandability and evolution of the framework core, better management of features, safe framework reuse, and pluggable/unpluggable crosscutting framework extensions.

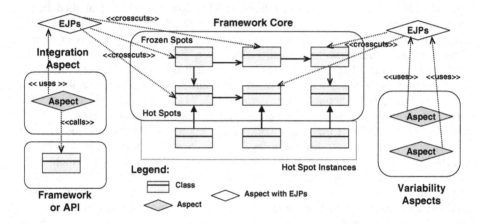

Fig. 1. Elements of our Framework Development Approach

2.2 JUnit Framework: An Ilustrative Example

The main purpose of the JUnit framework is to allow the design, implementation and execution of unit tests in Java applications. Figure 2 presents the main elements of the JUnit architecture. Its main functionalities are: the definition of test cases or suites to be executed (TestCase and TestSuite subclasses); the execution of a selected test case or suite (BaseTestRunner and TestRunner classes); and the collection (TestResult class) and visual presentation of the test results. However, different extensions can be implemented to add new functionalities into the JUnit framework core. Some examples of simple extensions are the following: (i) enable JUnit to execute each test suite in a separate thread (ActiveTestSuite aspect), and wait until all tests finish. In order to implement this extension we need to observe the event when the test suite starts running, the event when each test method runs, and the event when the test suite stops running; (ii) enable JUnit to run each test repeatedly (RepeatedTestGeneric aspect). In order to implement this extension we need to observe the event when each test method runs.

Figure 2 also presents the `TestExecutionEvents` aspect that works as an EJP. This aspect defines a set of public pointcuts that exposes relevant events of the JUnit framework, such as: (i) the beginning of test case execution; (ii) the beginning of test suite execution; and (iii) the initialization of test runners. Each of the extension aspects uses these pointcuts to extend the functionality of the framework core.

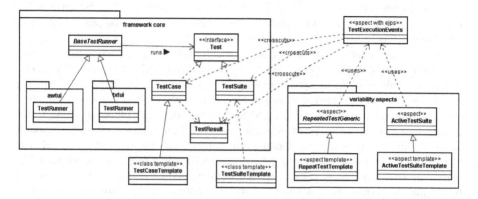

Fig. 2. JUnit Aspect-Oriented Architecture

3 Mapping Features to Aspect-Oriented Architectures

This section presents the model-based generative approach to mapping features to aspect-oriented implementation elements. It enables deriving members of an AO software family architecture through model-based generative support for customizing architecture variabilities. It can be used to complement our framework development approach described in Section 2. Our approach is presented in a stepwise fashion. First, the three main models of our generative approach are described by showing how the domain engineering team can develop and derive them during or after the architecture implementation (Sections 3.1-3.3). Later subsections detail the activities of template implementation (Section 3.4) and product derivation (Section 3.5).

3.1 Specifying an Architecture Model

The implementation of a software family architecture typically results in a set of implementation elements/artifacts, such as, classes, interfaces, templates, aspects, and extra files (e.g., configuration and image files). An aggregation of many of these heterogeneous elements realizes the components previously defined in design of the AO family architecture. For example, our aspect-oriented approach to framework implementation (Section 2) generates a set of well-defined implementation elements, such as: the framework core classes, OO hot-spots classes and interfaces, aspects in the core, extension join point aspects, variability aspects, and integration aspects.

The first step of our approach consists of the specification of an architecture model. It is used to relate the implementation elements from the software family with the specification of its architectural components. The main purpose of the architecture model is to create a representation of these implementation elements in order to relate them to feature models, where the component variabilities are expressed. It is developed to be used and processed by our model-based generative tool. An architecture model is composed by a set of components. Each component can aggregate different implementation elements, such as, classes, interfaces, aspects, templates and extra files. Templates are used to codify implementation elements (classes, interfaces, aspects and configuration files) which need to be customized during the software family derivation. A component can also be composed of a set of sub-components.

An architecture model can also be automatically generated by parsing the directory that maintains the implementation elements. Specialized AST (Abstract Syntax Tree) APIs available for many programming languages can be used to help the implementation of this parsing function. During this parsing process, every directory (e.g., a Java package) can be converted to a component with the same name in the architecture model. Each type of implementation element (classes, interfaces, aspects or files) must also have a corresponding representation in the architecture model. The functionality of reverse engineering from code to models (e.g., Java code to UML class diagrams) implemented by many IDEs (Integrated Development Environments) has a similar purpose to this functionality. Templates are the only implementation elements that need to be codified to specify the architecture model. They can be used to specify: (i) subclasses/subtypes of framework hot-spots (classes or interfaces); (ii) concrete subaspects that implement any implementation alternative for a crosscutting feature; or (iii) any class, aspect or configuration file that needs to be customized during the product derivation process.

Figure 3(c) shows an example of an architecture model implemented using the EMF (Eclipse Modeling Framework) [6] technology[1]. It partially represents the JUnit aspect-oriented architecture described in Section 2.2. It is composed of two main components: `core` and `extensions`. Each of them aggregates the implementation elements respectively for: (i) the framework core, including the graphical user interfaces available, and (ii) the extension aspects. The `TestExecutionEvents` aspect implements the JUnit EJP and is part of the core component. The following templates were also specified for the JUnit architecture model: (i) `TestSuiteTemplate` and `TestCaseTemplate` which are used to further derive specific test suite and test case classes; and (ii) `ActiveTestSuiteTemplate` and `RepeatedTestTemplate` which will be used to derive variability aspects that respectively address the concurrent and repeated execution of tests to be applied to test suites and test cases, respectively.

3.2 Specifying the Feature Model

The following step in the definition of the generative artifacts is to specify the feature model for the AO software family architecture. A feature model [7] is used to represent the common and variable features of a software family. Since the pivotal

---

[1] An instantiatiation tool which completely supports the definition of the models (architecture, feature and configuration) from the approach is under development. We are using Eclipse and EMF technologies as the base platform to define our instantiation tool. The specification of feature models in our tool is supported by the FMP plugin [3].

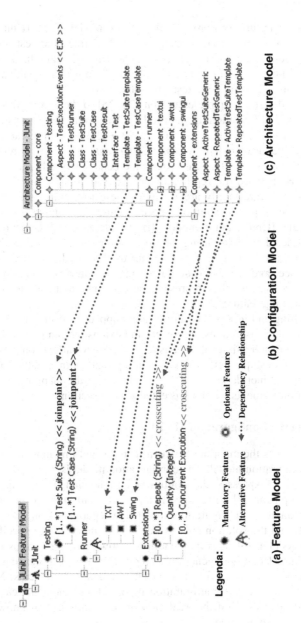

Fig. 3. JUnit Feature, Configuration and Architecture Models

purpose of the generative models is to automate product derivation, feature modeling focuses mainly on the specification of the software architecture variabilities. In our approach, we use the feature models proposed by Czarnecki et al [8], which allow modeling mandatory, optional, and alternative features, and their respective cardinality. The feature modeling plugin (FMP) [3] supports the modeling of feature models in Eclipse. Figure 3(a) presents the feature model of the JUnit framework. It defines three main features: (i) **Testing** – which defines the test suite and cases specific to an application; (ii) **Runner** – represents the graphical user interface alternatives provided by JUnit; and finally (iii) **Extensions** – which defines fine-grained extensions to be applied to test suites and cases.

Our approach defines a simple extension [26, 25] to the feature model in order to enable the aspect customization during product derivation. Our extension defines two properties, called <<crosscutting>> and <<joinpoint>>, which can be assigned to specific features being modeled. A *crosscutting feature* is used to represent aspects from the architecture model that can extend the behavior of other system features. A *joinpoint feature* is used to represent specific join points from implementation elements of the software family architecture. These join points are candidates to be extended by aspects in the solution space. Figure 3(a) shows examples of such properties in the JUnit feature model: (i) the **Repeat** and **Concurrent Execution** features are modeled as crosscutting, because they represent features that can extend the behavior of other JUnit features. They are used to model extension aspects from the solution space; and (ii) the **Test Suite** and **Test Cases** features are modeled as joinpoint features, because they represent the candidate elements to be extended by the JUnit crosscutting features.

The crosscutting and join point features are mapped, respectively, to the following implementation elements: extension aspects and extension join points (EJPs). In order to enable the customization of extension aspects to affect only specific EJPs, crosscutting relationships between crosscutting and join point features can be specified during product derivation [26]. Details about the mapping of these features to implementation elements will be presented in next sections.

3.3 Specifying the Configuration Model

Our approach defines the mapping between features and implementation elements by means of a configuration model. The configuration model is defined based on a set of mapping rules. It expresses the configuration knowledge existing in generative software development [7]. The specification of configuration models makes it possible to reason about configuration knowledge separately from the problem space (feature model) and the solution space (architecture model). The specification of the configuration model also brings the benefit to allow realizing various changes in the configuration knowledge of a generative approach, such as discarding or modifying the existing mapping between features and implementation elements. Next we detail the elements that define our configuration model. These elements can be explicitly created or modified based on the evolution of the configuration knowledge from a software family or product line.

Our configuration model is composed of three elements: (i) dependency relationships between implementation elements existing in architecture models and features in feature model specifications; (ii) definition of valid crosscutting relationships between join point and crosscutting features; and (iii) specification of the mapping between join point features and concrete join points existing in implementation elements from the architecture model. Table 1 presents the elements of the configuration model and their respective purpose for product derivation. In the following, we describe the guidelines to specify such configuration elements.

The dependency relationships between implementation elements (components, classes, aspects, templates and files) and features are used to determine which implementation elements must be instantiated when a specific set of features are selected in product derivation. They represent the accomplishment of decision models [32]. Table 2 describes the mapping rules between: (i) the kinds of existing features; and (ii) the elements from our AO approach to framework implementation (Section 2). Each line of Table 2 can be read as a rule that says: "If you have that specific kind of feature, it must be mapped to that specific implementation element from our approach". These mapping rules can be used as a base to derive the dependency relationships between implementation elements and features.

As we can see in Table 2, mandatory features are mapped to mandatory implementation elements (such as the framework core and the aspects in the core). In the configuration model, however, there is no need to create any dependency relationship between these elements, since these mandatory implementation elements must be found in every member/product of the software family/product line. As we mentioned in Section 3.2, the feature models are used to support the product derivation. It implies that they are mainly adopted to represent the software family variabilities. The representation of mandatory features is optional. However, if it is of interest to explicitly maintain the mapping between all the features to implementation elements, additional dependency relationships can be also created in the configuration model. Table 2 also shows that: (i) both optional and crosscutting alternative features are mapped to variability or integration aspects; and (ii) join point features are mapped to EJP implementation elements.

Besides using the mapping rules to define the dependency relationships, the following guidelines can be used to specify them: (i) if an implementation element must be instantiated to every member of a software family, there is no need to create a dependency relationship to any feature; and (ii) if an implementation element depends on any feature occurrence, a dependency relationship must be created between them. In the case of the template implementation element, the dependency relationships

Table 1. Configuration Model Elements

Configuration Model Element	Main Purpose
Dependency Relationships between Implementation Elements and Features	• Choice of Variabilities
Valid Crosscutting Relationships between Crosscutting and Joinpoint Features	• Restriction of Crosscutting Relationships in the Problem Space
Mapping between Joinpoint Features and Concrete Joinpoint from EJPs	• Customization of Pointcuts

define if they must be processed to generate any specific element to be included in the product/member generated. Thus, each template depends necessarily on a feature, which provides the useful information for the template processing.

Figure 3(b) defines a set of dependency relationships for the JUnit configuration model. The GUI alternative components (textui, awtui, swingui) and their respective implementation elements (classes, interfaces) will be instantiated based on the alternative feature selected for the Runner feature. Every template from the JUnit architecture model depends necessarily on a specific feature. The RepeatedTestTemplate, for example, will be processed only if the application engineer requests a Repeat feature during the product derivation stage.

Table 2. Mapping Rules between Features and Implementation Elements

Feature Type	Implementation Element
Mandatory Features	• Framework Core • Aspects in the Core
Alternative Features	• Hot-Spots Classes in the Framework Core
Joinpoint Features	• Extension Join Points (aspects)
Optional Features	• Variability and Integration Aspects
Alternative Crosscutting Features	• Variability and Integration Aspects

Our configuration model also defines a set of valid crosscutting relationships that can occur between crosscutting and join point features. These relationships are used to restrict which aspects (represented as crosscutting features) can affect which join points from the classes/aspects of the software family (represented as join point features). In our approach, a code generator uses such information to verify if application engineers are specifying valid relationships between crosscutting and join point features. Table 3 shows the valid crosscutting relationships for the JUnit case study. It specifies that: (i) the Repeat crosscutting feature can only extend the behavior of Test Case features; and (ii) the Concurrent Execution feature can only extend Test Suite features.

The last component of our configuration model is the mapping between the join point features and concrete join points existing on the implementation elements from the architecture model. This mapping is used by a code generator to customize pointcuts from extension aspects. If all the extension aspects have fixed pointcuts, there is no need to specify this mapping. The concrete join points can be directly

Table 3. Additional Elements of the JUnit Configuration Model

Configuration Model Element	JUnit Framework
Valid Crosscutting Relationships	Repeat feature <<crosscuts>> Test Case feature Concurrent Execution <<crosscuts>> Test Suite feature

Mapping between Joinpoint Features and Joinpoint from EJPs	Test Case feature <<maps>>
	    TestExecutionEventsEJP. testCaseExecution(...);
	
	Test Suite feature <<maps>>
	    TestExecutionEventsEJP.testSuiteExecution(...);

found and extracted from the EJPs defined for the software family architecture. Table 3 shows the joinpoint mapping of the Test Case and Test Suite features to concrete join points exposed by the EJPs of the JUnit framework.

3.4 Template Implementation

The last activity of product-line/domain engineering is to codify the templates for the architecture model (Section 3.1). During the specification of the architecture model, templates are defined to specify implementation elements which define any variability on their structure. After that, dependency relationships between templates and features are created in the configuration model specification (Section 3.3). The implementation of templates depends on the information provided by the feature model. The feature model is used to collect any data that helps to customize the template variabilities. For this reason, the complete codification of templates can only be completely realized after the specification of the architecture, feature and configuration models.

There are many tools which implement the template technology [9]. In our particular tool implementation, we are using JET (Java Emitter Templates) to codify our templates. JET is the template engine of the Eclipse Modeling Framework (EMF) plugin. It can be used to implement templates for any kind of implementation element (classes, aspects, configuration files). Figure 4 shows the implementation of the TestSuite template using JET. It contains initially basic configuration code of a JET template (lines 1-5). The FeatureElement type is used to store a reference to the feature which the template depends on the configuration model. This variable is suitably configured by the code generator during product derivation.

For example, the TestSuite template depends on the test suite feature. Because of that, the code generator will process this template for each test suite feature specified; it will also use the information from a specific test suite feature specified during this processing. The processing of the template TestSuite causes the code customization of test suite classes by using information from the FeatureElement

```
01  <%@ jet package="translated"
02      imports="org.eclipse.emf.common.util.Elist ..."
03      class="TestSuiteTemplate" %>
04
05  <% FeatureElement testSuite = (FeatureElement) argument;%>
06  import junit.framework.Test;
07  import junit.framework.TestSuite;
08
09  public class <%=testSuite.getName()%>TestSuite {
10
11      public static Test suite(){
12          TestSuite suite = new TestSuite("<%=feature.getName()%>");
13          <% EList features = feature.getChildren();
14            for (Iterator iter=features.iterator(); iter.hasNext();){
15              FeatureElement testCase= (FeatureElement) iter.next(); %>
16          suite.addTest(
17                  new TestSuite(<%=testCase.getName()%>Test.class));
18          <% } %>
19          return suite;
20      }
21
22  }
```

Fig. 4. The `TestSuite` template

attribute type, such as: (i) the class name of the test suite (line 9); and (ii) which test case classes will be part of this test suite (lines 13-18). Templates of aspects can also use the information about the join point mapping from the configuration model to customize pointcuts. This information is made available in the `FeatureElement` class[2] through a specific method (`getJoinPointFeatures()`).

3.5 Product Derivation

In the product derivation phase, an instance of the software family architecture is created based on the choice of variabilities by the software developers. It is supported in our approach by two main activities: (i) choice of variabilities through a feature model instance; and (ii) choice of valid crosscutting relationships between features. In order to generate a member of the software family architecture, a code generator uses the information collected by the derivation activities in addition to the architecture and configuration models.

The product derivation phase is composed of three steps: (i) initially an application engineer specifies a feature model instance and its respective crosscutting relationships; (ii) next, a code generator uses this feature model instance and a configuration model to decide which elements from the architecture model must be part of the generated application; and (iii) finally, after processing and customizing the architecture model, the code generator loads the implementation elements that will constitute the final product in a specific folder or project created in an IDE, such as Eclipse.

---

[2] The `FeatureElement` class is used in our plugin to store the subtree of a specific feature from a feature model configuration created using the FMP plugin.

The following actions must be performed by the code generator during the product derivation process:

(i) **verification of valid crosscutting relationships** – the code generator must initially guarantee that only valid crosscutting relationships were created by the application engineers. It must verify whether each crosscutting relationship created during product derivation is part of the set of valid crosscutting relationships specified by the configuration model. The current version of our tool [38] implements this verification functionality by manipulating the feature model instance and the configuration model of the SPL and comparing the crosscutting relationships specified by them. The detection of invalid crosscutting relationships would interrupt the product derivation process in order to avoid subsequent problems in code generation;

(ii) **processing of the architecture model** – the code generator processes the architecture model by traversing all the implementation elements. It proceeds as follows: for each component encountered, the code generator verifies in the configuration model if it depends on any special feature. In this case, the code generator only instantiates[3] that component (and processes its respective sub-elements) if there is an occurrence of that feature in the feature model instance. When processing implementation elements from each component the same process is applied; that is, it is verified if the implementation element depends on specific features as a condition to instantiate it. As we mentioned before, template elements always depend on some feature. They are processed by the code generator for each occurrence of that feature. During template processing, all the information about the feature and respective sub-features, which it depends, is used to support the template customization (Section 3.4);

(iii) **customization of pointcuts** – during the processing of aspect templates, pointcuts can also be customized. Every aspect template must depend on a specific crosscutting feature. If the aspect template has any pointcut to be customized, its join points can be obtained by looking at which join point features are affected by the crosscutting feature representing the aspect template. This information is obtained by the code generator in the configuration model and it is used by the template to customize its respective variable pointcuts.

4   J2ME Games Product Line

J2ME games are mainstream mobile applications of considerable complexity [1]. In this case study, we implemented the generative model of an industrial J2ME game Software Product Line (SPL) based on EJPs (Section 2). The case study implementation exposed game core EJPs in order to allow the composition of crosscutting extensions in its basic functionality. The detailed architecture model is described elsewhere [24]. The resulting generative model for this SPL is shown in Figure 5.

---

[3] In Java, for example, the component instantiation can be mapped to the creation of a package, which aggregates the implementation elements from that component.

According to Figure 5, there are EJPs in the core (ResourceEvents and DrawingEvents) as well as in specific extension components (BrightEvents, CloudEvents, and ScreenEvents in Components Bright, Clouds, and Image Loading, respectively). EJPs in the core are due to the mandatory features FLIP and ImageLoading, and are not necessarily linked to such features since they are in every SPL instance. On the other hand, the EJPs in extension components are due to specific alternative subfeatures of those features or the optional features Bright and Clouds, and need to be linked to such features since they are present in only some SPL instances.

Additionally, the dependencies for the Bright component have a peculiar behaviour: when the Bright feature is *not* selected, then the NoBright aspect has to be included. When such a feature is selected, the Bright Aspect is included, instead. This

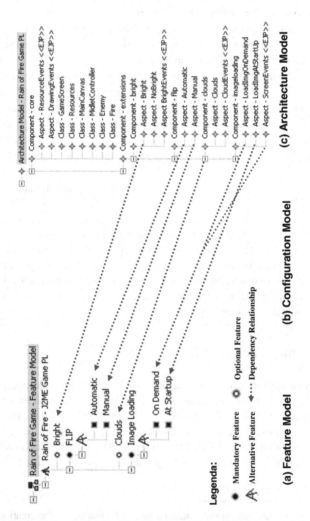

Fig. 5. J2ME Game Product Line Configuration and Architecture Models

occurs because the variability related to this feature could not be extracted into a single module (an aspect) to be composed with a base module representing non-brightness behavior. Therefore, the generative model for this feature has limited compositionality, which may lead to reduced scalability. Although not desirable, this phenomenon can arise frequently in SPLs. We further discuss this in Section 5.1.

In terms of granularity, the dependency relationships can depart from either fine-grained implementation elements such as aspects and EJPs, or from coarse-grained implementation elements such as components (Clouds and Bright). This reflects inherent levels of granularity in the SPL variability. Based on the lessons learned from new case studies, we intend to derive guidelines which help to reduce the total amount of dependency relationships, and consequently, facilitate the maintenance of the configuration model.

In this case study, we did not have occurrences of crosscutting relationships between crosscutting and join point features. The reason for this is that such relationships occur more frequently in the context of homogenous variability aspects, whereas in this case study most variability aspects were heterogeneous and with fixed pointcuts. For the same reason, this case study did not customize pointcuts, thereby not requiring mapping between joinpoint features and concrete joinpoints from EJPs.

5 Discussion and Lessons Learned

This section provides discussion and some lessons learned based on our experience on applying our approach. In particular, it shows the benefits that our implementation guidelines and mapping rules can bring: (i) to deal with the problem of feature interaction (Section 5.1); (ii) to specify traceability links between features, use cases and extension join points (Section 5.2); and (iii) to adopt proactive, reactive or extractive product line development strategies (Section 5.3).

5.1 Feature Interaction

The development of frameworks and product lines involves the modularization and composition of different features. The interdependence and interference between features can generate the problem of feature interactions. A feature interaction [36] occurs when a feature is modified or influenced by the behavior of other features. When features interfere with each other and are implemented by aspects, we say there is an aspect interaction. Different types of aspect interactions can occur. Sanen et al [37] proposes a classification of four types: (i) mutual exclusion - two or more aspects cannot coexist in the same application; (ii) dependency - an aspect depends on another one to execute correctly; (iii) reinforcement - there is a positive influence from one aspect to another one; and (iv) conflict - an aspect works correctly in isolation, but not in the presence of other aspects.

Different approaches can be used to deal with the problem of feature/aspect interaction during product line development. The mutual exclusion and dependency interactions, can be addressed, respectively, by the definition of <<excludes>> and <<requires>> constraints in a feature model [7]. On the other hand, conflicts and reinforcement between aspects need to be designed and implemented carefully.

Conflicts in the order of composition of aspects, for example, can require the definition of precedence statements (available in AspectJ). Our approach contributes in two ways to deal with feature interaction situations: (i) the specification of EJPs helps to identify possible join points of interactions between aspects from frameworks and product lines; and (ii) the explicit definition of valid crosscutting relationships between crosscutting and join point features in our configuration model allows to restrict undesirable aspect interactions.

Another potential problem of feature interaction is that the implementation element to which a certain feature is mapped may depend on the selection of another feature: if such other feature is also selected, then the implementation element to which the former feature is mapped might be different. In such case, there is reduced compositionality of the configuration model because functional composition at the feature model does not reflect into functional composition at the architectural model. Therefore, this may comprise the scalability of the resulting SPL. However, we note that compositionality, although desirable, is not always possible at the architectural level. Indeed, the very existence of EJPs indicates that interactions among the SPL core and its extensions constrain arbitrary composition.

5.2 Use Case Extensions

Use cases [17] are a largely adopted technique for requirements specification. It has been adopted by many modern development software processes. A use case is defined as a sequence of actions performed by the system to provide an observable result of value to a particular user. The use cases technique also provides an extension mechanism which can be used to describe extra (mandatory or optional) behavior. The extend relationship can be defined between use cases to achieve such extension purpose. An extension use case can add behavior to a specific set of extension points of other use cases. Jacobson [16] argues that the use case extension mechanism can be used to model aspects during the requirements specification. In his approach, extension use cases model aspects and the extension points represent join points at the requirements level.

This paper presented a set of mapping rules from features to implementation elements of our aspect-oriented framework development approach. We have also noticed that there is a strong synergy between our extension join points (EJPs) and the use case extension points proposed by Jacobson. The use case extension points are natural candidates to be implemented as an EJP. Alike, extension use cases can be implemented as extension aspects. The existence of mapping rules between feature models, use cases and implementation elements from our approach can help us to define and keep traceability links [18] between the different artifacts developed in the requirements, architecture and implementation stages. It can improve the development or evolution of frameworks and product lines by supporting relevant software engineering activities, such as change impact analysis and consistent variability management. We are going to develop new case studies to explore the synergies between these techniques and assess how their integration can be used to better support the management of traceability links between artifacts. These traceability links would also be specified as a set of mappings between the mentioned and other modeling notations in order to support round-tripping and, as a consequence, to address multi-level customization approaches [11] with the use of aspect-oriented abstractions, such as, EJPs and crosscutting/join point features.

5.3 Software Product Line Adoption Approaches

Different adoption strategies [21] can be used to develop software product lines (SPLs). The proactive approach motivates the development of product lines considering all the products in the foreseeable horizon. A complete set of artifacts to address the product line is developed from scratch. In the extractive approach, a SPL is developed starting from existing software systems. Common and variable features are extracted from these systems to derive an initial version of the SPL. The reactive approach advocates the incremental development of SPLs. Initially, the SPL artifacts address only a few products. When there is a demand to incorporate new requirements or products, the common and variable artifacts are incrementally extended in reaction to them.

Our approach has been used mainly in the aspect-oriented refactoring [29] of existing object-oriented frameworks and product lines [23, 24]. However, we believe that our guidelines to implement crosscutting features using aspects can be used in different SPL adoption strategies. Also, the mapping rules presented in this paper play an important role in the adoption strategies since they show clearly the relationships between features and implementation elements. In the extractive approach, our guidelines and mapping rules can be useful to determine which optional, integration and alternative features would be implemented using aspects. The reactive approach can benefit from EJPs previously specified to introduce new demands of optional and integration crosscutting features in the SPL or framework core. EJPs also promote a weak coupling between a SPL core and its respective crosscutting extensions. This can help in the incremental development or evolution of SPLs by allowing to (un)plug existing features and simplifying the core complexity. Finally, the proactive approach can benefit from the mapping between use case extensions, features and extension aspects presented previously (Section 5.2). Existing product-line development processes can use these mapping guidelines to help in the analysis and identification of candidate aspects to implement specific features.

6 Related Work

There are many feature-based tools to product derivation available in the industry, such as Pure::variants and Gears. Pure::variants [34] is a SPL tool for feature modelling and product derivation. It allows specifying a generative model, where features are modelled graphically in different formats such as trees and tables and constraints among features are expressed using first order logic in Prolog. Architecture modelling is also possible and conforms to a specific meta-model. The configuration model is specified in terms of rules relating elements of both models and can make use of a customizable transformation engine. Similarly, Gears [35] allows the definition of a generative model focused on product derivation. However, its language for expressing constraints within feature models uses propositional logic instead of full first-order logic. Additionally, Gears allows the definition of modular feature models, which can be combined hierarchically and support product line populations.

The Framed Aspects approach [27] explores the instantiation of AO architectures. It proposes the integration between Frame and AOP technologies. The main difference between our approach and the Framed Aspects is that they define many of the decision steps about the product derivation process in the template code of frames by means of meta-tags. In our approach, the decisions related to the architecture customization process are described separately by our configuration model. It makes it easier to adapt or evolve the decisions related to the architecture customization. We also use feature model instances to gather all information necessary for the resolution of AO variabilities.

Griss [14] presents some benefits of integrated use of aspect-oriented implementation technologies and feature engineering during development of product lines. He also outlines a general methodology for the combination of these two technologies. Our work can be seen as a concrete method of development and derivation of framework and product lines using aspect-oriented techniques, which follows the general guidelines presented by Griss.

There are also similarities between the mappings from our model-based generative approach and those proposed in the feature-based model templates approach [10]. The dependency relationship from our configuration model can be seen as a special kind of the "presence condition" annotation proposed by those authors. Our central idea, however, is to keep these relationships and other configuration knowledge information in a complete and separate model.

7 Conclusion

This paper presented a model-based generative approach to mapping features to aspects in order to enable the derivation of AO software family architecture. The approach defines a generative model, encompassing an extension for feature modeling to represent crosscutting relationship among features, mapping rules and guidelines for product derivation, and an architecture model complementary to a set of previously-proposed modularization guidelines to implement aspect-oriented frameworks. We illustrated the approach with case studies and discussed its benefits and drawbacks for handling feature interaction and SPL adoption strategies. We are currently incorporating the aspect-oriented generative model presented in this paper in our product derivation tool [38]. As future work, we plan to explore the synergies between use case extensions, features and extension aspects in the context of supporting the management of traceability links between artifacts.

Acknowledgements. This research was partially sponsored by FAPERJ (grant No. E-26/151.493/2005), CNPq (grants No. 552068/2002-0, 481575/2004-9 and 141247/2003-7), MCT/FINEP/CT-INFO (grant No. 01/2005 0105089400), European Commission Grant IST-2-004349: European Network of Excellence on AOSD (AOSDEurope), and European Commission Grant IST-33710: Aspect-Oriented, Model-Driven Product Line Engineering (AMPLE).

References

1. Alves, V., Matos, P., Cole, L., Borba, P., Ramalho, G.: Extracting and Evolving Mobile Games Product Lines. In: Obbink, H., Pohl, K. (eds.) SPLC 2005. LNCS, vol. 3714, pp. 70–81. Springer, Heidelberg (2005)
2. Anastasopoulos, M., Muthig, D.: An Evaluation of Aspect-Oriented Programming as a Product Line Implementation Technology. In: Proceedings of the International Conference on Software Reuse (ICSR), pp. 141–156 (July 2004)
3. Antkiewicz, M., Czarnecki, K.: FeaturePlugin: Feature modeling plug-in for Eclipse. In: OOPSLA 2004 Eclipse Technology eXchange (ETX) Workshop (2004)
4. Apel, S., Batory, D.: When to Use Features and Aspects? A Case Study. In: Proceedings of GPCE 2006, pp. 59-68, Portland, Oregon (October 2006)
5. Baniassad, E., Clements, P., Araújo, J., Moreira, A., Rashid, A., Tekinerdogan, B.: Discovering Early Aspects. IEEE Software 23(1), 61–70 (2006)
6. Budinsky, F., Steinberg, D., Merks, E., Ellersick, R.: Eclipse Modeling Framework. Addison-Wesley, Reading (2004)
7. Czarnecki, K., Eisenecker, U.: Generative Programming: Methods, Tools, and Applications. Addison-Wesley, Reading (2000)
8. Czarnecki, K., Helsen, S., Eisenecker, U.: Staged Configuration Using Feature Models. In: Proceedings of the Third Software Product-Line Conference (September 2004)
9. Czarnecki, K., Helsen, S.: Feature-Based Survey of Model Transformation Approaches. IBM Systems Journal 45(3), 621–664 (2006)
10. Czarnecki, K., Antkiewicz, M.: Mapping Features to Models: A Template Approach Based on Superimposed Variants. In: Proceedings of GPCE 2005, pp. 422–437 (October 2005)
11. Czarnecki, K., Antkiewicz, M., Kim, C.: Multi-level Customization in Application Engineering. Communications of the ACM 49(12), 61–65 (2006)
12. Fayad, M., Schmidt, D., Johnson, R.: Building Application Frameworks: Object-Oriented Foundations of Framework Design. John Wiley & Sons, Chichester (1999)
13. Filman, R., Elrad, T., Clarke, S., Aksit, M.: Aspect-Oriented Software Development. Addison-Wesley, Reading (2005)
14. Griss, M.: Implementing Product-Line Features With Component Reuse. In: Frakes, W.B. (ed.) Software Reuse: Advances in Software Reusability. LNCS, vol. 1844, Springer, Heidelberg (2000)
15. Griswold, W., Sullivan, K., Song, Y., Shonle, M., Tewari, N., Cai, Y., Rajan, H.: Modular Software Design with Crosscutting Interfaces, pp. 51–60, IEEE Software, Special Issue on Aspect-Oriented Programming (January 2006)
16. Jacobson, I.: Use Cases and Aspects-Working Seamlessly Together. Journal of Object Technology 2(4), 7–28 (2003)
17. Jacobson, I., Christerson, M., Jonsson, P.: Overgaard Object-Oriented Software Engineering: A Use Case Driven Approach. Addison-Wesley, Reading (1992)
18. Jarke, M.: Requirements Traceability. Comm. ACM 41(12), 32–36 (1998)
19. Kiczales, G., Lamping, J., Mendhekar, A., Maeda, C., Lopes, C., Loingtier, J., Irwin, J.: Aspect-Oriented Programming. In: Aksit, M., Matsuoka, S. (eds.) ECOOP 1997. LNCS, vol. 1241, pp. 220–242. Springer, Heidelberg (1997)
20. Kiczales, G., Hilsdale, E., Hugunin, J., Kersten, M., Palm, J., Griswold, W.: Getting Started with AspectJ. Comm. ACM 44, 59–65 (2001)
21. Krueger, C.: Easing the Transition to Software Mass Customization. In: Proceedings of the 4th International Workshop on Software Product-Family Engineering, pp. 282–293 (2001)

22. Kulesza, U., Garcia, A., Lucena, C., Alencar, P.: A Generative Approach for Multi-Agent System Development. In: Choren, R., Garcia, A., Lucena, C., Romanovsky, A. (eds.) SELMAS 2004. LNCS, vol. 3390, pp. 52–69. Springer, Heidelberg (2005)
23. Kulesza, U., Alves, V., Garcia, A., Lucena, C., Borba, P.: Improving Extensibility of Object-Oriented Frameworks with Aspect-Oriented Programming. In: Proceedings of the 9th International Conference on Software Reuse (ICSR-9), pp. 231–245 (June 2006)
24. Kulesza, U., Coelho, R., Alves, V., Neto, A., Garcia, A., Lucena, C., von Staa, A., Borba, P.: Implementing Framework Crosscutting Extensions with EJPs and AspectJ. In: Proceedings of the ACM SIGSoft 20th Brazilian Symposium on SoftwareEngineering (SBES 2006), pp. 177–192, Florianópolis, Brazil (October 2006)
25. Kulesza, U., Garcia, A., Bleasby, F., Lucena, C.: Instantiating and Customizing Product Line Architectures using Aspects and Crosscutting Feature Models. In: Proceedings of the Workshop on Early Aspects, OOPSLA 2005, San Diego (2005)
26. Kulesza, U., Lucena, C., Alencar, P., Garcia, A.: Customizing Aspect-Oriented Variabilites using Generative Techniques. In: Proceedings of SEKE 2006, pp. 17–22, San Francisco (2006)
27. Loughran, N., Rashid, A.: Framed Aspects: Supporting Variability and Configurability for AOP. In: Bosch, J., Krueger, C. (eds.) ICOIN 2004 and ICSR 2004. LNCS, vol. 3107, pp. 127–140. Springer, Heidelberg (2004)
28. Mezini, M., Ostermann, K.: Variability Management with Feature-Oriented Programming and Aspects. In: Roy, B., Meier, W. (eds.) FSE 2004. LNCS, vol. 3017, pp. 127–136. Springer, Heidelberg (2004)
29. Monteiro, M., Fernandes, J.: Towards a Catalog of Aspect-Oriented Refactorings. In: Proceedings of AOSD 2005, Chicago, pp. 111–122 (March 2005)
30. Rashid, A., Moreira, A., Araújo, J.: Modularisation and Composition of Aspectual Requirements. In: Proceedings of AOSD 2003, Boston, pp. 11–20 (March 2003)
31. Sullivan, K., Griswold, W., Song, Y., Cai, Y., Shonle, M., Tewari, N., Rajan, H.: Information Hiding Interfaces for Aspect-Oriented Design. In: Proceedings of ESEC/FSE' 2005, Lisbon, Portugal, pp. 166–175 (September 5-9, 2005)
32. Weiss, D., Lai, C.: Software Product-Line Engineering: A Family-Based Software Development Process. Addison-Wesley Professional, Reading (1999)
33. Zhang, C., Jacobsen, H.: Resolving Feature Convolution in Middleware Systems. In: Proceedings of OOPSLA 2004, October 24-28, 2004, Vancouver, BC, Canada pp.188–205
34. Pure::Variants (July 2007), http://www.pure-systems.com/
35. Gears/BigLever (July 2007), http://www.biglever.com/
36. Jackson, M., Zave, P.: Distributed feature composition: A virtual architecture for telecommunications services. IEEE Transactions on Software Engineering 24(10), 831–847 (1998)
37. Sanen, F., Truyen, E., Joosen, W., Jackson, A., Nedos, A., Clarke, S., Loughran, N., Rashid, A.: Classifying And Documenting Aspect Interactions. In: Proceedings of the 5th AOSD Workshop on Aspects, Components, and Patterns for Infrastructure Software (ACP4IS) at AOSD 2006, Bonn, Germany (March 2006)
38. Cirilo, E., Kulesza, U., Lucena, C.: GenArch – A Model-Based Product Derivation Tool. In: Proceedings of the First Brazilian Symposium on Components, Architecture and Reuse (SBCARS 2007), Campinas, Brazil (August 2007)

Metamodel for Tracing Concerns Across the Life Cycle

Bedir Tekinerdoğan, Christian Hofmann, Mehmet Akşit, and Jethro Bakker

Department of Computer Science,
University of Twente, P.O. Box 217, 7500 AE Enschede, The Netherlands
{bedir, c.hofmann, m.aksit, j.bakker}@cs.utwente.nl

Abstract. Several aspect-oriented approaches have been proposed to specify aspects at different phases in the software life cycle. Aspects can appear within a phase, be refined or mapped to other aspects in later phases, or even disappear. Tracing aspects is necessary to support understandability and maintainability of software systems. Although several approaches have been introduced to address traceability of aspects, two important limitations can be observed. First, tracing is not yet tackled for the entire life cycle. Second, the traceability model that is applied usually refers to elements of specific aspect languages, thereby limiting the reusability of the adopted traceability model. We propose the concern traceability metamodel (CTM) that enables traceability of concerns throughout the life cycle, and which is independent from the aspect languages that are used. *CTM* can be enhanced to provide additional properties for tracing, and be instantiated to define customized traceability models with respect to the required aspect languages. We have implemented *CTM* in the tool *M-Trace*, that uses XML-based representations of the models and XQuery queries to represent tracing information. *CTM* and *M-Trace* are illustrated for a Concurrent Versioning System to trace aspects from the requirements level to architecture design level and the implementation.

1 Introduction

Several aspect-oriented approaches have been proposed to specify aspects at different phases in the software life cycle. At the programming level it appears that almost for every popular programming language there is now an aspect-oriented version in which crosscutting concerns are represented using dedicated language constructs. The early aspects domain has focused on defining approaches for modeling aspects at the level of requirements engineering and architecture design. Several design notations for representing aspects have been proposed in the context of aspect-oriented modeling using, for example, UML-based approaches. Aspects rarely occur in isolation. They are related to other artifacts within a phase or across multiple phases. Aspects can appear within a phase, be refined or mapped to other aspects in later phases, or may even disappear. Changes to an aspect can have consequences for other artifacts, which are directly or indirectly related to it. To assess the impact of a change to an aspect before it is made, it is necessary to have tool support for the storage and analysis of dependency relationships. Tracing aspects is necessary to support understandability and maintainability of software systems.

The concept of tracing implies usually following dependency relationships between artifacts. When developing large systems it is hard to identify the dependency relations.

A. Moreira and J. Grundy (Eds.): Early Aspects 2007 Workshop, LNCS 4765, pp. 175–194, 2007.
© Springer-Verlag Berlin Heidelberg 2007

Improving the traceability of artifacts supports not only the understandability but also is important for maintainability, adaptability and managing complexity. Traceability is a topic that is considered relevant and discussed in various domains. In requirements engineering lots of work has been done on tracing requirements from the stakeholders and in the design process [1,2,3,4]. In the model-driven engineering approach [5,6] traceability is considered important for tracing model elements. A reference model for requirements traceability is provided in [3]. Here a simple metamodel for traceability models is defined and elaborated for requirements traceability. In [7] a UML-based metamodel for requirements traceability is presented that is translated into a UML profile. In [6] a traceability model and a UML profile is presented that include both requirements and model elements. In [5] a metamodel is defined for traceability of models in model-driven development. Hereby, tracing is defined in the transformation specification.

The problem of traceability has recently also been addressed by the AOSD community [8]. The AOSD community encompasses the adoption of aspects throughout the lifecycle and for each phase aspects are specified. Although several initial approaches for traceability have been introduced to address traceability of aspects, two important limitations can be observed. *First*, tracing is tackled within a phase or does not cover the entire life cycle yet. For example, tracing of aspects has been defined within the requirements analysis phase [9], from requirements to architecture [10] and from architecture to design [11]. *Second*, the traceability model that is applied usually is focusing on elements of specific aspect languages. The selection of tracing properties, however, might be dependent on the corresponding project requirements. The traceability model must be therefore sufficiently generic to cope with the different aspect-oriented approaches.

We propose the concern traceability metamodel (CTM) that enables traceability of aspects throughout the life cycle, and which is independent from the aspect languages that are used. CTM can be enhanced to provide additional properties for tracing, and instantiated to define customized traceability models with respect to the required aspect languages. We have implemented CTM in the tool M-Trace, that uses XML-based representations of the models and XQuery queries to represent tracing information. CTM and M-Trace are illustrated for a Concurrent Versioning System to trace aspects from the requirements level to architecture design level and the implementation.

The remainder of the paper is organized as follows. In section 2 we will shortly discuss the background on traceability. In section 3 we present as an example a concurrent versioning systems (CVS) and illustrate on it the need for tracing crosscutting concerns. In section 4 we define the requirements for concern traceability. Based on these requirements we will propose the concern traceability metamodel that will be explained in section 5. The CTM can be implemented in various ways. In section 5.3 we will present an implementation using XML. We will discuss then the application of CTM to trace aspects in and accross phases of the software development lifecycle in section 7. Section 8 will finalize the paper with the conclusions.

2   Terminology

In the following we describe the basic terms that we adopt throughout the paper.

- *Artifacts* – We adopt here the view from [12] in which artifacts are defined as workproducts of the software development lifecycle, such as models, source code or other documents related to the development of a software system.
- *Units* – Units are used to represent artifacts and can have different granularity, ranging from, for example, a sourcecode-file to a single statement. In essence, the structure of the artifacts can also be reflected in units.
- *Concerns* – Concerns can be generally defined as a matter of interest, or design intentions of corresponding stakeholders [13]. Concerns are usually implemented in artifacts.
- *Crosscutting concern* – Concerns that cannot be easily mapped to a single artifact and are scattered over multiple artifacts are called crosscutting concerns. Typical examples for crosscutting concerns are security, reliability and concurrency concerns.
- *Aspect* – An aspect is an artifact that implements a crosscutting concern.
- *Dependency relation* – Artifacts are conceptually dependent on the concerns. As such a change to a concern, for example, will impact also the artifacts that are dependent on the concern.
- *Traceability Link* – To enhance traceability of artifacts the dependency relations among them need to be recorded. We call a recorded dependency relation a traceability link.

3 Example: Concurrent Versioning System (CVS)

To analyze the impact of concerns a Software Configuration Management (SCM) example will be used as a case study. The SCM deals with control of software changes, proper documentation of changes, the issuing of new software versions and releases, the registration and recording of approved software versions. An important functionality in SCM forms the concurrent version control system (CVS), which keeps a history of the changes made to a set of files that can be concurrently accessed.

3.1 The Life Cycle Phases of CVS

To illustrate the traceability throughout the life cycle we have defined (1) requirements model, (2) architecture design, (3) design, and (4) implementation of the concurrent version control system. Figure 1(a) shows the requirements for the CVS and Figure 1(b) the layered architecture. This architecture consists of three major layers: client's layer, session layer, and data layer. The client layer represents the programmer's environment and provides a set of programming tools, such as compilers, interpreters and debuggers, editors and tools for integrating program modules into a consistent program. When a programmer wants to edit a file which is stored in the project repository, a request is made to the session manager in the session layer. The session manager associates a timestamp with it, and initiates an editing session by calling on the request handler in the data layer. The session layer also includes administration functions providing a set of management tools. The administrator further includes a performance monitoring module that is used to generate reports on the average time of accesses, the effect of data size and simultaneous accesses to performance, number of aborts, etc. The request

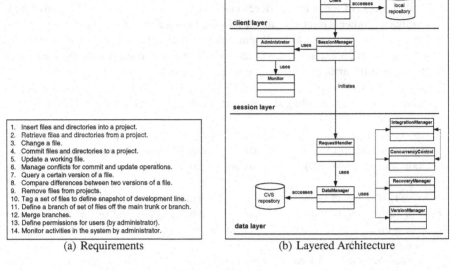

1. Insert files and directories into a project.
2. Retrieve files and directories from a project.
3. Change a file.
4. Commit files and directories to a project.
5. Update a working file.
6. Manage conflicts for commit and update operations.
7. Query a certain version of a file.
8. Compare differences between two versions of a file.
9. Remove files from projects.
10. Tag a set of files to define snapshot of development line.
11. Define a branch of set of files off the main trunk or branch.
12. Merge branches.
13. Define permissions for users (by administrator).
14. Monitor activities in the system by administrator.

(a) Requirements   (b) Layered Architecture

Fig. 1. Requirements and Layered Architecture for the CVS

handler in the data layer *checks out* the requested file and passes it to the programmer's environment. When files are checked out they can be edited and compiled and *check in* the modifications to the file. Checking out a file does not give a programmer exclusive rights to that file. Other programmers can also check it out, make their own modifications, and check it back in. The concurrency control module administrates all the simultaneous accesses to the same file.

This module is also responsible in identifying the read/write conflicts in accessing the files. If a conflict is detected, the integration manager is called. The integration manager provides a set of functions to resolve the conflicting accesses. The version

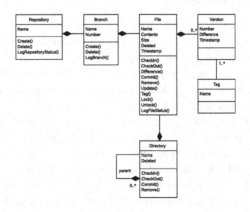

Fig. 2. Object-Oriented Design of the CVS System

manager generates version ID's, compares versions of files and notifies if there are inconsistent versions in the same configuration. Based on this architecture (part of) an object-oriented design of the CVS system is shown in Figure 2. Besides of the requirements specification, architecture design and the design we have also an implementation of the system in AspectJ [14]. The program includes nine classes and two aspects implementing the concerns versioning and monitoring.

4 Requirements for Concern Traceability

Based on the work on the literature on traceability and the concern modeling in AOSD we provide a set of requirements for traceability of concerns. To illustrate the problem we will first define a set of change scenarios for the CVS in section 4.1. In sections 4.2 to 4.4 we list the requirements for traceability of concerns throughout the lifecycle.

4.1   Change Scenarios for CVS and Observed Traceability Problems

We consider the following change scenarios for the CVS system we described in the last sections:

- *Update Versioning*
  In the current design, versioning is only implemented for files but this should be enhanced to support versioning for directories as well. With file versioning, the system allows you to track every change made to any file by saving a copy (version) of a file each time that file is saved. However, versioning on a directory merely represents the default versioning setting for all files created within that directory. This scenario will impact the artifacts in the different phases. For the requirements analysis this will impact at least the requirements 4, 7, 8 as listed in Figure 1(a). In the architecture in Figure 1(b) it will impact the *VersionManager* module but also other modules that are directly or indirectly related to versioning. In the object-oriented design and the implementation this will require changing several classes.
- *Add Security*
  In the initial design the session manager starts an editing session by calling on the request handler in the data layer. To ensure that data is only accessed by the corresponding authorized person security needs to be added to the CVS. This means, that for example, before the session manager initiates a session it should authorize the request of the client. All the artifacts in the phases that depend on the security concern, that is, authentication and authorization in this case, will need to be enhanced to implement the required concern.

The above scenarios indicate that in the given (object-oriented) design it is hard to follow all the dependency relations within and across phases. The following sections define the requirements for achieving traceability of concerns in general and aspects in particular.

4.2 Explicit Modeling of Concerns

In order to explicitly reason about traceability of the concerns it is necessary that the corresponding concerns are explicitly modeled as first class abstractions. The detail of concern model could range from just a description of its name to a full semantic model including attributes such as stakeholder, the domain of the concern, the date it was raised at, the impact that it has, etc.

Harrison et al. [12] define the following requirements for concern modeling: (a) providing modeling concepts for *concerns* and their organization (b) Neutrality and open-endedness with respect to the kind of artifacts, (c) and specification that captures intended structure of material rather than simply reflecting existing structure.

If we decide to explicitly model concerns then the question arises whether to provide a uniform model for both the concerns and artifacts, or explicitly separate these using dedicated language constructs. In general these two different approaches are identified as symmetric and asymmetric approach [15]. In the symmetric approach one adopts a single concern model to represent both the concerns and the artifacts. Note that hereby concerns are still represented explicitly, and this is different from a language which only provides uniform modeling notations for artifacts but which does not consider concerns explicitly. In the asymmetric approach separate from the artifacts, concerns are modeled using their own abstraction mechanisms.

4.3 Explicit Modeling of Dependency Relations

Assuming that concerns are related to concerns or artifacts, it is necessary to make these relations explicit. This can be only done when dependency relations are recorded as traceability links. For this traceability should be specified as first class abstractions in the adopted traceability model. The choice for a symmetric or asymmetric approach has also an impact on the traceability links. In the asymmetric model, the traceability links will need to be established for both artifacts and concerns. On the other hand, in the symmetric approach the traceability links need to refer to one type of concern. This simplifies the traceability specification but could reduce understandability because the user has to explicitly distinguish between concerns and artifacts.

4.4 Support for Traceability Within and Across Phases

Obviously, concerns can occur in various phases of the life cycle such as requirements analysis, architecture design, design or programming. Tracing should be supported within and across life cycle phases, as we will explain in the following.

Intra-phase Traceability. To understand the relations among the concerns and artifacts within the same phase it is necessary to model traceability for the given phase. Figure 3(a) shows the abstract model for traceability within a phase t. Here we have shown the case of an asymmetric model and distinguished between an artifact and a concern. We define two types of intra-phase traceability: *intra concern to artifact traceability* and *intra artifact to concern traceability*.

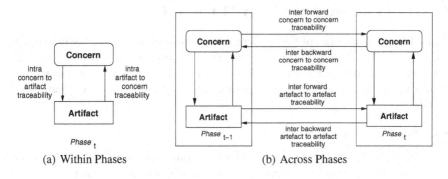

(a) Within Phases   (b) Across Phases

Fig. 3. Traceability Relationships

Inter-phase Traceabiltiy Figure 3(b) presents the abstract model for traceability across software development lifecycle phases. Four types of relations are defined that we think are necessary. In alignment with the literature on traceability we make here a distinction between *forward* and *backward traceability*. Forward traceability defines traceability relationships between a concern or artifact in one phase to another concern or artifact in a *later* phase. Backward traceability defines the traceability relationships between a concern or artifact in one phase to another concern or artifact in a *previous* phase. To distinguish from intra phase traceability we use the term *inter* referring to relations across different phases.

Traceability relationships accross different phases can also be distinguished into forward and backward traceability relationships. These relations are defined from a concern to an artifact, or from an artifact to a concern. It should be noted that, for example, *inter forward concern to artifact* traceability relationships can be traced, even if corresponding trace-links are not explicitly specified. The trace-link can be inferred, for example, from the existence of an *intra concern to artifact* trace-link and an *inter forward artifact to artifact* trace-link for an artifact in a given phase. From this perspective we can state that the traceability relations of Figure 3 represent the primitive traceability relations.

4.5   Support for Automated Tracing Using Queries

The explicit models for concerns and traceability links help to automatically determine relationships between the different concerns and artifacts. Although relationships among concerns can only be determined in an implicit manner by following the trace links between concerns and artifacts. Following the traceability links manually might not be trivial for a complex system, even though the traceability links are made explicit. The management of models and dependencies, as well as tracing the dependencies between model elements and concerns should be automated. In order to minimize the amount of trace data presented to the user and to select only relevant concerns, it should be possible to define generic queries that determine the set of elements for which a trace is calculated.

5 CTM: Concern Traceability Metamodel

In the following we present the concern traceability metamodel for tracing concerns throughout the life cycle. CTM is symmetric with respect to making no distinction between crosscutting and non-crosscutting concerns, but asymmetric in distinguishing between artifacts and concerns, though artifacts may introduce new concerns, as we will discuss later.

5.1 The Traceability Metamodel

The concern traceability metamodel CTM, which is shown in Figure 4, models concerns as parts of a concern model. The concern model is represented in our metamodel by the meta-class *ConcernModel* that consists of one or more instances of *ConcernGroup* and *UnitModel*, as shown on the left. An instance of *ConcernModel* would be, for example, a concern model like the one used in the Concern Modeling Environment (CME), which is described in [12]. We assume in our metamodel that concerns, which are modeled by the meta-class *Concern*, are grouped into concern groups. A concern group corresponds in AspectJ, for example, to a package that contains a set of aspects. We consider aspects in our metamodel as a kind of concern. *CrosscuttingConcern* is therefore a subclass of *Concern*. The source of concerns, as we required for traceability, is explicit in our model. Each concern is associated with one or more stakeholders, represented by the meta-class *Stakeholder,* and a stakeholder has one or more concerns.

The right hand side of Figure 4 shows the part of our metamodel that is used to trace units and concerns. Before we explain this part of the metamodel, however, we need to take a closer look at the unit model. An instance of meta-class *UnitModel* is a model used in a phase of the lifecycle. For example structured text documents, for the requirements engineering phase, Architecture Description Languages (ADLs) and UML-class diagrams, for the architectural design phase, and Java sourcecode files, for the implementation phase. Several such models may be used simultaneously in one phase, like in the Rational Unified Process, where UML-Class Diagrams, UML-Sequence Diagrams, and so on, are used to model the units interesting for architectural design.

The unit model consists of one or more instances of the meta-class *Unit,* like usecase, connector, class, and import-statement, to name only one example for each lifecycle phase. As we already mentioned, are units representations of artifacts. Therefore has the meta-class *Unit* the attributes *reference* and *name* that allow referring to the artifact. Sub-units may be associated through the *parent* relationship. Examples for units and their corresponding sub-units in an object-oriented design document are: class, classvariables, instance-variables, methods and so on.

5.2 Traceability of Crosscutting Concerns

Supporting traceability of crosscutting concerns in our metamodel requires, besides explicit trace-links, also an explicit model of aspects. Our metamodel should be independent of the implementation of aspects and the particular aspect model (symmetric or asymmetric) that was chosen. Therefore we distinguish crosscutting concern from aspect specification[1] and pointcut model.

---

[1] The way the crosscutting concern is specified in a specific aspect language like AspectJ.

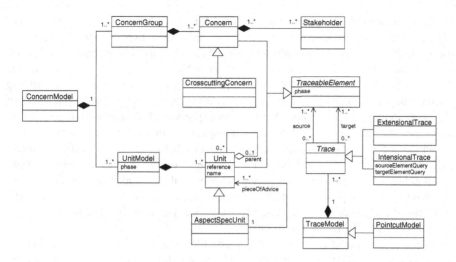

Fig. 4. Concern Traceability Metamodel

An aspect specification is a unit of the artifact model and is represented in Figure 4 by the meta-class *AspectSpecUnit*, which is a subclass of *Unit*. An instance of an *AspectSpecUnit* would be, for example, a piece of Java code containing an AspectJ aspect declaration, or an aspect class in an AODM model [16] of a system's design. The relationship *pieceOfAdvice* represents a piece of advice (which is also a unit in terms of our metamodel) that implements a crosscutting concern of the system or model of the system.

We stated in Section 4 that traceability of concerns throughout the lifecycle requires an explicit representation of traceable elements and trace links. We represent these in our metamodel by the abstract meta-classes *TraceableElement* and *Trace*. Each instance of the meta-classes *Unit*, *AspectSpecUnit*, *Concern* or *CrosscuttingConcern* is a kind of traceable element. We explicitly model the phase in the software development lifecycle the traceable element belongs to. Also the trace relation is modeled explicitly by the meta-class *Trace* and the relations *source* and *target*. These relate one or more traceable elements that are in the domain of the relation to one or more traceable elements that belong to the codomain of the relation. Traces can be specified extensionally by listing all source-target mappings between traceable elements, or intensionally by a query. A query can compute, for example, the set of target elements associated with a source element. Extensional and intensional traces are represented in the metamodel by the meta-classes *ExtensionalTrace* and *IntensionalTrace*, which are sub-classes of *Trace*. The queries associated with an instance of meta-class *IntensionalTrace* are represented by the attributes *sourceElementQuery* and *targetElementQuery*. This allows us to effectively represent *m:n* traceability relationships by queries that compute the source and target elements. Still, *1:n* and *n:1* traceability relationships can be represented easily in our meta-model, without having to write queries for single source- or target elements. For example, the target elements of a *1:n* relationship can be calculated by a query and the reference to the single source element can be simply listed.

Traces are modeled as parts of a trace model, represented by the meta-class *Trace-Model*, which makes it possible to specialize it. This can be used to explicitly represent the different traceability relationships we identified in Section 4.4. We also regard pointcut models, represented by the meta-class *PointcutModel* in Figure 4, as a kind of trace model. A pointcut model is a model of a pointcut designator that allows identifying the units to which the piece of advice from an aspect specification unit applies. Part of the aspect declaration is a pointcut designator expression, formulated in some pointcut language. The semantics of the pointcut in a specific pointcut language is modeled by instantiating the meta-class *PointcutModel*. Because both units and concerns are traceable elements, the metamodel poses no restrictions on the type of elements that are composable. It is therefore element symmetry neutral [15] and therefore all kinds of compositions of components, aspects, or aspects and components can be modeled. The meta model is also neutral with respect to join-point symmetry, because *any element* of a model can be related with a trace link.

Selecting any model element with a query allows also to establish a mapping between the aspect specification and the units into which the piece of advice is woven. As a result remains the relation between an aspect specification and the woven artifacts, like model or code, traceable. Together with the trace link from the crosscutting concern to the aspect specification unit it is possible to determine the units to which a crosscutting concern applies. Crosscutting concerns remain therefore traceable; even in later lifecycle stages, where they would have normally become invisible after weaving. The pointcut model is not explicitly part of an aspect specification in our metamodel. Instead, remains the element where the pointcut specification resides implicit. Our meta model is therefore also neutral with respect to the symmetry of the composition relationships. This allows to instantiate the meta model for aspect languages where composition relationships can be part of another element. For example Hyper/J, where composition rules are at least conceptually not part of the crosscutting concern. They are, however, part of the aspect specification. In a truly composition relationship symmetric aspect language, aspect specification and pointcut designator declaration would be separate. Furthermore would be pointcut designators needed that can compute join-points for arbitrary element types. These can also be expressed in our meta-model by using the meta-class *IntensionalTrace*. The queries associated with this meta-class are formulated for instances of type *TraceableElement*, which can be concerns and arbitrary units of some artifact of the software development lifecycle.

5.3 Utilizing CTM

Figure 5 represents the process for utilizing the CTM. Traceability models can be instantiated directly from the CTM without restrictions to a specific syntax. It is also possible to first enhance CTM, resulting in a customized meta-model that is then later on instantiated. New types of dependencies between traceable-elements, for example, can be added by specializing the meta-class trace-link. This way we can explicitly representat relations like, specializes, includes, eliminates or supports in the traceability meta-model. If such a restriction is not wanted, then all these relations can be introduced at the model level by first instantiating CTM and enhancing the resulting model.

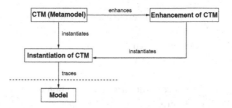

Fig. 5. The Process for Utilizing CTM

6   M-TRACE: Implementation of CTM

We have implemented CTM in our tool M-TRACE that uses XML models to instantiate CTM and represent concerns, artifacts and trace links. Using the eXtensible Markup Language (XML) to instantiate CTM has the advantage that the instantiated model can be easily used together with standard tools for creating, editing and transforming XML files. Such tools can also be used to transform the representation into other models. We instantiate CTM by defining the XML-document structure according to the meta-model in the Document Type Definitions (DTD) shown in Fingure 6-9. These document type definitions also contain enhancements with respect to the meta-model. They introduce, for example, comments to ease readability, unit types to distinguish between different kinds of artifacts, and unique identifiers that are needed to represent units and concerns. We will now explain the instantiation and representation of CTM using XML, as well as the enhancements we added.

A concern model element (Figure 6) consists of an optional description, one or more unit models, and concern groups, one or more unit models, and concern groups.

```
1 <!ELEMENT concernmodel (description?, concerngroup+, unit-
model+)>
2 <!ELEMENT description (#PCDATA)>
```

Fig. 6. Concernmodel Structure

The comma identifier, called a sequence, specifies the order in which the elements must occur. The plus indicates that one or more elements are required. We declare that several unit models may be used, because an architectural model of the system, for example, may be comprised of several architectural views.

6.1   (Crosscutting) Concerns

The element type declaration for the element concerngroup is shown in Figure 7, Lines 1-4. A *concerngroup* element consists of one or more crosscutting- or non-crosscutting concerns. To make the XML-model more readable, an optional name (Lines 3-4) may be given to the concern group. This is actually an extension of CTM. We will also extend the instances of the meta-classes *Concern* and *CrosscuttingConcern*; namely the

```
1      <!ELEMENT concerngroup ((concern | crosscutting-
concern)+)>
2  <!ATTLIST concerngroup
3    name CDATA #IMPLIED>
4
5  <!ELEMENT concern (description, stakeholder+)>
6  <!ATTLIST concern
7    id CDATA #REQUIRED
8    phase CDATA #REQUIRED
9    name CDATA #REQUIRED>
10
11 <!ELEMENT crosscutting-concern (description, stakeholder+)>
12 <!ATTLIST crosscutting-concern
13   id CDATA #REQUIRED
14   phase CDATA #REQUIRED
15   name CDATA #REQUIRED>
16
17 <!ELEMENT stakeholder (#PCDATA)>
```

Fig. 7. Concerngroup Structure

element type definitions *concern* and *crosscutting-concern* in Lines 6-17. The definition states that a concern element consists of a description and one or more stakeholder elements. The description is the first extension with respect to the meta-model. Another extension is adding an *id* attribute (Line 8). We need this attribute, because it is not possible to specify an XML model in an object-oriented manner. Thus, we have to use an explicit identifier to mimic the object identities of the traceable elements. Explicit modeling of the inheritance relationship is also not possible. We therefore just duplicate inherited relationships, and all inherited attributes like *phase* in the definition of the element attributes in Line 8-10 and Line 14-17. The fact that a crosscutting concern is a kind of concern remains implicit.

6.2   Unitmodel

The element type definition for the element *unitmodel*, which is an instance of the correspondingly named CTM meta-class, is shown in Figure 8 in Line 1. It states that the unit model element must contain one or more *unit* elements or *aspect-specunit* elements. Because a unit model is used in a specific phase of the software lifecycle, for example, ADLs in the software architecture design phase, we have to define a *phase* attribute (Lines 2-3) in the XML model as well. Lines 5-11 describe the *unit* element and Lines 13-20 the element for defining an aspect specification unit. Both may have child units, which are defined in the *child-units* element definition in Line 22 and 23. *Child-unit* elements consist of one or more *unit* or *aspect-specunit* elements. Again, it becomes not apparent that an aspect specification unit is a kind of unit.

This means, we also have to mimic object identities with an *id* attribute. We define it for *unit* and *aspect-specunit* elements in the Lines 7 and 16 respectively. The element

```
1   <!ELEMENT unitmodel ((unit | aspect-specunit)+)>
2   <!ATTLIST unitmodel
3     phase CDATA #REQUIRED>
4
5   <!ELEMENT unit (child-units?)>
6   <!ATTLIST unit
7     id CDATA #REQUIRED
8     phase CDATA #REQUIRED
9     reference CDATA #REQUIRED
10    name CDATA #REQUIRED
11    type CDATA #REQUIRED>
12
13  <!ELEMENT aspect-specunit (child-units?, piece-of-advice+)>
14  <!ATTLIST aspect-specunit
15    id CDATA #REQUIRED
16    phase CDATA #REQUIRED
17    reference CDATA #REQUIRED
18    name CDATA #REQUIRED
29    type CDATA #REQUIRED>
20
21  <!ELEMENT child-units (unit | aspect-specunit)+)>
22
23  <!ELEMENT piece-of-advice (unit | aspect-specunit)>
```

Fig. 8. Unitmodel Structure

type definitions define phase, reference and name attributes, as required in the meta-model. We extend CTM again, by adding an attribute *type* to the element *unit* and *aspect-specunit*. The element *aspect-specunit* may also contain child elements.

As presented so far, do *aspect-specunit* elements not differ much from the *unit* elements according to their definition. The only differences are, that *aspect-specunit* elements may contain one or more pieces of advice represented by a *piece-of-advice* element. The relation between pieces of advice and the units that it applies to is represented as a traceability-relationship. We will explain this later when we define the XML-representation of the trace model.

A *piece-of-advice* element (Lines 25-26) can consist of a unit or an aspect specification unit. As mentioned before, allows this the specification of arbitrary compositions and makes therefore also the instantiation of CTM as XML model, element-symmetric.

6.3   Queries

One of our goals was to model traceability of aspects independent of the aspect model used. This requires to separate the pointcut model from the aspect specification units, and to model traces explicitly and independent of the traceable elements. The trace model is defined in Figure 9. A *tracemodel* element consists of at least one *intensional-trace* or *extensional-trace* element, as we define in line 3. The *ExtensionalTrace* meta-class in CTM has references, called source and target, to the meta-class *TraceableEle-*

```
1   <?xml version="1.0" encoding="ISO-8859-1" ?>
2
3   <!ELEMENT tracemodel ((extensional-trace I intensional-trace)+)>
4
5   <!ELEMENT extensional-trace (source, target)>
6   <!ELEMENT intensional-trace ((source I source-query), (target I target-
query))>
7
8   <!ELEMENT source (traceable-element+)>
9   <!ELEMENT target (traceable-element+)>
10
11 <!ELEMENT traceable-element (description?)>
12 <!ATTLIST traceable-element
13   id CDATA #REQUIRED>
14
15 <!ELEMENT description (#PCDATA)>
16
17 <!ELEMENT source-query (#PCDATA)>
18 <!ELEMENT target-query (#PCDATA)>
19
20 <!ELEMENT pointcutmodel ((extensional-trace I intensional-trace)+)>
```

Fig. 9. Trace Model DTD

ment. The corresponding element definitions are shown in Line 6, where we define that an *extensional-trace* element consists of a source and target element. The source and target elements contain one or more elements *traceable-element*. We can identify the traceable elements referenced by the trace using the attribute *id*, as defined in Line 13. To make manual editing easier we allow an optional description that can be added to a traceable element. Intensional trace-links, where we calculate the elements belonging to the trace-link, are modelled in XML as defined in Line 6. An *intensional-trace* element consists of a *source* or *source-query* and a *target* or *target-query* element. The source-query and target-query elements contain the text that describes the XQuery, which cal-

```
1  f:getUnitByName("RA"," ","Insert File")
2
3  declare function f:getUnitByName($phase,$root,$name) as element()* {
4    let $units := f:check($phase,$root)
5    for $i in $units
6      return if($i[@name=$name]) then $i else f:getUnitByName($phase,$i,$name)
7  };
8
9  declare function f:check($phase,$root) as element()* {
10   if($root instance of element())
11     then $root/unit union $root/aspect-specunit
12     else /concernmodel/unitmodel[phase=$phase]/unit union
13     /concernmodel/unitmodel[@phase=$phase]/aspect-specunit
14 };
```

Fig. 10. Query of an Intensional Trace

culates the source- and target elements. XQuery is a technology under development by the W3C, that is designed to query collections of XML-data.

Intensional- and extensional trace are also part of the *pointcutmodel* element and are used there as a kind of pointcut mechanism. The query is then used to select the units out of the unitmodel to which a piece of advice should be applied. We will usually use queries as pointcut designators, although, the pointcut could be designated by enumerating all the elements. Queries are a very powerful mechanism, since XQuery is a full-blown functional programming language with strong typing. The evaluation of the query expression reads a sequence of XML fragments or atomic values and returns a sequence of XML fragments or atomic values that are the query result. The simplest kind of query is an XPath expression.

For example, *'/concernmodel[@phase=RA]/unitmodel/unit'* selects all units of the concern model from the requirements analysis phase, which we will introduce in Section 7. To compute the trace links, we have defined queries that can be used to select parts of the unit and concern model. Figure 10 shows in Line 1, for example, a query statement that returns all units corresponding to the requirement statements about the insertion of files into the CVS. The parameter *"RA"* indicates that we want to search the unitmodel of the requirements analysis phase. A unit can correspond to a section in the requirements document, which describes the insertion of files for example, because it can reference an artifact. To query all units with a name equal to *"Insert File"*, we have to specify the function: *'f:getUnitByName'* as depicted in Lines 3 to 11. This function recurses over all units (Line 6) until a unit with the same name as the parameter *'$name'* is found. It returns then the selected unit. The function *check* (Lines 9-13) is used to test if the parameter *$root* is an XML-element or just plain text. If the root element has been determined, all unit-elements starting from the element *$root* are returned. If no valid XML-element was passed, and all aspect-specunit elements in the unitmodel are returned that were defined for the phase *$phase*.

7   Application of CTM

After defining the structure of the XML-documents, we will show in the following how they can be used to model concerns and artifacts of the requirements analysis phase. Furthermore, we will show how they can be used to define intra-phase traceability links for the CVS case we introduced in Section 3. Architecture design, aspect-oriented design, and aspect-oriented implementation can be modeled accordingly. Due to space limitations we will only show an excerpt of the whole XML-model that was made for the first change scenario, i.e. updating versioning. In Section 7.3 a short summary is given, of how the presented models can be used to trace the impact of change scenarios.

7.1   Concern Modeling and Tracing Within a Phase

Listing 6 shows the concern model for the requirements of CVS. The example shows only show two concerns of that concern group: *retrieve file or directory*, and the crosscutting concern *synchronization*. These are examples for concerns that the requirements related to information stored in files and directories depend upon. The unitmodel that follows the concern group, shows an example of a unit for a requirement from Figure

1(a). The dependencies between concerns and requirements are specified by the trace links in Figure 11(b). We use XQuery statements or explicitly list the units that are related to each other. The first intensional trace link, for example, specifies that the concern *"Retrieve file or dir"* with identity *id="r2"*, is addressed by the requirement corresponding to the unit with *id="2"*.

```
<concernmodel phase="RA">
<concerngroup>
  <concern id="r2"
    phase="RA" name="Retrieve file or dir">
    <stakeholder> User </stakeholder>
  </concern>
  <crosscutting-concern id="r16"
    phase="RA" name="Synchronization">
            <description>Synchr.   activi-
ties</description>
    <stakeholder> Admin </stakeholder>
    <stakeholder> User </stakeholder>
  </crosscutting-concern>
  ...
</concerngroup>
<unitmodel phase="RA">
  <unit id="2" phase="RA"
    reference="-//RequFileRetrieval.doc"
    name="Retrieve file"
    type="requirements statement">
  </unit>
  ...
</unitmodel>
...
</concernmodel>
```

(a) Concern Model

```
<tracemodel>
<intensional-trace>
  <source>
    <traceable-element id="r2">
    </traceable-element>
  </source>
  <target-query>
  f:getUnitStartsWith("RA","statement",
    "Retrieve")
  </target-query>
</intensional-trace>
...
<intensional-trace>
  <source>
    <traceable-element id="r16">
    </traceable-element>
  </source>
  <target-query>
  f:getUnitStartsWith("RA","statement",
    "Concurrent usage")
  </target-query>
</intensional-trace>
...
</trace-model>
```

(b) Intra-Phase Trace Model

Fig. 11. Concern Model and Trace Model for the Requirements Analysis Phase

7.2   Tracing Across Lifecycle Phases

To trace concerns across the lifecycle phases, units and concerns have to be defined for each phase in the same way as shown for the requirements phase. The architectural module *VersionManager* from the architectural model of the CVS (Figure 1(b)), for example, can be represented with our XML model as shown in Figure 12(a). The reference to an XMI representation of the UML model depicting this architecture, could also contain the full path to the *VersionManager* element. Due to space limitations the example only shows a link to the whole document.

Figure 12(b) shows an XPath expression that defines a trace link between the requirements analysis phase and the architecture design phase. The query defines a backward traceability link that states that *VersionManager* realizes the requirements related to

```
<unit id="a12"
  phase="AD"
                reference="-
//CVSArchModel.xmi"
  name="VersionManger"
  type="architectural element">
</unit>
```
(a) Architectural Module

```
f:getUnitContains("RA", "statement", "Commit")
  union  f:getUnitContains("RA",  "statement",
"Branch")
```
(b) Intensional Trace Link

Fig. 12. XML and XPath Representations

committing and branching. Trace links and units can be defined in the same way for the remaining phases of the software development lifecycle. Modeling artifacts using unit elements allows us to decouple the trace model from a specific implementation language or modeling formalism.

7.3 Application of CTM for Impact Analysis

The information represented in the concern models and trace models for the CVS can be used to trace the impact of the change scenarios listed in Section 4.1. We use the XML database 'eXist' [17] to execute queries over our models. The queries calculate a trace containing all elements that are impacted by the change. In the following we will describe shortly how to trace the impact of the first change scenario *Update Versioning*.

Determining the Initial Set of Changed Elements. The change scenario Update Versioning adds new requirements that impact the concerns and requirements that we defined in the requirements analysis phase. Apparently all requirements making statements about files or directories will be influenced by the new requirement that the version mechanism should be extended to directories as well. This can be formulated as a query over concerns and units from our trace model. Figure 13 shows the corresponding queries.

```
f:getUnitContains("RA",      "statement",
"File")
  union
    f:getUnitContains("RA", "statement",
"Dir")
```
(a) Changed Requirements

```
f:getConcernContains("RA",     "statement",
"File")
  union
    f:getConcernContains("RA", "statement",
"Dir")
```
(b) Changed Concerns

Fig. 13. Queries for Impact Analysis

The union of the elements calculated by these queries, is the initial set of elements that are impacted by the changed requirements. This first step is the only step that has to be done individually for each change scenario and cannot be re-used for other change scenarios.

Calculating the Impact. The impact on the other lifecycle phases can be automatically calculated by following the forward-traceability links that are defined in the tracemodel. If a trace-link exists for an element of the initial element set, then all the target elements listed in the trace-link are indirectly impacted by the change scenario. These elements are added to the result set of the trace. All elements in the next phase are then determined for which a trace link exists that has one of the elements in the result set as source. This proces is repeated for all models from each phase. All query definitions that were used to follow the trace-links can be re-used for other change scenarios.

7.4 Enhancing the Metamodel

As we depicted in Figure 5 can CTM be (1) directly instantiated or (2) first enhanced and then instantiated, to customize it for a particular context. The context can be defined by, for example, tracing through different phases, application of different modeling approaches, using different joinpoint models, etc. CTM is generic and can be applied for at least the following cases:

Symmetric vs. Asymmetric Paradigms. Although an explicit distinction is made between unit and concern, CTM can express both symmetric and asymmetric composition paradigms. Since units can represent any type of artifact, both paradigms can be represented by defining the DTD's accordingly. It does not matter whether this distinction is made or not in the model. Only the mapping between the model elements represented by the units of the concern model and the artifact that contains these model elements will differ. If concerns are explicit in the models then exists a mapping between the concern model and these concerns. Otherwise, are the traceability links between model elements and concerns only defined in the concern model that was derived from CTM.

Adoption of Different Aspect Languages. CTM abstracts from the languages applied. Concerns and units are represented in a declarative way independent from the artifacts. No assumptions are made for using a particular aspect-oriented language. In fact, it even does not make a difference whether we are dealing with an object-oriented language or an aspect-oriented language.

Adoption for Different Phases and Life Cycle Models. CTM abstracts from phases in the life cycle or even the adoption of a particular life cycle model such as the waterfall model, iterative model or agile model. In many cases the instantiation of CTM will be sufficient to define the concerns and the mappings of these to the artifacts. The element *UnitModel* in the metamodel in Figure 4 can be enhanced to represent models of different phases.

Expression of Existing Traceability Models Using CTM. The recent work on traceability of aspects have resulted in several traceability models [9, 8, 11]. Since CTM abstracts from phases and the adopted aspect specification languages these models can be represented either through instantiation or through first enhancing the metamodel. The latter approach can be used if, for example, different models (enhancement of *UnitModel*) or different joinpoint models (enhancement of *PointcutModel*) are required.

The problem that is basically addressed in this paper is the traceability of aspects *throughout the lifecycle phases* and as such it provides a general framework for this. In another paper that we have written [18] we have shown that this general metamodel can indeed be enhanced for tracing concerns within and across architectural views. Software architecture modeling includes the description of different views that represent the architectural concerns from different stakeholder perspectives. In case of evolution of the software system the related architectural views need to be adapted accordingly. To synchronize the architectural views it is necessary that the dependency links among the architectural concerns in the architectural views can be easily traced. Unfortunately, despite the ongoing efforts for modeling concerns in architectural views, the traceability of concerns remains a challenging issue in architecture design. This problem of architectural view synchronization is of course quite different from tracing concerns throughout the life cycle for impact analysis. Moreover, the tracing of concerns is hereby within one phase only and not across phases. Nevertheless, we were able to reuse and extend the metamodel for defining a metamodel for tracing architectural concerns and as such support the architecture view synchronization. This required that we had to model the architectural views in the metamodel explicitly and update the tracemodel which had to process views instead of phases. The concern model in the metamodel, however, is general and could be reused as is. Besides of the extension of the metamodel the implementation of the DTDs and the related queries for defining queries for tracing concerns within and across architectural views are different. A challenging issue for the future would be to integrate the tracing of concerns through the phases in this paper with the tracing of concerns within and across architectural views in [18].

8   Conclusions

Traceability is an important quality factor that has been addressed in various domains to improve other quality factors such as understandability, maintenance and adaptability. Recently traceability has recently also been addressed by the AOSD community [8] to improve the traceability of aspects and as such support the maintenance throughout the life cycle. Although several initial approaches for traceability have been introduced to address traceability of aspects, we can observe that still lots of work needs to be done to achieve a complete traceability approach. First of all it appears that there is no tracing approach for the entire software life cycle yet. It is beneficial to enhance and complement existing work to include tracing for the entire life cycle. Second, it is important to provide a generic traceability model that is independent of the various approaches for specifying concerns and the way aspects are declared in a specific language.

In this paper we have built on the general literature on traceability, concern modeling and the recent work on traceability of concerns. We have proposed the concern traceability metamodel (CTM) that enables traceability of concerns throughout the life cycle, and which is independent from the aspect languages that are used. We have defined a case study on Concurrent Versioning System and defined a set of scenarios to illustrate the problem of traceability of concerns. Based on our observationsand the literature on traceability we have defined a set of requirements that are realized by CTM. CTM has been implemented in our tool M-Trace, that uses XML-based representations of the models and XQuery queries to represent tracing information. It is possible to enhance the meta-model CTM to define various traceability models.

References

1. Gotel, O., Finkelstein, A.: An analysis of the requirements traceability problem. In: First International Conference on Requirements Engineering (ICRE'94), pp. 94–101 (April 1994)
2. Pinheiro, F.A.C., Goguen, J.A.: An object-oriented tool for tracing requirements. IEEE Softw. 13(2), 52–64 (1996)
3. Ramesh, B., Jarke, M.: Toward Reference Models for Requirements Traceability. IEEE Trans. Softw. Eng. 27, 58–93 (2001)
4. Ramesh, B., Stubbs, C., Powers, T., Edwards, M.: Requirements traceability: Theory and practice (1997)
5. Bondé, L., Boulet, P., Dekeyser, J.-L.: Traceability and interoperability at different levels of abstraction in model transformations. In: Forum on Specification and Design Languages, FDL 2005, Lausanne, Switzerland (September 2005)
6. Gérard, S., Babau, J.-P., Champeau, F.J. (eds.): Model Driven Engineering for Distributed Real-time Embedded Systems. ISTE Ltd (2005)
7. Torres, P.L.: A framework for requirements traceability in uml-based projects. In: Edinburgh, U.K., pp. 32–41 (September 2002)
8. Workshop on Early Aspects: Traceability of Aspects in the Early Life Cycle (held with AOSD 2006), (Bonn, Germany)
9. Chitchyan, R., Rashid, A.: Tracing requirements interdependency semantics. In: Workshop on Early Aspects (held with AOSD 2006), Bonn, Germany (2006)
10. Katz, S., Rashid, A.: From aspectual requirements to proof obligations for aspect-oriented systems. In: Proceedings of the 12th IEEE International. Requirements Engineering Conference, pp. 48–57. IEEE Computer Society Press, Los Alamitos (2004)
11. Jackson, A., Sanchéz, P., Fuentes, L., Clarke, S.: Towards traceability between ao architecture and ao design. In: Workshop on Early Aspects (held with ASOD 2006), Bonn, Germany (2006)
12. Harrison, W., Ossher, H., Sutton Jr., S.M., Tarr, P.: Concern modeling in the concern manipulation environment. In: MACS 2005. Proceedings of the 2005 workshop on Modeling and analysis of concerns in software, pp. 1–5. ACM Press, New York (2005)
13. Kandé, M.M.: A Concern-Oriented Approach to Software Architecture. PhD thesis, Ecole polytechnique fédérale de Lausanne (2003)
14. Laddad, R.: AspectJ in Action: Practical Aspect-Oriented Programming. Manning Publications Co., (2003)
15. Harrison, W.H., Ossher, H.L., Tarr, P.L.: Asymmetrically vs. symmetrically organized paradigms for software composition. Tech. Rep. RC22685, IBM Research (2002)
16. Stein, D., Hanenberg, S., Unland, R.: A uml-based aspect-oriented design notation for aspectj. In: AOSD 2002. Proceedings of the 1st international conference on Aspect-oriented software development, Enschede, The Netherlands, pp. 106–112. ACM Press, New York (2002)
17. http://www.exist-db.org
18. Tekinerdoğan, B., Hofmann, C., Akşit, M.: Modeling traceability of concerns in architectural views. ACM Digital Library 209, 49–56 (2007)

Early Aspects: Are There Any Other Kind?

Awais Rashid

Computing Department, Infolab21, Lancaster University, Lancaster LA1 4WA, UK
awais@comp.lancs.ac.uk

Abstract. This article summarises the discussions that took place as part of a panel at the 10th Early Aspects workshop held in conjunction with the 6th International Conference on Aspect-Oriented Software Development (AOSD '07), Vancouver, BC, Canada. The panel was chaired by Awais Rashid. The panelists included: Maja D'Hondt, Anthony Finkelstein, Gregor Kiczales and Ana Moreira. The discussions focused on understanding the relationship between early aspects and those that are tackled by aspect-oriented designs and programs. The panel concluded that there was a gap between *problem understanding* that is the focus of early aspects and *problem solving* which is the goal of aspect-oriented design and programming approaches. This gap needs to be bridged in order to address the modularity mismatch problem which compounds the complexity of modern software-based systems.

1 Introduction

Early Aspects [1, 3] is a term used to denote crosscutting concerns that need to be addressed during requirements engineering and architecture design. Recently, some researchers have suggested that aspects are properties of the program and do not represent problem domain concepts [4]. The Early Aspects community representatives, on the other hand, have argued that crosscutting concerns first manifest themselves in requirements; this is where developers must start to identify and address them using aspect-oriented techniques to avoid costly refactorings and maintenance later on in the lifecycle [2]. This begs the question as to what is the relationship between *Early Aspects* and their *Late* counter parts? Are the solution domain aspects simply refinements of requirements-level aspects? In other words, do crosscutting concerns arise due to the concern dependencies and interactions inherent to a problem or are there additional ones that may arise due to our chosen solutions? These were the questions posed to the panelists.

2 Panel Members

The panel comprised of leading experts in aspect-oriented software development and multi-perspective engineering of software systems. The panel members were as follows:

- Awais Rashid, Lancaster University, UK (Panel Chair)
- Maja D'Hondt, Universite des Sciences et Technologies de Lille, France

A. Moreira and J. Grundy (Eds.): Early Aspects 2007 Workshop, LNCS 4765, pp. 195–198, 2007.

- Anthony Finkelstein, University College London, UK
- Gregor Kiczales, University of British Columbia, Canada
- Ana Moreira, Universidade Nova de Lisboa, Portugal

Awais Rashid opened the panel by posing the above-mentioned questions to the panel. The panelists then presented their individual positions. This was followed by open discussion between the panel members and questions from the audience.

3 Relationships Between *Early* and *Late* Aspects

Each panel member highlighted the relationship between Early and Late aspects from different perspectives. These are summarised below.

3.1 Reasoning About the Problem Domain

Ana Moreira argued that Early Aspects are motivated by the need to improve reasoning about the problem domain or problem space. In her opinion they represent stakeholders' *real* concerns and offer a means to reason about the dependencies and interactions amongst broadly-scoped requirements. She also highlighted the potential traceability benefits of using Early Aspects techniques as they can facilitate tracing stakeholders' concerns through subsequent refinements to design and implementation. She concluded that aspects are not concerns that magically appear during development. Instead they are concerns of the stakeholders, design- and implementation-level aspects being solution domain realisations of Early Aspects.

3.2 Crosscutting is Inherent

Gregor Kiczales pointed out that there is no doubt that crosscutting exists in non-implementation models. He noted that, in fact, a lot of the driving factors in the original PARC project on aspect-oriented programming were based on treating crosscutting concerns as part of the design. He also highlighted that crosscutting is a well-accepted notion in other engineering disciplines—organisations work through crosscutting processes. He concluded that crosscutting manifests itself both before implementation and during implementation.

3.3 Crosscutting in a Process Context

Anthony Finkelstein started his position by noting his dislike for the word "Early". He felt that it implied a traditional waterfall lifecycle. He noted that crosscutting concerns are intertwined all the way through the life of a system. So if we ignore the word "Early", there aren't other kinds of aspects. In his view, another way of understanding the relationship between problem domain and solution domain aspects is to go to the question of how they fit in the process context. There are no other kind of aspects but Early Aspects in the sense that the activities of requirements and architecture have the responsibility of identifying the stakeholders and their concerns. So they are the critical lead in to identifying aspects. On the other hand, there are other kinds of aspects beyond Early Aspects as there are emergent concerns that arise as you proceed through development by virtue of elaboration.

3.4 Modularisation Mismatch

Maja D'Hondt noted that requirements analysis is about *problem understanding* while design and implementation is about *problem solving*. So everything could be simplified to boxes and arrows, where boxes represent concepts and arrows the relationships. However, the purposes of these boxes and arrows are different when it comes to problem understanding and problem solving. Using various examples including business rules and UML design models, amongst others, she highlighted that there was a modularisation mismatch between the so-called Early and Late phases. She concluded that the key issue facing us is how to solve the modularisation mismatch. In her view this requires new aspect-oriented programming languages and development processes? She also asked the question whether there is something like too much analysis and proposed to add elements from aspect-oriented programming languages to the early phases to combat this *analysis overload*.

4 Discussion and Conclusion

The panelists' statements were followed by lively discussions where the panel members responded to each other's initial statements and to questions from the audience. It is impossible to capture the full discussion in a short report. Therefore, only the main conclusions are summarised here.

Anthony Finkelstein noted that modularisation mismatch, as noted by Maja D'Hondt, is a general problem in software engineering and not something specific to aspect-orientation. Similarly, too much analysis is the same point as being made by the agile software development community. He felt that one could indeed argue that probably there is too much analysis but it would be hard to find examples where one can say "enough".

Ana Moreira agreed with the distinction between problem understanding and problem solving. In her view, the former is there to help us understand how to do the latter. Gregor Kiczales complemented this point by noting that modularisation mismatches are inevitable. They may arise due to different reasons, for instance, due to the need to represent more or less detail or different types of modularity. Anthony Finkelstein added that analytical representability is another factor. They agreed that a mismatch is, therefore, inevitable. Gregor Kiczales pointed out that the mismatch happens when we switch between different types of modularity, that is, when concepts in representation A get forcibly squashed into representation B. He argued that join point models and a correspondence calculus may give us a better handle on representation mismatch and hence a means to reason about this correspondence.

Anthony Finkelstein added that such capabilities could help us express and understand controversial concepts such as obliviousness. Ideally a developer chooses representations suited to his/her analytical goal. Then s/he draws the relevant information. However, we don't have the magic to do that so we end up making compromises on either side of the problem solving and understanding divide.

The panel concluded that it was this gap that we urgently need to bridge in order to address the modularity mismatch problem which compounds the complexity of modern software-based systems.

References

[1] Baniassad, E.L.A., Clements, P., Araujo, J., Moreira, A., Rashid, A., Tekinerdogan, B.: Discovering Early Aspects. IEEE Software 23(1), 61–69 (2006)
[2] Rashid, A., Moreira, A.: Domain Models are NOT Aspect Free. In: Nierstrasz, O., Whittle, J., Harel, D., Reggio, G. (eds.) MoDELS 2006. LNCS, vol. 4199, pp. 155–169. Springer, Heidelberg (2006)
[3] Rashid, A., Sawyer, P., Moreira, A., Araujo, J.: Early Aspects: A Model for Aspect-Oriented Requirements Engineering. In: IEEE Joint International Conference on Requirements Engineering, pp. 199–202. IEEE Computer Society Press, Los Alamitos (2002)
[4] Steimann, F.: Domain Models are Aspect Free. In: Briand, L.C., Williams, C. (eds.) MoDELS 2005. LNCS, vol. 3713, pp. 171–185. Springer, Heidelberg (2005)

Author Index

Akşit, Mehmet   175
Alves, Vander   155
Amyot, Daniel   19

Bakker, Jethro   175
Batista, Thais V.   75
Borba, Paulo   155
Boucké, Nelis   115

Carvalho, Fabiano Costa   55
Cirilo, Elder   155

de Freitas, Edison Pignaton   55
de Lucena, Carlos J.P.   155

Easterbrook, Steve   1

Fuentes, Lidia   94

Garcia, Alessandro   75, 115, 155

Hilliard, Rich   139
Hofmann, Christian   175
Holvoet, Tom   115

Kulesza, Uirá   155

Medeiros, Ana Luisa   75
Minora, Leonardo   75
Mussbacher, Gunter   19

Neto, Alberto Costa   155
Niu, Nan   1

Pereira, Carlos Eduardo   55
Pinto, Mónica   94

Rashid, Awais   195

Salvaneschi, Paolo   39
Silva Jr., Elias Teodoro   55
Silva, Lyrene F.   75

Tekinerdoğan, Bedir   175

Wagner, Flávio Rech   55
Wehrmeister, Marco Aurélio   55
Weiss, Michael   19
Whittle, Jon   19

Yu, Yijun   1

Lecture Notes in Computer Science

Sublibrary 2: Programming and Software Engineering

For information about Vols. 1– 4257
please contact your bookseller or Springer

Vol. 4902: P. Hudak, D.S. Warren (Eds.), Practical Aspects of Declarative Languages. X, 333 pages. 2007.

Vol. 4888: F. Kordon, O. Sokolsky (Eds.), Composition of Embedded Systems. XII, 221 pages. 2007.

Vol. 4849: M. Winckler, H. Johnson, P. Palanque (Eds.), Task Models and Diagrams for User Interface Design. XIII, 299 pages. 2007.

Vol. 4839: O. Sokolsky, S. Taşıran (Eds.), Runtime Verification. VI, 215 pages. 2007.

Vol. 4834: R. Cerqueira, R.H. Campbell (Eds.), Middleware 2007. XIII, 451 pages. 2007.

Vol. 4829: M. Lumpe, W. Vanderperren (Eds.), Software Composition. VIII, 281 pages. 2007.

Vol. 4824: A. Paschke, Y. Biletskiy (Eds.), Advances in Rule Interchange and Applications. XIII, 243 pages. 2007.

Vol. 4807: Z. Shao (Ed.), Programming Languages and Systems. XI, 431 pages. 2007.

Vol. 4799: A. Holzinger (Ed.), HCI and Usability for Medicine and Health Care. XVI, 458 pages. 2007.

Vol. 4789: M. Butler, M.G. Hinchey, M.M. Larrondo-Petrie (Eds.), Formal Methods and Software Engineering. VIII, 387 pages. 2007.

Vol. 4767: F. Arbab, M. Sirjani (Eds.), International Symposium on Fundamentals of Software Engineering. XIII, 450 pages. 2007.

Vol. 4765: A. Moreira, J. Grundy (Eds.), Early Aspects: Current Challenges and Future Directions. X, 199 pages. 2007.

Vol. 4764: P. Abrahamsson, N. Baddoo, T. Margaria, R. Messnarz (Eds.), Software Process Improvement. XI, 225 pages. 2007.

Vol. 4762: K.S. Namjoshi, T. Yoneda, T. Higashino, Y. Okamura (Eds.), Automated Technology for Verification and Analysis. XIV, 566 pages. 2007.

Vol. 4758: F. Oquendo (Ed.), Software Architecture. XVI, 340 pages. 2007.

Vol. 4757: F. Cappello, T. Herault, J. Dongarra (Eds.), Recent Advances in Parallel Virtual Machine and Message Passing Interface. XVI, 396 pages. 2007.

Vol. 4753: E. Duval, R. Klamma, M. Wolpers (Eds.), Creating New Learning Experiences on a Global Scale. XII, 518 pages. 2007.

Vol. 4749: B.J. Krämer, K.-J. Lin, P. Narasimhan (Eds.), Service-Oriented Computing – ICSOC 2007. XIX, 629 pages. 2007.

Vol. 4748: K. Wolter (Ed.), Formal Methods and Stochastic Models for Performance Evaluation. X, 301 pages. 2007.

Vol. 4741: C. Bessière (Ed.), Principles and Practice of Constraint Programming – CP 2007. XV, 890 pages. 2007.

Vol. 4735: G. Engels, B. Opdyke, D.C. Schmidt, F. Weil (Eds.), Model Driven Engineering Languages and Systems. XV, 698 pages. 2007.

Vol. 4716: B. Meyer, M. Joseph (Eds.), Software Engineering Approaches for Offshore and Outsourced Development. X, 201 pages. 2007.

Vol. 4709: F.S. de Boer, M.M. Bonsangue, S. Graf, W.-P. de Roever (Eds.), Formal Methods for Components and Objects. VIII, 297 pages. 2007.

Vol. 4680: F. Saglietti, N. Oster (Eds.), Computer Safety, Reliability, and Security. XV, 548 pages. 2007.

Vol. 4670: V. Dahl, I. Niemelä (Eds.), Logic Programming. XII, 470 pages. 2007.

Vol. 4652: D. Georgakopoulos, N. Ritter, B. Benatallah, C. Zirpins, G. Feuerlicht, M. Schoenherr, H.R. Motahari-Nezhad (Eds.), Service-Oriented Computing ICSOC 2006. XVI, 201 pages. 2007.

Vol. 4640: A. Rashid, M. Aksit (Eds.), Transactions on Aspect-Oriented Software Development IV. IX, 191 pages. 2007.

Vol. 4634: H. Riis Nielson, G. Filé (Eds.), Static Analysis. XI, 469 pages. 2007.

Vol. 4620: A. Rashid, M. Aksit (Eds.), Transactions on Aspect-Oriented Software Development III. IX, 201 pages. 2007.

Vol. 4615: R. de Lemos, C. Gacek, A. Romanovsky (Eds.), Architecting Dependable Systems IV. XIV, 435 pages. 2007.

Vol. 4610: B. Xiao, L.T. Yang, J. Ma, C. Muller-Schloer, Y. Hua (Eds.), Autonomic and Trusted Computing. XVIII, 571 pages. 2007.

Vol. 4609: E. Ernst (Ed.), ECOOP 2007 – Object-Oriented Programming. XIII, 625 pages. 2007.

Vol. 4608: H.W. Schmidt, I. Crnković, G.T. Heineman, J.A. Stafford (Eds.), Component-Based Software Engineering. XII, 283 pages. 2007.

Vol. 4591: J. Davies, J. Gibbons (Eds.), Integrated Formal Methods. IX, 660 pages. 2007.

Vol. 4589: J. Münch, P. Abrahamsson (Eds.), Product-Focused Software Process Improvement. XII, 414 pages. 2007.

Vol. 4574: J. Derrick, J. Vain (Eds.), Formal Techniques for Networked and Distributed Systems – FORTE 2007. XI, 375 pages. 2007.

Vol. 4556: C. Stephanidis (Ed.), Universal Access in Human-Computer Interaction, Part III. XXII, 1020 pages. 2007.

Vol. 4555: C. Stephanidis (Ed.), Universal Access in Human-Computer Interaction, Part II. XXII, 1066 pages. 2007.

Vol. 4554: C. Stephanidis (Ed.), Universal Acess in Human Computer Interaction, Part I. XXII, 1054 pages. 2007.

Vol. 4553: J.A. Jacko (Ed.), Human-Computer Interaction, Part IV. XXIV, 1225 pages. 2007.

Vol. 4552: J.A. Jacko (Ed.), Human-Computer Interaction, Part III. XXI, 1038 pages. 2007.

Vol. 4551: J.A. Jacko (Ed.), Human-Computer Interaction, Part II. XXIII, 1253 pages. 2007.

Vol. 4550: J.A. Jacko (Ed.), Human-Computer Interaction, Part I. XXIII, 1240 pages. 2007.

Vol. 4542: P. Sawyer, B. Paech, P. Heymans (Eds.), Requirements Engineering: Foundation for Software Quality. IX, 384 pages. 2007.

Vol. 4536: G. Concas, E. Damiani, M. Scotto, G. Succi (Eds.), Agile Processes in Software Engineering and Extreme Programming. XV, 276 pages. 2007.

Vol. 4530: D.H. Akehurst, R. Vogel, R.F. Paige (Eds.), Model Driven Architecture - Foundations and Applications. X, 219 pages. 2007.

Vol. 4523: Y.-H. Lee, H.-N. Kim, J. Kim, Y.W. Park, L.T. Yang, S.W. Kim (Eds.), Embedded Software and Systems. XIX, 829 pages. 2007.

Vol. 4498: N. Abdennahder, F. Kordon (Eds.), Reliable Software Technologies - Ada-Europe 2007. XII, 247 pages. 2007.

Vol. 4486: M. Bernardo, J. Hillston (Eds.), Formal Methods for Performance Evaluation. VII, 469 pages. 2007.

Vol. 4470: Q. Wang, D. Pfahl, D.M. Raffo (Eds.), Software Process Dynamics and Agility. XI, 346 pages. 2007.

Vol. 4468: M.M. Bonsangue, E.B. Johnsen (Eds.), Formal Methods for Open Object-Based Distributed Systems. X, 317 pages. 2007.

Vol. 4467: A.L. Murphy, J. Vitek (Eds.), Coordination Models and Languages. X, 325 pages. 2007.

Vol. 4454: Y. Gurevich, B. Meyer (Eds.), Tests and Proofs. IX, 217 pages. 2007.

Vol. 4444: T. Reps, M. Sagiv, J. Bauer (Eds.), Program Analysis and Compilation, Theory and Practice. X, 361 pages. 2007.

Vol. 4440: B. Liblit, Cooperative Bug Isolation. XV, 101 pages. 2007.

Vol. 4408: R. Choren, A. Garcia, H. Giese, H.-f. Leung, C. Lucena, A. Romanovsky (Eds.), Software Engineering for Multi-Agent Systems V. XII, 233 pages. 2007.

Vol. 4406: W. De Meuter (Ed.), Advances in Smalltalk. VII, 157 pages. 2007.

Vol. 4405: L. Padgham, F. Zambonelli (Eds.), Agent-Oriented Software Engineering VII. XII, 225 pages. 2007.

Vol. 4401: N. Guelfi, D. Buchs (Eds.), Rapid Integration of Software Engineering Techniques. IX, 177 pages. 2007.

Vol. 4385: K. Coninx, K. Luyten, K.A. Schneider (Eds.), Task Models and Diagrams for Users Interface Design. XI, 355 pages. 2007.

Vol. 4383: E. Bin, A. Ziv, S. Ur (Eds.), Hardware and Software, Verification and Testing. XII, 235 pages. 2007.

Vol. 4379: M. Südholt, C. Consel (Eds.), Object-Oriented Technology. VIII, 157 pages. 2007.

Vol. 4364: T. Kühne (Ed.), Models in Software Engineering. XI, 332 pages. 2007.

Vol. 4355: J. Julliand, O. Kouchnarenko (Eds.), B 2007: Formal Specification and Development in B. XIII, 293 pages. 2006.

Vol. 4354: M. Hanus (Ed.), Practical Aspects of Declarative Languages. X, 335 pages. 2006.

Vol. 4350: M. Clavel, F. Durán, S. Eker, P. Lincoln, N. Martí-Oliet, J. Meseguer, C. Talcott, All About Maude - A High-Performance Logical Framework. XXII, 797 pages. 2007.

Vol. 4348: S. Tucker Taft, R.A. Duff, R.L. Brukardt, E. Plödereder, P. Leroy, Ada 2005 Reference Manual. XXII, 765 pages. 2006.

Vol. 4346: L. Brim, B.R. Haverkort, M. Leucker, J. van de Pol (Eds.), Formal Methods: Applications and Technology. X, 363 pages. 2007.

Vol. 4344: V. Gruhn, F. Oquendo (Eds.), Software Architecture. X, 245 pages. 2006.

Vol. 4340: R. Prodan, T. Fahringer, Grid Computing. XXIII, 317 pages. 2007.

Vol. 4336: V.R. Basili, H.D. Rombach, K. Schneider, B. Kitchenham, D. Pfahl, R.W. Selby (Eds.), Empirical Software Engineering Issues. XVII, 193 pages. 2007.

Vol. 4326: S. Göbel, R. Malkewitz, I. Iurgel (Eds.), Technologies for Interactive Digital Storytelling and Entertainment. X, 384 pages. 2006.

Vol. 4323: G. Doherty, A. Blandford (Eds.), Interactive Systems. XI, 269 pages. 2007.

Vol. 4322: F. Kordon, J. Sztipanovits (Eds.), Reliable Systems on Unreliable Networked Platforms. XIV, 317 pages. 2007.

Vol. 4309: P. Inverardi, M. Jazayeri (Eds.), Software Engineering Education in the Modern Age. VIII, 207 pages. 2006.

Vol. 4294: A. Dan, W. Lamersdorf (Eds.), Service-Oriented Computing – ICSOC 2006. XIX, 653 pages. 2006.

Vol. 4290: M. van Steen, M. Henning (Eds.), Middleware 2006. XIII, 425 pages. 2006.

Vol. 4279: N. Kobayashi (Ed.), Programming Languages and Systems. XI, 423 pages. 2006.

Vol. 4262: K. Havelund, M. Núñez, G. Roşu, B. Wolff (Eds.), Formal Approaches to Software Testing and Runtime Verification. VIII, 255 pages. 2006.

Vol. 4260: Z. Liu, J. He (Eds.), Formal Methods and Software Engineering. XII, 778 pages. 2006.